The Burn Journals

BRENT RUNYON

PENGUIN BOOKS

PENGUIN BOOKS

Published by the Penguin Group
Penguin Books Ltd, 80 Strand, London WC2R 0RL, England
Penguin Group (USA) Inc., 375 Hudson Street, New York, New York 10014, USA
Penguin Group (Canada), 90 Eglinton Avenue East, Suite 700, Toronto, Ontario, Canada M4P 2Y3
(a division of Pearson Penguin Canada Inc.)
Penguin Ireland, 25 St Stephen's Green, Dublin 2, Ireland (a division of Penguin Books Ltd)
Penguin Group (Australia), 250 Camberwell Road, Camberwell, Victoria 3124, Australia
(a division of Pearson Australia Group Pty Ltd)
Penguin Books India Pvt Ltd, 11 Community Centre, Panchsheel Park, New Delhi – 110 017, India
Penguin Group (NZ), cnr Airborne and Rosedale Roads, Albany, Auckland 1310, New Zealand
(a division of Pearson New Zealand Ltd)
Penguin Books (South Africa) (Pty) Ltd, 24 Sturdee Avenue, Rosebank, Johannesburg 2196, South Africa

Penguin Books Ltd, Registered Offices: 80 Strand, London WC2R 0RL, England

penguin.com

First published in the United States by Alfred A. Knopf 2004
First published in Great Britain in Penguin Books 2005
Published in this edition 2006
1

For Christina Egloff.

She said I should write everything I could remember and call it *The Burn Journals*. We spent four years working together on this book. She developed the structure. She shaped the tone, rhythm, and pacing. She pursued perfection in all the details.

This book wouldn't exist without her.

February 4, 1991
Falls Church, Virginia

I'm awake, listening to the radio, and Mom is yelling at me to get out of bed. I don't want to get out of bed. I don't want to go to school. Maybe I should play sick, but I've done that too many times this year already.

The bathroom is right next to my bed, so I don't have to put on a robe or anything. I go in and lock the door behind me, and then the door that leads to the hallway, and then the one that separates the shower and toilet from the sink. It's weird that this bathroom has three locking doors, but I like it. If I ever have to hide from anyone, like a burglar or something, or just really want to be by myself, I can come in here and lock all the doors.

The shower is warm when I get in and I suck a little water into my mouth and spit it out again. I'm going to be in such trouble. It's like a black cloud hanging over my head, like in cartoons when it's only raining on the one guy and it follows him around wherever he goes, even indoors. That guy is me.

I run the whole thing back in my head. I did so many things wrong, I can't even believe it. I shouldn't have taken the matches from Adam. I shouldn't have lit that match. I shouldn't have set the whole pack on fire. I shouldn't have thrown them into that locker. And I really shouldn't have put that lock on the locker.

"I'm so stupid," I say out loud, and turn off the shower. I reach out and grab my big black bathrobe, like the ones boxers wear but without a hood, put it on, and step out into the cold air.

I'm going to wear all black today. I always do. I like my black button-down shirt the best, the cotton one, not the silk one. The black sweater my mom bought for me last week is kind of cheesy, but I like the black dress pants they gave me for Christmas. I've only worn the really hip baggy black pants once. I wore them when my parents took me into D.C. to see the Vincent van Gogh exhibit. I had to read a book in French class about a famous person, and I chose *Lust for Life*, all about van Gogh and how fucked up his life was. I got so obsessed with him when I was reading it. That story about how he cut off his ear and sent it to his girlfriend. God, that's so great. After that, I had my parents take me into D.C. to see that movie *Vincent and Theo*, about how screwed up his relationship was with his brother. I thought it was awesome, but my parents didn't understand it.

I finish getting dressed and go downstairs. My dad would be drinking coffee, staring at the paper, but he's on a business trip in Arizona or Arkansas or something, so there's a big hole at the breakfast table. My mother is moving around the kitchen, cleaning things up, putting my sandwich in a brown paper bag, along with fifty cents for a carton of milk.

She says, "How'd you do on that science test?"

"I don't know." I do know. I failed it.

"How about that algebra test?"

"I don't know." Got a C minus.

She walks over and looks at the calendar on the wall with the picture of the volcano exploding and lava flowing like red water down the side. She says, "You have basketball practice after school today."

"Okay."

"It's at four-thirty."

I hate it when she talks about schedules. She lives her whole life by that calendar on the wall.

My brother is still in his room, getting ready for high school, but he can leave late because his friend Schmed picks him up. If I wait any longer, I'll be late for the bus. I grab my black book bag and head out the door. The three Jennifers are already there when I walk up. I nod at them and stand on the other side of the bus stop. I shove my hands way down in my pockets and wait. It's cold and raining.

The bus comes. I get on and walk all the way to the back. There's still a seat next to Abby, a girl from down the street. I sit down and turn my body just enough so I can slide my right hand under Abby's sweater. At first she doesn't move, but when my hand touches her belly, she exhales really loud and whispers, "It's too cold."

I take my hand back, rub it, and blow on it until it's warm, and then I slide it back under her sweater and rub my thumb against the fabric of her bra and the top of her breast. Once I asked her how it came undone and she said, "It's a latch in the front," and I spent the rest of the ride trying to figure out what that meant. And one time I noticed a hole in the crotch of her pants and tried to put my finger in it, but she said it tickled too much. Today I'm happy just to feel the warmth of her skin.

When we get to school, I pull my hand from under her sweater and get off the bus as fast as I can.

My best friend, Stephen, and I are in homeroom together because both of our last names begin with R, and that makes it the most fun class of the day, which sucks because it's also the first. The homeroom teacher is Mrs. Clagg, the drama teacher, and because she likes us and knows we're the funniest kids in school, she lets us entertain the class occasionally. Last week, we did Abbott and Costello's "Who's on First?" which I screwed up royally because I couldn't remember which one I was supposed to be.

Stephen is Australian and I do an impression of him that is very good. I like to joke him about the time he asked Mrs. Parker, our science teacher, for a rubber, which is what they call an eraser in Australia.

"Excuse me, Mrs. Parker, may I borrow a rubber?" Everyone always laughs at that.

Today Stephen and I don't perform. We sit in the back

6

row, holding copies of *The Catcher in the Rye*, which I haven't read, but I might read because I like books about baseball, and whisper about Megan, the girl we both like.

I say, "Did you call her?"

"Yeah."

"Did you ask her out?"

"Yeah."

"What did she say?"

"She said maybe."

"Maybe?"

"She said she kind of likes someone else."

"Who?"

"You."

"Me?"

This is bad. This is bad because I know how much Stephen likes her. Why do I have to screw this up for him? I hate myself.

Mike and I sit in the back row of Mr. Wolf's civics class, figuring out how to spin a pencil between our fingers like Iceman does in *Top Gun*. I know it's something to do with putting the pencil between your middle finger and ring finger and then you somehow flick it and it winds up between your index and middle fingers.

Mr. Wolf never pays attention to us or asks us any questions because he knows we're smart enough to figure out the answer even if we haven't paid attention for the whole period. Leah sits in front of us and pays attention the whole time. She used to write notes to me, asking who I liked, and drop them onto my desk. I would write back asking her if she wanted to join my religion, the Ace of Spades.

Last year, in seventh grade, I had a lot of time on my hands and I'd come up with crazy ideas just to freak people out. I came up with this idea about a religion based around a god called the Ace of Spades, and we'd all worship the Ace and make sacrifices to him and stuff, and he'd be the one true creator and always wear black. But I never really figured out how to make people believe that he was the one true creator, so I sort of gave up the whole thing. Although, sometimes I still draw the Ace on my papers and tell people about it if I don't have anything else to do.

Leah always thought I was a freak for talking about things like that, but at least she used to pay attention. Now she just ignores me. Maybe because of the time she got a B plus on her report card and started crying because it was the first time she'd gotten anything lower than an A and I called her a stupid bitch for crying about something so stupid.

I used to get all A's too. When we moved here, I was in second grade, and the first thing they did was take me out of class and start testing me. They gave me IQ tests and all sorts of other things to see how smart I was.

I hated that because I'd just moved, and I didn't even have time to make any friends before they took me out of the class and made me feel different. They talked about taking me out of normal school and putting me in a school for smart kids, but I talked them out of it. They put me in this program for smart kids called GT, which stands for Gifted and Talented.

I thought it was okay. I got to learn a lot of different things. We learned about suspension bridges and did all these cool puzzles. I even got to meet an actor that was on *Gilligan's Island* once.

After that, though, I really started to hate GT. I started calling it Goobers and Twerps because all of the kids that were in it were real dorks. None of the cool kids were in it. None. Well, one, if you count me.

I started begging my parents to let me out of the program because it was so stupid, but they didn't want to let me out because it was such a great opportunity. I kept begging and begging, and then, finally, this year, they let me out of GT, and for some reason this is the year I started doing really badly. Now I'm getting F's in a couple of classes.

I meet up with my friend Adam halfway down the main hall and we walk to gym together.

He says, "I swear, man, did you see Catherine's tits in that sweater? She's so stacked, especially for a seventh grader."

"Yeah, I guess." I'm thinking about last Friday in gym, when me and a bunch of guys were changing, dropping our pants and pulling up our green gym shorts as fast as we could, and Adam pulled out a book of matches he'd gotten from the 7-Eleven and showed them to me. I don't know why, but I grabbed them and lit one of them on fire and then, because I thought it would be funny to see everybody's reaction, I set the whole pack on fire, and all of a sudden there was a big ball of fire in my hand and I didn't know what to do, so I opened one of the lockers and threw the burning thing in. Then I realized there was a shirt in the locker. I panicked when the shirt caught fire too and I grabbed a loose lock from the bench and put it on the locker, thinking that it would put out the flames. All the other guys were just standing there staring at me. Then I ran over to the water fountain, cupped some water between my hands, and carried it back to the burning locker. I tried to throw it through the metal slats, but the shirt had just about burnt itself out and now my problem was the smoke. By that time all the other guys had gone out to the gym and I was the only one left in the locker room. So I just opened all the windows to get the smell of burning cotton out and then went out and played volleyball. When we came back in at the end of the period to change, you could still smell the smoke, but the gym teacher just thought somebody had been smoking.

But when I walk into gym today, I see that I didn't get away with it. Mr. Huff is standing in the back of the locker room, right next to the locker that was on fire. He's wearing shorts and a white T-shirt, just like he always does, but he's got his arms folded and he keeps moving his bottom lip over his mustache like he's trying to eat it.

He says, "Okay, boys, settle down. On Friday, there was

an incident in the locker room, which I'm positive occurred during this period. Some arsonist among you purposefully set a shirt on fire and then opened the windows to cover his crime. We had the fire chief come over and investigate. He took some fingerprints and we expect the results later today. Boys, whoever did this is in an enormous amount of trouble. Charges will be pressed. He'll be expelled. But now, I'm prepared to give the guilty party a chance to confess. So whoever did it, or if you know who did it, come see me in my office before the end of the period." His eyes lock with mine on the last word and I feel a cold sickness all over my body, but somehow I manage to keep my eyes from showing that I know he knows it's me.

"What am I going to do? What am I going to do?" I say over and over as we walk out into the gym and start stretching. We're playing dodgeball. Kevin picks up the purple ball and wings it, nailing me in the back, and I go sit on the sidelines for the rest of the game.

Nick beans Adam and he comes over and sits next to me. They were his matches. His fingerprints were on them too.

"What are you going to do?" he says.

"I don't know," I say.

"Are you going to turn yourself in?"

"No."

"You're not?"

"No."

"Then what are you going to do?"

"I'm going to kill myself."

"You are?"

"Yeah."

"But how will they know that it was you and not me?"

"I don't know. I guess I'll write a note saying I did it."

"You will? Okay."

He gets up and starts to walk away and then calls out, "Hey. Thanks."

Brian and I sit in the back row during English. Sometimes we draw Mötley Crüe and Aerosmith symbols in our notebooks. Brian likes me because I tell him what the books are about when he doesn't read them. I like the Suicidal Tendencies patch on his denim jacket.

"Brian?"

"Brent."

"The cops couldn't get fingerprints from a book of matches if it was all burnt up, could they?"

He thinks for a second. He knows this kind of thing. "Yeah, they could."

"They could?"

"Yeah, because fire doesn't burn away fingerprints."

"It doesn't?"

"No, unless the person who lit the matches also poured lighter fluid or some other emollient, like gasoline or something, on the matches. Then they wouldn't be able to find anything."

"But, like, the school doesn't have our fingerprints on file, does it?"

"Yeah, of course they do. They have everybody's finger-prints on file."

"They do?" I slide a little lower in my seat.

"Yeah. Don't you know anything?"

I am so fucked.

These days in algebra, I sit up front with the fucking brains. I used to sit in the back with Nick and Kevin, two of the coolest kids in school. We'd open Mrs. Loftus's file cabinets when she wasn't looking and steal school supplies. We got Wite-Out, and pencils, and big yellow legal pads, and we'd take them back to Kevin's locker and store them there. We never used them or anything. We just liked stealing. I don't know how they figured out it was us. Kevin thinks they installed a security camera, but I'm not sure.

The day before we got caught, Mrs. Loftus threatened the whole class with in-school suspension if we didn't tell her who did it. She said, "Class"—she has the world's most annoying lisp and she's always using words with S's in them—"class, someone has been stealing school supplies from my supply closet. Whoever you are, you have a con-science. You're not kleptomaniacs."

I raised my hand and asked what a kleptomaniac was. I thought maybe that would throw her off the trail, but it didn't. She knew it was us.

That night, I got dressed up in my best outfit, a black blazer, black silk shirt, black dress pants, and a black tie, and lay in my bed listening to Warrant's *Cherry Pie* album.

I took my knife from its hiding place between the mattress and the box spring and held it against my wrist. When the music got really loud, I sliced as fast as I could and bit my lip from the pain. I hung my arm between the two twin beds pushed together from when my brother used to share the room with me and let it bleed. I was surprised when I woke up in the morning. My blood had clotted into the carpet. I had to find a Band-Aid big enough to cover the wound and told my parents I'd scratched my wrist on a locker.

We got three days in-school suspension for stealing and my parents were pissed. They grounded me for two weeks with no TV. They said, "We've never been so disappointed in you."

I wonder how they'll feel when I get expelled.

I see Stephen in the hall on the way to lunch. I pull him out of the way of the crowd and say, "I'm in big trouble."

"Why?"

"I lit a book of matches on fire in gym and burned somebody's shirt up."

"That was you?"

"Yeah."

"That was my shirt."

"It was?"

"Yeah, why did you do that?"

"I don't know, I was just playing around. It was your shirt? Maybe you could tell them that it was just an accident? What did you tell them?"

"I just showed it to Mr. Huff and he said he'd take care of it."

"Shit. I wish I'd known it was your shirt."

"Yeah. What are you going to do? They took fingerprints."

"I don't know what I'm going to do. See you after seventh period." I walk down the hall toward the cafeteria and I know that I'm completely screwed.

At lunch, I sit near a few guys I know and eat my sandwich.

"Did you hear about the guy who went to the doctor with a red ring around his dick and the doctor gave him lipstick remover?"

"Dude, I heard Nick and Deanna did it in the ditch next to her house."

"Kevin told me that he fingered Sonja and she got her period all over his fingers."

"Did you hear about Jennifer L.? She got caught fingering herself in the bathroom."

I think about that movie we saw in English class, about the guy who's standing on the bridge waiting to get hung. As soon as the rope snaps his head back, he's dead.

I wonder why all the ways I've tried to kill myself haven't worked. I mean, I've tried hanging. I used to have a noose tied to my closet pole. I'd go in there and slip the thing over my head and let my weight go. But every time I started to lose consciousness, I'd just stand up.

I tried to take pills. One afternoon, I took twenty Advil, but that just made me sleepy. And all the times I tried to cut my wrists, I could never cut deep enough. That's the thing—your body tries to keep you alive no matter what you do. I've got to think of a way to kill myself that I can't turn back from.

In Mrs. Parker's science class, I sit in the back with Sean and Moira. He's really funny and she's really beautiful, so we spent all of last quarter trying to make her laugh until she started going out with a guy in high school and I started failing this class. Now we just sit here.

Today I stare at the black lab table and use my house key to scrape things into it. I scrape a big Ace of Spades into the black surface and wait to go home.

I sit in the back of Miss Guppie's French class and wait for the office to call me in. I'm sure they will. They have to. I think about what will happen when I get home. Where the matches are, and where the gas can is, and how I'll blow into a million pieces like in the movies. I wait for them to call me in, but nothing happens.

Mrs. Clagg's drama class is usually fun. We do theater sports, which is like improvisational comedy, and staged readings, but today we read silently from this play called *Arsenic and Old Lace*. I think it's just about the saddest thing I've ever read, even though I haven't really been paying attention.

Fifteen minutes into the class, the hall monitor comes to the door with a note for Mrs. Clagg. She reads it and says, "Brent, you're to go directly to the office."

I say, "Okay." I stand up and walk out of the room, but I can hardly feel my legs, they're so numb.

It takes me a second to realize that the hall monitor is Chris, one of my friends from elementary school. We used to play soccer together, and I can't figure out why I didn't recognize him before. We walk down the hall and he asks me what I did this time.

I say, "Lit some matches in gym."

"That was you? Oh, you're in deep shit, dude."

"I know," I say, and I walk into the office.

Mrs. Robins is the vice principal for the eighth grade and I go sit in a chair outside her office. Adam is already there, waiting.

Pretty soon, she opens the door and calls him in and I sit waiting and my stomach gets tighter and tighter, like something is eating me from the inside.

Finally Adam opens the door and kind of half smiles at me as he walks out. Mrs. Robins is still sitting behind her desk and she calls out for me to come in. She's wearing a red dress that I can't stop staring at.

She says, "Do you know why you're here?"

I say, "I don't know. I'm not sure."

"Do you want to take a guess?"

"Um, the thing in gym?"

17

"Yes, the arson in second-period gym on Friday. Do you know anything about that?"

"No. I don't know anything about that."

"Did you see what happened?"

"No, I didn't see what happened."

"Do you know who did it?"

"No, I don't know who did it."

"Brent, if you know anything or if you were somehow involved, it would be much better for you to say so now. It would be much better. So, do you know anything?"

"No. I don't know anything."

She stares at me for a few seconds. "Okay, you can go." I get up and walk out of the office.

She knows that I did it.

When seventh period is finally over, I run to my locker and put all my books inside. I won't need them anymore. I grab my lock-picking set and a spare Ace of Spades that I have lying around.

At the end of the hallway, I can see Stephen talking to Megan, the girl we both have a crush on. I walk up to them and say hi. She smiles at me and I try to smile back. He looks a little suspicious.

I don't really want to say anything, I don't want to tell them what I'm going to do. I hand him the Ace of Spades and say, "Good-bye," and I walk away. I hope they'll be happy together.

I see my friend Jake at his locker and give him the lock-picking set. "Use them wisely," I say, and head toward the bus.

Laura walks with me down D hall. She says, "Hey, I heard you set that fire in gym class."

"Yeah."

"What are you going to do?"

"I'm going to set myself on fire." She stops at her locker, and I keep walking.

On the bus ride home, I sit by myself. I lean my head against the cold glass window and try not to think about all the stupid things I've done, all the bad things I've done, and all the pain I've caused everyone.

My brother is playing basketball outside the house when I get home. He's shooting free throws.

I rebound the ball for him and throw it back. I don't want to take any shots. I tell him the whole story, about what I did and what they're going to do to me. I don't tell him what I'm going to do to myself.

When I'm done talking, he says, "That sucks," and I go inside the house. I don't have to write a note anymore. Craig knows everything.

I walk out to the shed to get the gas can. I bring it inside to the bathroom at the top of the stairs because that's the room with the most locks. I go back downstairs and get the matches from the kitchen.

I take off all my clothes and put on the pair of red boxers with glow-in-the-dark lips that my mom bought for me at the mall last weekend. I bring my bathrobe into the shower and I pour the gasoline all over it. The gas can is only about a quarter full, but it seems like enough.

I step into the bathtub and I put the bathrobe over my shoulders. It's wet and heavy, but there's something kind of comforting about the smell, like going on a long car trip. I hold the box of matches out in front of me in my left hand.

I take out a strike-anywhere match and hold it against the box.

Should I do it?

Yes. Do it.

I strike the match, but it doesn't light. Try again.

I light the match. Nothing happens. I bring it closer to my wrist and then it goes up, all over me, eating through me everywhere. I can't breathe. I'm screaming, "Craig! Craig!"

I fall down. I'm going to die. I'm going to find out what death is like. I'm going to know. But nothing's happening.

This hurts too much. I need to stop it. I need to get up. I stand. I don't know how I stand, but I do, and I turn on the shower. I'm breathing water and smoke. I unlock the door and open it. My hand is all black. I walk out. There's Craig with Rusty, our dog, next to him. They have the same expression on their faces.

Craig yells something and runs downstairs. I think he's calling 911. I'm following him. He hands me the phone and runs off. There's a woman on the phone asking me questions. I try to tell her what's happened, but my voice sounds choked and brittle. There's something wrong with my voice.

The woman on the phone says the fire trucks and ambulances are on their way. Somehow she knows my address. Craig is gone now, gone to get Mom, and Rusty is hiding somewhere. Smoke is coming from the bathroom upstairs and I can see that the whole room has turned black. I look down and see my flesh is charred and flaking and the glow-in-the-dark boxer shorts are burnt into my skin.

The woman on the phone says everything is going to be all right, and I believe her. She has a nice voice. She keeps asking me if I'm still on fire and I say, "I don't think so."

I'm walking around the kitchen, waiting for the ambulance to come. I can see my reflection in the microwave. Where's my hair? Where did my hair go? Is that my face?

We used to put marshmallows in the microwave. We used to watch them get bigger and bigger and then shrink down.

"Oh God, just tell them to get here, just tell them to get here, okay?"

She says, "It's okay. They're coming. They're almost there."

"I'm so sorry. I'm so sorry."

"It's okay, that's okay."

I can hear the sirens in the distance now.

I say, "I want to lie down. I'm going to lie down." It hurts to talk. I think there's something wrong in my throat.

"You can't lie down."

"But I have to."

"Okay, you can lie down."

The men are here. The firemen are here. They're putting me on a plastic sheet. They say I'm going to be okay. One of them puts something over my face. That feels good. That feels so good. The cold air feels so good going into my lungs.

What are they talking about? What are they saying? They're giving me a shot. They say it's going to make the pain go away. Make the pain go away.

I'm looking at the faces of all the men who are gathered around me. Their eyes are so blue and so clear.

I turn my head and see Craig in the front hall. He's yelling and punching the walls. He's angry.

And my mom is here, and she's smiling and saying she loves me, and her eyes, which are green like my eyes, are the most beautiful things I've ever seen.

I'm being lifted. They're rolling me through the front door, down the path, and into the ambulance.

I wonder if anybody in the neighborhood is watching. I don't want them to know.

I can feel that we're going to the ball field down the road, where I play soccer, and I hear something about a helicopter—that should be fun. I'm so tired. I keep trying to close my eyes and sleep, but this woman with red hair is yelling at me to stay awake.

I'm outside now, and people are running. It's windy and the mask over my face smells like plastic and I'm so tired.

And now we're flying, but I can't see anything because I'm lying down and that woman is still yelling at me to stay awake, and I wonder where my mom went, is she here? I don't think she's here.

I was in a helicopter once in Hawaii, we flew over volcanoes and along these big cliffs and saw waterfalls. It was beautiful.

We must be over Washington, but I can't see the monuments or the White House or anything. This is probably the only time I'll get to fly over the city like this unless I get to be president someday, but I don't think I'm going to be president.

That woman is still yelling. Please stop yelling. I don't want to stay awake, I want to sleep. Why won't she let me sleep?

I wonder if I'm going to the hospital near where my dad works. I could get a ride home with him later, oh, but he's in Arkansas or something. I wonder where he is.

I try to say something, ask the woman with red hair if my mom is here, but I can't move my mouth, and my throat is dry from all the cold air they're making me breathe. I'm so cold. I wish I had a blanket or a sweater. I guess I do have a blanket, but I'm still so cold. Maybe when we get to the hospital, they'll give me another blanket or a pair of sweatpants. My body hurts, everything everywhere hurts. I close my eyes.

Something's different, I'm outside again. It's windy. No, it's not. I'm in an elevator, I can tell because of the doors and the lights. Who is that woman talking to me? How does she know my name? She looks like that other woman on that TV show I saw.

And now there are even more lights and lots of people wearing masks. They're putting me on a metal table. And it's so cold, it's so cold. And everybody's talking, but nobody's talking to me. Somebody just said my urine is red. I don't want red urine. I want to cry and I want to sleep.

I want to go back.

February 5, 1991
Children's National Medical Center
Washington, D.C.

There's a balloon and a room.

There's a balloon and something funny with breathing.

Why is there so much noise and so much trouble breathing? Why is it always night?

Stop tearing. They are tearing at me. Tearing away my skin. Please stop. Please.

Boys like in algebra. Trouble with the boys. We're standing in the parking garage. Let's go down into the garage. Let's burn. Let's set fires. Let's set me on fire. I don't want to be on fire. I want to be home. Woman with the black curly hair here to save me. Woman with the black curly hair carries me away. Save me.

I think the woman brought me waffles, the woman that takes care of me. She brings me waffles and says I'll be okay and I don't have to worry about anything. Except I don't remember eating them. I think there's something in my mouth and I can't open my eyes.

Stop. It's not time to do this now. Stop trying to unwrap me. Everything hurts. Please don't do this now. I wish I could talk and say something so she'd understand me.

There's something plastic in my mouth keeping me from saying anything.

I can't talk. They give me a big marker so I can write. I'm supposed to write what I want to say. But the marker is too hard to hold and I forget what most of the letters look like.

I try to write. I try to write what I'm thinking, but to write, you have to remember the beginning of the word and the ending of the word you're writing so that you can write down the whole word at the same time.

There's a camera in the balloon. I know because every time the balloon moves, there is a sound like a hidden camera and that means that they're watching me, but I don't know who they are yet.

Now they want me to talk to them with this board? They point at the letters and I blink when I want them to stop. And I spell out the words, but it's hard to remember what I'm trying to say. I want to say, I want to go home. I want to go home. They tell me that home is fine and I'll be home soon. But I want to be home now.

I feel like there's a rod in my side.

If they unplug me, I'll die. If they unplug me, I'll die. I could die. Maybe I should ask them to unplug me. But I don't want to die anymore.

Mom and Dad are always here. And I think I saw Grandma and Grandpa and Nanny and Grandpa and Uncle Tom or somebody that looked like Uncle Tom, but I haven't seen Craig. Where is Craig?

Mom says there's a girl next door who's hurt like me. She says the girl is my age and she got hurt the same day as me. The girl's name is Maggie.

The Hispanic boy comes and lifts my arms. He has brown hair, brown eyes, and he's very nice. Everyone is nice.

Sometimes they come into my room and pull out the tubes and I can't breathe, and they pour salt water down my throat and I still can't breathe. Then they suck the salt water out and put the tubes back in my mouth and I can breathe again.

Mom says that they're going to do surgery on my hands and that I'm lucky to have such a good doctor. He'll use my skin to fix my hands up, the skin from my stomach will be on my hands. They have to fix my hands because my hands are so important, but my back is what hurts. Can they fix my back too?

Doctors and nurses come to move me. Mom and Dad wave and all the beeping machines are following me down the hall and I can see different lights now. This must be surgery. I'll have new hands. Then maybe I can go home soon.

My throat hurts. I'm back in the room with the balloons and Mom and Dad and my new hands. Is everything okay, Mom? Is everything okay, Dad? I try to say it with my mouth, but I've still got the breathing tubes in, so I say it with my eyes. "Everything's okay, honey," says my mom. She heard me.

There are lots of cards and pictures in my room, lots from people I don't know. Pictures of girls with teddy bears and pictures of Florida. Every day there are more cards and pictures. Mom and Dad like to show me all the pictures and tell me about how everybody cares about me.

Mom says Maggie is too sick to have surgery. Maggie and I are the same because we both got hurt the same day and we have the same problems, but I'm doing a little better. That's good. I'm winning.

More tearing.

The woman with black curly hair is Tina. She's a nurse. I've never met anyone who's so beautiful and kind. She likes me. I like her. I know by the way we smile at each other.

They get the message board so I can ask a question and I ask about basketball. It's easier now to remember what I'm trying to say, and they are better about guessing what I want to know. They say they'll tape the All-Star Game for me so I can watch it. Someday soon, they'll take the tubes out and let me breathe on my own. Then I can have ice and juice and waffles.

Barbara with the red hair, different than Barbara with the blond hair and the other one they call Barb. Kerry, the young one. Lisa, the night nurse. Janice, like a model. Calvin, funny guy. Amy, Calvin's girlfriend. Reggie, tall guy.

Every day they give me morphine and something they call a Mickey, and then I fall asleep. I wake up when they're cleaning my legs. They always start at the legs. They clean each part three times. And it hurts so bad, but they keep cleaning and cleaning, all the way up my legs, and my arms, and my chest, but they don't touch my face, they say my face isn't bad. They turn me over and start cleaning my back. That hurts the worst. When they're done, they change the sheets and turn me over again.

Mom says they're going to take some of my skin and fly it to Boston to grow in a lab, like the Six Million Dollar Man, and then fly it back and put it on me. She's really happy about that because I don't have enough skin to cover my body. She says they want to cover my body with dead people skin and skin from pigs while I wait for the Boston skin. I don't want the dead people on me.

Mom says Maggie is going to get off the respirator soon. I want to get off the respirator. I'm going to try and get off the respirator.

They take the tubes out and I'm breathing on my own and I can tell Dad is really happy. He keeps telling me that if I can keep the tubes out, I can eat and drink and go home sooner. I try to eat waffles, but it's hard to swallow and it's hard to breathe. It's so hard to breathe. Dad says I have to keep my oxygen saturation up to ninety-eight or ninety-nine, and he shows me the machine that has that number on it. He says if I breathe deeply, then the numbers will stay up and they won't put the tubes back in. But it's so hard to breathe, I forgot how hard it was. I try to talk, but I can't say much, so I just keep trying to breathe deep so the number is high. The cold air feels good on my face, and Dad is reading, this is so much harder than I remember it. Maybe the tubes aren't so bad. Maybe they should put the tubes back in so I can breathe again.

Surgery again. They're putting skin on my legs, but it's not my skin. It's from a pig, and they're supposed to take my skin off me and send it to Boston.

I hurt. I need something. Lisa gives me something to stop hurting, and it's working, but now I can't see, everything is double.

Ice. Mom is giving me ice, and I never realized this before, but ice is the best-tasting thing in the entire world. I could eat ice for breakfast, lunch, dinner, and dessert. I wish I could live on ice. They didn't take my skin off. Maybe tomorrow.

The nice old doctor is here, Dr. Randolph, I think his name is, and the scary-looking tall guy with the glasses. I want to make a joke, but I can't figure out how to say, What's up, Doc? with these tubes in my mouth. They've come to take my skin. They're going to put me to sleep for a little while.

I'm standing. I don't know how, but I'm standing in the street and Tina is there and we're walking together.

I'm awake. Tina is standing over me, and she's so beautiful. She says it's Valentine's Day and I want to ask her if she'll be my valentine, but I'm worried that she doesn't think I'm handsome enough, so instead I ask if I can see my face in the mirror. She holds it up and says it looks so much better than when I first came in, but I don't like to look at it. I hate the way it looks and I cry. She puts the mirror down and puts her face near mine and says she thinks my face looks so good now, and it's going to keep getting better and I won't hardly believe it when I see myself in a few weeks, I'll be so handsome. And when I get better and I can walk again, we'll go out on the town together and get some ice cream because she knows I like ice cream. Do I like Ben & Jerry's? When we get the tubes out, we'll have Ben & Jerry's together, how about that?

I tell Mom with the message board about my dream about standing, and she's really happy about that. I don't tell her I was with Tina.

My friends from school are sending me stuff all the time. Stephen sent me a tape, and they put it on the stereo for me. He put all these Aerosmith songs on it because he knows how much I like them. I miss him and Megan. I hope they're happy.

Dad is reading the comics when I wake up. It's the Sunday comics because it's in color. He holds up the pictures so I can see and starts reading what Charlie Brown says to Lucy and what Lucy says to Charlie Brown and what Garfield says to Odie. I'm getting frustrated with the way he's reading to me like a baby, so I make him get the message board and I write, I can still read, you know.

He laughs and says he's sorry and we read the rest of them together, silently.

They're taking me to surgery. This big bed can fit inside this elevator. But why are we going up? The operating room is down. We're up on the roof now, where the helicopter lands. I remember what it was like up here, flying. I remember the wind. Now we're going back down to surgery. We got lost.

Mom and Dad are holding my hands. I can't talk because the tubes are still in from the surgery, but they ask me how

I am and I say, I hurt, with the message board. That makes them sad. They're looking at me with so much love in their eyes, which is so much better than when they look scared. They say they love me, and I use the message board to say I love them too.

Everything hurts, and it's so much worse than before. All I want is for there to be less pain and for them to stop hurting me. I know they mean well. I know it. But God, it hurts.

Mom says they're going to try and bring Maggie down to surgery again. I see the nurses going in and out of her room. Sometimes I wish they came and saw me as much as they see her.

Dad is sitting next to my bed again when I wake up. He's reading and he smiles at me and asks if I need anything. I try to say something, but I always forget that I can't talk, so I try to ask him with my eyes if he'll put the cool cloth on my forehead, and at first he doesn't understand. He grabs the message board, but I don't want to use that stupid thing, I just want him to understand me. I say again with my eyes, Cloth, and this time he hears me and gets the cloth from the bedside table and puts it on my forehead.

He says, "Brenner, you've got the most expressive eyes I've ever seen."

The old doctor comes by, Dr. Randolph, and says he's really happy with my progress, and my parents start asking questions with very serious voices and taking notes, but he stops them and starts talking to me. He tells me that I have an infection in my lung and that it's nothing to worry about and I'll get better soon, but I'll have to stay on the ventilator until I get a little stronger. He says I can't eat or drink anything for a while, but that'll change too. He says he's really proud of me and he knows I'm going to get better.

I just realized how many tubes are coming out of me. There's a big one in my mouth, a smaller one in my nose, something in my shoulder they inject medicine and blood into, a thick plastic one in my rib cage that drains fluid into a little yellow bag, and then there's a little one coming out of my penis. I'm glad my penis didn't get hurt in the fire.

During burn care, Tina puts on some music. She says it'll help relax me. Piano, some guy named George Winston. She really likes it, and I like it too. We have a lot in common.

I'm waking up from surgery. They were supposed to cover part of my back and my left shoulder. The tubes are out and I'm awake, but something's wrong. I feel dizzy and I can't talk and my chest hurts and my lung feels like someone is standing on it. I can't talk. Someone needs to help me. Get help. My chest, I can't breathe. Mom is here, she's asking me what's wrong, but I can't talk. I try to say, My chest hurts, but there's no air to say it with. She's yelling for the nurses. Now there's a doctor here. They're pushing my parents out of the room. Mom calls out that she loves me. I still can't breathe. This guy is asking me questions. I don't know. I don't know. Just fix it. Just fix it. They're yelling at each other and someone is sticking something through my rib cage. Oh God, that hurts. I can feel it pushing through the skin and the muscle between my ribs and into my lung. Oh God. This hurts too much. I'm so scared.

Mom says I had a punctured lung from something they did wrong in surgery and my lung collapsed and that's why they had to put the tubes through my rib cage, but I'm better now and that shouldn't happen again. I hope that never happens again.

Everybody is worried because my temperature is so high, but forty doesn't seem very high to me, or maybe it is because it's not Celsius or it is Celsius, I'm not sure which.

The tube in my throat is out, and my voice works again. But my voice sounds so scratchy and old now. It hurts to say too much, so I'm not going to say much. I sound like a smoker.

Dad is here, Mom's not. I want to talk and I want to tell him about what I did and that I'm so sorry, but I can't figure out how to say that, so I ask him if he ever wanted to kill himself, and he says that he must have once, a long time ago, and I feel better because even if he's lying, then it's nice of him. I try to tell him about what happened, but it's so hard to say out loud. I don't even remember why I did it now. Because of school and because of my friends, but those don't seem like good reasons anymore. Because I was going to be expelled, but I think I'd rather be expelled than be here. Dad seems like he understands, and he cries and I cry. I'm so sorry, Dad. I'm so sorry.

Craig still hasn't come to visit me. I ask my mom why and she can't really answer me and I ask if he hates me, and she says no, of course he doesn't hate me, but the way she says it, I can tell he really does.

Barbara the nurse who calls me Gorgeous is here. I like the way she says that because it sounds like she really means it. She's going to clean my wounds. She puts on some music, she says it's from *Dances with Wolves* and that I should imagine I'm in the middle of a field with horses and buffalo and there are wide-open spaces and mountains in the distance and I should explore the field in my mind and tell her what I'm seeing. I tell her I see a field with grass up to my waist, everything is waving in the wind and I can sort of float through it like I don't have any legs, and the mountains in the distance are huge icy peaks with sharp rocks sticking out. There's a beautiful black horse in front of me that looks like he wants me to ride him, and I float over to him and I see that someone has shot him and there's a big hole in his side from where the shotgun blast was, and the hole goes all the way through so I can see the mountains out the other side.

I open my eyes and look down and I see everything. I see the purple skin and the big open wounds. I lay my head back, close my eyes, and try to think of something else.

Mom says the night Maggie died I saw angels in my room. She says that Tina was there changing my ventilator and I looked up at the ceiling and said, "There are people flying around my room looking for someone who died, but it's not me." Now Mom and Dad wear little angel pins on their shirts every day.

Craig is here and Mom and Dad are going to leave us alone for a while. He doesn't seem so mad at me anymore. He talks about his job at the movie theater and his new girlfriend, Valerie, who works at the movie theater with him. He thinks I'll like her. She thinks he wears too much blue, and every time he doesn't wear anything blue, she gives him a kiss. So now, every time he goes to work, he gets a kiss. That's nice for him, that he's getting kisses. He says he hasn't had sex yet, but they're going to. It's too bad that no one will ever want to have sex with me, but I don't really care. I hope Craig can love me again.

Mom sits by my bedside and I can tell that she wants to talk about the fire and everything about it. So I start by asking her the same question that I asked Dad, and she says she wanted to kill herself too a long time ago when she was a girl, which I don't think is true, but I know she's trying to make me feel better. And I try to say why I was so sad, and how I thought that the principal was going to expel me and how I didn't want them to be mad at me because they both wanted me to be so smart and I'm sorry I couldn't be what you wanted. And she says, "You are everything we wanted." And we both cry together.

Surgery. They took part of my scalp and moved it to my left leg, over that big gaping wound, the one as big as a mailbox. They almost didn't take me in because my fever came back and I've got a lot of stuff in my lungs, but then they changed their minds and took me. They had to shave my head to cut the skin off. Then they put this stuff on my scalp called scarlet or crimson, I can never remember which, and they say it will help the skin grow back in a few weeks. I'm worried about my hair. My parents are happy that I'm not on the ventilator anymore.

The thing about being in the hospital is that people come into your room in the middle of the night, take your blood and urine, and leave again. People stick things to your chest, hook you up to machines, and don't even introduce themselves.

Becky is here to stretch my arms and hands. She tells me about an episode of *Monty Python's Flying Circus* that she just saw, about a guy who buys a dead parrot. She's very funny and does a great English accent. I wonder why I thought she was a Hispanic boy.

Dad wants to stay during burn care because he wants to see what I look like, but I don't want him to see what I look like. I'm afraid he'll get sick or get scared and he won't want to come visit me anymore.

I think we used to say we loved each other too much. Mom and Dad used to make us say we loved each other every night before we went to bed, and since we said it all the time, it was like it didn't mean anything, but now when we say it, it feels like we really mean it.

This short woman just came to visit me, her name is Dr. Rubinstein and she's a psychologist. I don't like her. The first thing she did was sit down at my bedside and start asking me questions about what happened in the fire and what I was thinking about. She asked me about drugs and my friends and whether I told them I was going to do it. Most people who come to visit me lean forward in the chair, but she leans away.

Surgery. They took more skin from my stomach and moved it to the spots that were open on my arms and legs. When I wake up, the tubes are already out of my mouth, extubated, which is good, I hate those fucking tubes. Everyone says I'm becoming an old pro. I've done this five or six times already. They said I'll have at least ten before I'm done.

Today is the day that Tina and I will eat Ben & Jerry's together. Mom and Dad are here too, but they're not going to have any. Tina brings her favorite flavors—Heath Bar Crunch, Cherry Garcia, and New York Super Fudge Chunk. She pushes a button so the bed makes me sit up a little bit and gives me a spoonful of Heath Bar Crunch. Oh

49

God, that's good. I forgot how good ice cream was. I'm feeling a little dizzy, but I ask Tina for another bite, this time New York Super Fudge Chunk.

I forget that people are watching me for a second while I'm enjoying the ice cream and then I remember and so I try to ham it up and look really, really happy. Everyone laughs when I raise my eyebrows and look like I'm going to faint from pleasure. But then I realize that I actually am going to faint from sitting up so straight and I make them put me back down flat.

The doctors are here to look at my hands. Mom and Dad are here too, and a couple of nurses, and everybody seems really excited to see how my hands are doing. The doctors unwrap the bandages. They're purple and spotted and covered with blood and staples. They start talking about how great my purple skinny hands look and how I'm going to get full range of motion back. It makes me feel sick to look at them. God. I close my eyes.

When all the doctors leave, Mom sits close to my bed and starts talking really softly and quietly to me. She says, "This is just the first day. Everything is going to look so much better in a few weeks. And in a few months your hands will almost be back to normal. You're going to be okay, honey."

I'm crying a little, but it's not because of my hands. It's because of this other thing that I'm afraid of, that I haven't said to anybody yet. "Mom, no one's ever going to love me, are they?" And I can't help it, I just start crying all over the place like a baby.

But Mom puts her hand on my fingertips and whispers, "Brent, listen to me, honey, you are so smart and so kind. You will fall in love, and someone will fall in love with you. I promise."

It makes me feel better to hear her say that, but I can tell that she's not really sure. It'll be okay, I tell myself, I can live in the basement when I get older so people don't have to look at me.

Carol, the social worker, got me a phone so I can call my friends. I can't use a regular phone because of the bandages over my ears, so they had to get me this bear speaker phone. When the person on the phone talks, the bear's face lights up and its mouth moves like it's talking. It's pretty cool.

The first person I want to call is Stephen, to see how he's doing and to see if he's dating Megan or what. Carol sits the bear on a table in front of me and moves the head of my bed up a little. When she pushes the dial tone button, the bear's eyes and mouth open and it looks like it's ready to talk. I tell her the phone number and she dials for me. I'm excited. I haven't talked to anyone at school since I got into the hospital. Stephen answers the phone and I try to think of something really funny to say, but I can't come up with anything, so I just say, "Stephen, it's Brent."

The bear lights up a little, blinks, and says, "Brent," with an Australian accent, but I can tell from how he says my name that something's different. His voice is tight and he doesn't sound as excited as I thought he would.

I say, "What's up?"

The bear says, "What's up, dude?"

So I say, "How's it going?"

And he says, "How's it going with you?" The bear's mouth is a little behind the words and it blinks in all the wrong places, but it's still kind of cool.

"Going good. How about with you?"

"It's good. It's good. What's new?"

"Not much. What's new with you?"

"Nothing," says the bear.

"How's Megan?"

"Megan's good. She misses you."

"I miss her too. I miss all you guys."

The bear blinks but doesn't say anything for a second, then says, "When are you coming home?"

"Soon. Soon."

"Good. Well, get better."

"I will. See you, dude."

"Bye, dude." When he hangs up, the bear's mouth closes, the eyes close halfway, and the little light inside its face goes out.

Some girls from school made me a tape of their everyday life and sent it to me. It sounds weird listening to all the noises of school all smacked together. I wonder why no guys talk on the tape.

"Hi, Brent, it's Jennifer reporting from D hall and there's a bunch of us here who just want to say hi."

"Hi."

"Hi."

"Hi."

"Hi, Brent!"

"You're my hero, Brent."

"Hi, Brent, I hope you do well and we all really miss you."

"Hi, Brent, it's Leah, your favorite person in the world. We're going to civics and we're really going to miss you there, so bye."

"Brent, this is Mrs. Clagg. I sure hope you're feeling better. We miss you a whole lot. Remember the funny time you put all those rubber bands in your hair and you walked down the hall like that? You sure have a tremendous amount of confidence in yourself and I'm sure I'm going to see you again walking down the hall with the rubber bands in your hair. All right, take care, get well, we sure care about it. Love and prayers, Mrs. Clagg."

"Hi, Brent, we're in algebra right now. Do you want to hear Mrs. Loftus's lisp?"

"Brent, come back and do your Elvis impression."

"Hi, Brent, this is Julie and Jenny. Do the weasel. Every time we hear 'Blue Suede Shoes,' we think of you."

"Hi, Brent, this is Victoria Key. I really miss you and really love you and I hope you get better soon."

"Hey, Brent, get well, come back to us soon, Brent."

"I got my brother some wrapping paper for Christmas. I told them to wrap it but in a different print so when he opens it, he'll know when to stop. Remember when you told me that joke? Now I get it."

"I know this guy who has a car phone and an answering machine on the car phone. The message on the machine says, 'Sorry, I'm at home right now, I'll call you when I go out.' Ha ha ha."

"Nobody forgot your jokes."

"Hi, Brent, this is Miss Guppie, it's noisy in here because

we're working on conversation. Get well, come back soon, we miss you."

"Hi, Brent, you're walking into the girls' dressing room right now. You're in the girls' dressing room. Hey, look at Jennifer. Hey, Brent, we're going to try and tape some Jane Fonda for you. Hey, Brent, we're all changing right now."

"Don't look."

"Yeah, don't look, Brent."

"Are we boring you? I hope we're not boring you."

"Hi, Brent. Well, I hope you've enjoyed our tape. We really, really, really, really miss you and we really, really hope you get better real, real soon, okay, so you can come back and tell us some more of your jokes that I don't understand but now I finally do and you can sing some more Elvis songs and put your hair in some more weird styles and just, you know, be yourself. Okay, bye."

More surgery today. They're going to put that special skin on me, the skin that they took off me a couple of weeks ago and flew to Boston. It's been growing there, and now there are fifty postage-stamp-size pieces of skin and they're going to spread them on my right leg and my right shoulder and anywhere else that needs it.

I ask Mom if this means I can go home soon, but she says there's still a lot of work to be done and that it will probably be a few more months before I can go home again.

I've been here exactly one month.

Tina says there's a phone call for me and sets up the bear phone. She pushes the button on the bed to make me sit up a little.

I say, "Hello?"

"Hello, is this Brent?" It's a little hard to hear what the guy on the phone is saying.

"Yes. Who's this?"

"It's Magic Johnson. How you doing, buddy?"

"Magic Johnson?"

"Yup, how's it going, man? How you feeling?"

"Okay."

"I want you to work real hard and get better, okay, buddy?"

"Okay."

"If you're gonna play ball with me, you're gonna have to work real hard, okay?"

"Okay."

"All right, I've got to go, but keep working hard and get better soon. I'm sending you a pair of my shoes and a workout suit. What size shoes do you wear?"

"I don't know. Nine?"

"Okay, man. Good luck. See you this summer."

"Okay. Bye."

He hangs up and I look up at Tina. She's laughing. I can't believe it. I really can't believe it. Magic Johnson.

Tina says that I'm eighty-five percent burned and I don't really have enough good skin on my body to cover the burned-up parts. She says they're going to shave my head and take the skin from my scalp because that's good thick fresh skin.

She says they'll cut the skin off my scalp in a big rectangular chunk, about as big as an envelope, and put it on a meshing machine. The machine pokes holes in it and spreads it out. They can change the settings on the machine so it'll spread the skin out a lot or a little. Like for my hands, they spread it only a little, that's why the little holes on my hand are only as big as the dimples on a golf ball, but the ones on my shoulders are as big as raindrops. Then they staple it in place, probably with a big old staple gun like we used in Boy Scouts to build those baskets for Mother's Day.

After a week, it's healed enough to take out the staples and see how well the grafts have taken. That's the only part that hurts really because for the rest I'm asleep. But when they take out the staples, they have to push really hard on the skin and kind of pop the staple out with this tool they have. And there are always one or two that are in so deep, the nurses have to really work at them, bending them back and forth, like pulling bent nails out of a two-by-four. That's the only part that hurts.

Dr. Rubinstein, that short psychologist woman, is back. I like her even less than the first time. She asks, "Brent, was this your first suicide attempt?"

"No." I hate her accent.

"How many times have you tried to commit suicide?"

I say, "I don't know, maybe three or four."

"And what were the circumstances of those attempts?"

"Once was before they caught me for stealing school supplies in algebra. And another time when my parents were about to find out about me failing science."

"And are your parents aware of these suicide attempts?"

"No. I don't think so."

"Do you understand that you must tell them about these attempts?"

"Why?"

"You must tell them because it is imperative that they understand the condition of your mental health in order to prevent you from attempting suicide again."

"But I'm not going to do that again."

"Regardless, you must tell your parents about your previous attempts at suicide."

"Why?" I'm starting to get upset.

"Brent, as I've already explained to you, this is absolutely necessary for your recovery."

"Why?" I'm starting to cry.

"Brent, you must understand this is for your own good. And for your parents' good."

"Why?" I'm really crying now.

"Your parents must understand how critical your mental health was at the time of your suicide attempt."

"But they don't need to know. Will you tell them?"

"You have to tell them. It's very important."

I can't talk anymore. I'm just crying and crying. I want her to go away and leave me alone.

My favorite part of burn care is when they put the morphine into my blood. I know that they're supposed to drip it through the IV, but when they do it that way, I can barely feel it at all, and it just sort of makes me sleepy. Some of the nurses do me a favor and push the shot all at once into my bloodstream. That's the best feeling in the world, the way it comes into my body and warms me up from the inside and all of a sudden my eyes don't work anymore but I don't care and there's pleasure all through my body, nothing but pleasure for miles and miles, and then it starts to fade and they tear into my skin and there's nothing but pain forever.

Tina says they're going to reduce my medication during burn care because they're worried that I'm going to get addicted to the stuff. She says I should start to work on meditation and relaxation techniques to help with pain management.

I hate Dr. Rubinstein. My problems aren't anything to do with her. I don't even have any problems, now that I think about it. I'm happy and I've got friends and family and they understand me and I don't need her to understand me or to ask me questions and I wish she'd just leave me the fuck alone.

I got another tape in the mail. This one is from Alida, this girl that used to go to Kilmer with me. She's in high school now, but we always had this kind of special connection. We had gym together, and instead of playing dodgeball we used to walk around the field and talk about our feelings. Anyway because we had this special psychological connection we called each other Psycho.

The tape is marked *Psycho's Mix*. Mom raises her eyebrows at the title. I'm not going to explain it to her. That's stupid.

She puts it in the tape player and presses play. Alida's voice is the first thing I hear. "Hi, Psycho. This is Alida, or Psycho, or whatever. And I'm just here with a bunch of friends, and we're all really hyper because we've been eating ice cream like all night."

A bunch of girls giggle in the background.

"And we all brought our favorite music over, and we're making you a tape. So, Jenna's here, remember, you helped kidnap her? Say hi, Jenna."

"Hi." That girl sounds nervous.

Alida says, "Louder."

"Hi!"

"That's better. And Katie's here. You don't know her."

"Hi."

"And Cecilia."

"Hi."

"Louder."

"Hi!"

"And my mom's here too. She misses you at the school store."

A lady in the background says, "Hi, Psycho."

"Mom always really liked it when you came and visited her in the school store because even my brother doesn't visit her. Anyway, we're going to put on a bunch of songs and stuff. So enjoy."

The tape clicks and then there's the sound of a needle on an old record, and this piano, and a voice singing that sounds so clear and beautiful, like water.

> When you're weary, feeling small,
> When tears are in your eyes, I will dry them all;
> I'm on your side. When times get rough
> And friends just can't be found,
> Like a bridge over troubled water
> I will lay me down.
> Like a bridge over troubled water
> I will lay me down.

I close my eyes and listen to the music because I feel tired and because the music sounds so good to listen to.

They're bringing in a burned kid to see me. His name's Tony, and he's a few years younger than I am, maybe ten or eleven. His right arm is amputated above the elbow.

He walks into my room. He's got a big limp and he holds his amputated arm really close to his stomach, like he's afraid it'll bump into something. He's got a little sock over the end of his arm. I wonder if that's to keep it warm or what.

He says, "Hi."

I say, "Hi."

He's looking at me, down at my skinny legs all wrapped in bandages and then up at my stomach and chest, but he doesn't look at my face. I think maybe he's just shy.

He says, "I got burned too."

I say, "Yeah."

"I grabbed on to a power line that fell when a tree hit it."

"Yeah?"

"It shocked me and burned up my whole arm and that's why they had to amputate it." He says everything like it happened to someone else.

"Yeah?"

"Yeah." He pulls up his sleeve and shows me the graft sites and how they stretch up to his shoulder. He's black, but the graft sites are a bunch of different colors like tan and off-white. They aren't purple or oozing like mine. They swirl up his arm and stop near his shoulder, almost like they belong there. "It hurt, but then it stopped hurting."

"Hmm." I can tell he wants to hear my story, about what happened to me, but I can't say it because if I told him, then he'd want to know why and I wouldn't know what to say.

He says, "You got burned real bad too."

"Yup."

"But you're getting better?"

"Yeah, I guess so."

"That's good."

We're quiet for a long time.

"Hey, it was really nice to meet you, Tony."

"Yeah. Nice to meet you too."

He walks out and shuts the door behind him with his one arm.

I'm calling Alida because she made me that great tape.

"Hello."

"Hello, Alida?"

"No, this is her mother. Can I ask who's calling?"

"This is Brent."

"Oh my God, Psycho. How are you, sweetie? We've all been thinking about you and praying for you. All right, you just hang in there. You just hang in there, all right, honey?"

"Okay."

Her mom yells, "Alida, it's Psycho!" I can hear some moving around in the background. They're whispering something I can't hear.

"Hi, Psycho." She sounds cheerful. Not too weird.

"Hi."

"Did you get our tape?"

"Yeah, I got it. Thanks. It was great."

"You sound so good."

"I do?"

"Yeah, you sound great."

"Oh."

"So, when can I come visit you?"

"I don't know. Pretty soon."

"That would be so much fun. I could come and sit with you and we could have dinner and everything."

"Yeah, and watch a movie."

"That would be so much fun."

"Yeah."

"Yeah."

"Okay, well, I'll tell my parents and they'll figure out when would be a good time to come, okay?"

"Okay. It's great to talk to you."

"It's great to talk to you too. See you."

"Bye."

Wow, so I'm going to have a visitor. That's weird. At least she didn't sound scared. She sounded like she used to sound. We're going to have dinner and watch a movie, but I don't think we're going to have sex because I don't think I'm up for it.

They want to take me outside the Intensive Care Unit, but I'm not really sure how. First, Barbara with the short red hair slips a hospital gown over my arms and pulls it down over my chest and then wheels in a big blue chair that looks like a La-Z-Boy and puts it next to my bed. I think I know what they're going to do next because it's the same thing they do when they put me on a stretcher to go to the operating room. Barbara, Amy, Janice, and Kerry each grab a corner of my sheet and lift me all at once up and over onto the blue chair. I feel dizzy, so I can't quite say the words that I want to say, which are, Why can't I just lie in bed and watch television? Barbara grabs my IV and wheels me out the door into the hallway. My room is the last one in the Intensive Care Unit, the corner suite, and the whole unit is in front of me now. It's different than I pictured it, smaller and with less fancy equipment everywhere.

There's a picture of a bear with a stethoscope around his neck on the wall to my right, a bunch of patients' rooms on the left, and the nurses' station is up there on the right. Lisa is talking on the phone behind the desk and she smiles and waves as they wheel me by. There are two big double doors in front of us and my dad goes and opens them up so we can get the chair through. There's green carpet everywhere and a bunch of big Easter Bunny cutouts on the walls and a lot of people walking around wearing striped shirts. I can hear some kids playing together somewhere and a baby crying and lots of telephones and conversations all at once, like you hear in a train station. I sort of want to go back to bed.

They wheel me out into an open space and put the brakes on. Barbara adjusts my pillow and asks me if I'm warm enough. I say, "Sure."

Carol leans down to talk to me. "Brent, we've got a very special visitor to the hospital today and she would like to meet you, if that's all right."

"Madonna?"

She laughs, "No, it's not Madonna. It's Danuta Walesa, the first lady of Poland. She's married to the president of Poland, Lech Walesa."

"Who?"

"The first lady of Poland."

"Of Poland?"

"Yes. Of Poland. She's in town while her husband is meeting with President Bush."

"So she's coming to meet me here, in the hallway?"

"Well, she's coming to tour the hospital and you're one of the planned stops."

"Is she bringing Mrs. Bush?"

"No."

"Is she bringing President Bush?"

"No." I can tell she's getting kind of annoyed at my questions, so I stop and try to be nice about it.

"Oh, cool."

We wait for a few minutes in the hallway like that. My mom is talking to Barbara, who looks really nervous and is saying something about how the kid that she adopted is from Poland. Finally a lady comes down the hallway with a bunch of Secret-Service-looking people and a translator and a photographer. The lady looks at me and says something to the translator, who says to me, "Mrs. Walesa is very pleased to meet you."

I'm not sure what to say, and my dad pipes up, "He's very pleased to meet you too."

Mrs. Walesa looks a little confused as to why my dad is answering when she spoke to me, but the translator explains and then Mrs. Walesa takes a doll from her assistant and hands it to me and says something in Polish. "Mrs.

Walesa extends this gift to you and wishes you continued success in your recovery."

I take the doll from her hand as best I can and look at it. It's a little doll made of plastic in a purple wool coat. I don't think the arms even move or anything. I try to look happy and to kind of smile at her and my dad says, "He's very pleased," in a voice that is just a little too loud. I look at him and try to say with my eyes, She's Polish, not deaf, but he doesn't notice.

Barbara is talking to Mrs. Walesa now through the translator, talking about her kid and how she adopted him from Poland. Mrs. Walesa is smiling and shaking her hand. I look at the doll again and at my hand that's holding it. My hands are purple, almost as dark as the doll's wool coat.

Becky, my occupational therapist, comes in every other day and stretches the scars on my arms and hands. Becky says that I'm going to get full range of motion back in my hands. She can tell because I can touch my thumb to each of my fingers. She says my right shoulder is tighter than my left one, but if I work hard and keep stretching, I should get full range of motion or almost full range in a few months.

They call the scars over my arms and shoulders bands. And that's what they feel like. Really thick and strong rubber bands that keep me from moving the way I used to. It's sort of like that except that the rubber bands are made out of my skin.

Dawn, my physical therapist, is coming in the other days

now to stretch my legs. She says I'm getting stronger and soon she'll have me up and walking. I don't know about that.

Alida is on her way over here for dinner and a movie, our big date thing. Tina suggests that they bring in the big blue La-Z-Boy chair and put me in it and then they can wheel me into this other room where there's a TV and a VCR and enough space to sit and have dinner. Dad picks up his newspapers and leaves the room.

Tina brings in the chair, puts it close to my bed, and says, "Do you want to try to get in yourself or do you need some help?"

I say, "Some help."

She gets Calvin, Reggie, and Mary from the nurses' station and they grab the sheet I'm lying on and lift me up and into the chair. I try to think of something funny to say about Superman, but I can't think of anything. Tina wheels me out of my room and the nurses at the nurses' station are smiling at me and I wave like Queen Elizabeth.

We go into a room on the left, the playroom, I guess. There's a bunch of toys and a big yellow mattress and a TV and VCR. My dinner is here too, waiting for me. Chicken and potatoes and a carton of milk.

Alida walks in. She looks exactly the same. Curly brown hair, bangs, and a big smile. She looks happy to see me. I think I was worried that she would be scared or something. Maybe I don't look that bad. My head is shaved from where they took the grafts and I still have a nose tube and I'm covered in Ace bandages, but at least I'm not on the ventilator anymore, and my hands are starting to work better, I don't even have to wear bandages on them anymore. They're still purple but not as bad as they used to be. My dad is cutting up my chicken and says, "Maybe we should get a bottle of wine and some candles?"

I say, "This is the Burn Unit, Dad." He laughs and says he'll leave us alone for a little while and come back to see if we need anything.

Alida leans down to give me a hug, but she barely touches me and then sits down in a chair near mine. She says, "You look great."

I say, "So do you."

She says, "How are you?"

I say, "Great. How are you?"

"Great."

"Yeah?"

"Yeah."

I say, "How's the Thomas Jefferson School for Brainiacs?"

"It's good. I'm taking Russian now."

"Cool."

"Yeah, it's really cool. I never knew how different it was from English," she says.

"Really."

"Yeah, like, there's a bunch of different letters that are completely different from English. It's so cool."

"It sounds cool."

"It is."

"It sounds like it."

"Yeah." She stops talking for a second and looks at me. I hope she doesn't ask me anything.

"Are you hungry?"

"Yeah," I say.

She puts a piece of chicken on a fork and puts it in my mouth. Somebody must have told her that she was going to have to feed me since I can't get my hand up that far yet. It feels like I'm wearing a coat that is way too small.

I chew slowly. I'm not quite used to this whole solid food thing. I swallow.

I say, "My dad got a movie."

"Oh yeah?"

"Yeah, it's a comedy. It's called *Things Change*."

"Oh yeah?"

"Yeah. Do you want to watch it?"

"Sure. Do you want another bite?"

"Yeah, thanks. Have you tried it?"

"No, is it good?"

"Kind of."

Neither one of us says much of anything. Then she says, "Have you heard about Stephen?"

"What?"

"He's dating Megan."

"Oh yeah?"

"Yeah, they started going out a few weeks ago."

"That's good."

"I'm surprised he hasn't told you." So am I, but I don't say that.

My dad pops his head in the door and asks if we need anything. I say I'd like some ice, and I ask if he'd start the movie. He says sure and goes out for the ice.

"Your dad is so nice."

"Yeah."

"So is your mom."

"Yeah."

"Do you want another bite?"

"No thanks."

My dad comes in and hands Alida the ice, pops in the video, and leaves the room. I close my eyes to try and rest a little while the previews are going.

When I wake up, the nurses are lifting me into my bed. I try to ask where Alida went, but I'm too tired to talk.

Dr. Rubinstein is here again with her annoying voice. I really don't like her. I really don't.

She says, "Brent, how are you feeling today?" I know she doesn't care. She's just setting me up for questions that come later.

"Brent, how are you feeling today?" she asks again. I see how it works. If I don't answer, she'll be stuck on the first question and she won't be able to work up into the more complicated ones.

I take the knob that says Dr. Rubinstein and turn it all

the way down and now I can't even hear her voice. Oh, there's that card from Aunt Katie and Uncle Ara with a picture of me and all my cousins making a sand horse on the beach in December. Taran rides horses and that sand horse, which is really pretty good now that I look at it, is an almost exact replica of her horse, whose name is, I can't remember the name, but it's some kind of stallion that she owns and tries to ride every day after school. Dr. Rubinstein's still sitting there, but I don't have to talk to her, I don't even have to look at her. Taran told me all about horses when we were making that, about how if you cut off their balls, you call them geldings. Mares are female. Stallions are male, of course. Colts are young males. I was so happy making that sand horse and I kept thinking, If I can only remember how it feels to be this happy, then when I go back home, I won't try to hurt myself again, but it's so hard to remember something like that in a month like February. February is so long. I look so stupid in those pink shorts. I'm never going to wear those ever again. Everything here smells like plastic. Plastic and raisins. Has anyone else noticed that? Doesn't it smell like plastic and raisins? I wonder what movie I'm going to get to watch later, or maybe Mom will read to me from a book. Hey, Brent, what do you call an overfull mental hospital? What? Chock full o'Nuts. That's funny. That's very funny.

"What are you smiling at, Brent?" says stupid Dr. Rubinstein.

I didn't realize that I was smiling. Oh well, no harm no

foul, as they say. They say that all the time to people who listen. I don't have to listen. In fact, I think I'm one of the better nonlistening types here. What's your favorite color? Oh, favorite color. I would say black, it used to be black, but I'm not sure it's black anymore. Maybe some other color. I like green. I've always liked green. And navy blue. Navy blue is good.

She closes the door behind her.

Today's the day I take a bath. They're going to put me on a stretcher and wheel me into the bathroom and use some sort of contraption to lower me into the not-too-hot water. It'll be so much better than the other way we do burn care. No wiping every wound three times and screaming. And they won't have to change the sheets on my bed while I'm still lying on them. That totally sucks, rolling me onto my side and sliding the new sheet under me. I hate the feeling of my back scraping against the sheets.

Tina comes in with a stretcher and a student nurse named Kerry. They're wearing scrubs and hairnets and masks. Tina's so cute, she can never quite get all her curly black hair into the hairnet. There're always at least a few pieces sticking out somewhere.

"Ready, Brent?"

"I'm ready."

God, I love her voice, so high and a little squeaky. The way she says my name. God. She makes it sound like it has three or four syllables. My dad says she's from North

Carolina. I think he has a little crush on her, like he does on every waitress that serves him food.

They lift me onto the stretcher and wheel me down the hall to the bathroom. I've never been in here before. There's the big bathtub. I didn't know it was going to be all metal. I thought it was going to be like a spa.

They start at my feet, unwrapping the Ace bandages. They can do it fast because there's not usually any skin stuck to that. Next there's a layer of white gauze that they have to be really careful with. Tina uses water to loosen all the scabs and the hard spots and then she pulls the gauze off quick. This is when it starts to hurt.

When they get all the gauze off, they have to pull off the Xeroform, the yellow dressing that goes right over the wound. This is the worst part. When they put it on, it feels so wet and moist and comforting, but when they take it off the next day, it's dried and stuck to the wound. Tina's good at pulling the old Xeroform off. She knows when to let it sit there and pull it slowly, she knows when to add some water, and she knows when to just rip it off and let me scream for a few seconds.

Finally they get me completely unwrapped, and I'm lying naked on the stretcher, with all the old burn dressings and gauze and Ace bandages around me. Tina puts a washcloth over my penis, and she and Kerry slide me onto the canvas stretcher. I have to lift my head up a little as I get on the stretcher and I accidentally see my whole purple body down below me. Skinny and purple.

74

Tina uses the mechanism to lower me into the bathwater. It stings at first, but then it's so warm, and I guess I'm smiling pretty big because Tina and Kerry start to laugh and Kerry says, "I guess that feels good, huh?"

I'm so light, I can move my hands and feet around again just like I was a real person. Tina puts some George Winston on the little boom box she brought with her. I close my eyes. There's nothing quite as beautiful as a piano.

Tina comes over and I open my eyes. She's looking at my legs. "You're looking so much better. Kerry, did you see this new skin? They grew this in a tank in Boston and flew it back here to put on Brent. Have you ever been to Boston, Brent?"

"No."

"Well, part of you has."

I laugh and close my eyes again. They both reach their hands into the water and start pulling off the little scabs, like barnacles, on my legs.

An hour later, Tina says I have to get out and uses the scaffold to raise me up. They put more Xeroform on and more white gauze and then the layer of Ace bandages. They roll me back onto the stretcher and wheel me down the hallway, past the nurses' station, and into my room at the end of the hall. While they get my bed ready, I look at all the cards and pictures on the walls, some from family, some from friends, and a lot from people I don't even know. I don't think I've ever been this happy.

I got a letter today in a manila envelope, the return address just said the White House. Inside was a letter from President Bush, written on this really nice stationery with the White House seal on it, that said how he'd heard about me from some congressman and was sorry to hear about my accident and that he and Mrs. Bush would keep me in their thoughts and prayers. I've never really liked President Bush. I remember when they started dropping the bombs on Baghdad and my family was watching CNN with Bernard Shaw talking on a telephone underneath a table in a hotel room somewhere and how stupid and sad and meaningless it all seemed. It was just so sad. I went upstairs and changed into all black clothing, socks and everything, and I went to school the next day like that. I found a bullet on the bus that day, a big long one. I don't know how it got there, but it was sitting on my seat when I sat down, like it was waiting for me. I picked it up and put it in my pocket and I remember thinking that I wished I had a gun because if I had a gun, I'd put that bullet in it and put it in my mouth and squeeze the trigger and make it all go away.

Here's how my day goes. Every morning, I wake up and watch TV, the morning shows mostly, but if it's a weekend, I watch the cartoons. My mom gets here at about nine and brings me my breakfast. I can get anything I want, but I always get the same thing: cornflakes, milk, a banana, and a carton of orange juice.

After breakfast, Mom usually reads a chapter from a book.

About eleven, Tina comes in and tells me it's time to get ready for burn care and my mom leaves. Tina slips me a Mickey, like they say in all those old gangster movies, and I fall asleep. When I wake up, I'm usually naked. Before she starts cleaning the wounds, she gives me a shot of morphine. I always ask her to push the stuff right into my bloodstream so I can get that rush and whitewash my vision, and sometimes she does. Mostly she just lets it drip through the IV, which is still good, but I like to feel it all at once.

That's when she starts cleaning the wounds. Every hole on my body has to be cleaned three times with a sterile cloth. She starts with my feet. Counting each swipe out loud. One, two, three. And I scream because Tina says I should if it hurts too much. One, two, three. Scream.

She goes all the way up my legs. She does my hands and arms. Then she rolls me onto my stomach and does my back. My back is what hurts the most. She says that's because the burns aren't as deep back there. I wish they were deeper so it wouldn't hurt so much. I don't know why people need backs. I don't think I need mine. I'd be happy if they just removed the whole thing and left me alone.

When she finishes my back, she rolls me back over, changes the sheet underneath me, and puts on the new bandages. Everything is wrapped in three layers. First the Xeroform, that's the wet yellow stuff that helps the skin grow. Then the gauze, a thick layer of white, and then Ace bandages, thousands of feet of Ace bandages wrapped all the way up my legs and up around my chest. I try and think of new jokes every time about the Mummy or the Invisible Man or something. I think Tina's heard them all before, but she laughs anyway.

After burn care, I rest. Sometimes I take a nap. Sometimes my mom comes in and holds my hand while I sleep. She's gotten really good at reading a book with one hand and holding my hand with the other. When I wake up, even if I don't move, she's always looking at me when I open my eyes. Sometimes I try and trick her by opening only one eye, but she always catches it.

We have lunch together, Mom and I. She brings a salad from home and I get chicken soup. If I want a glass of juice or some ice chips, she goes and gets it from the nurses' station.

After lunch, Mom gets the VCR and puts on a movie. Some Hitchcock thing or a goofy comedy, and I usually fall asleep in the middle.

Becky and Dawn come in the afternoon and stretch my arms and legs for me.

When it starts to get dark, Mom goes home to make dinner for Craig. But pretty soon after she leaves, Dad comes from work and has dinner with me in his suit. He still smells the way he used to when he came home from work, like he's been smoking his pipe.

When the good stuff comes on TV, Dad goes home and then they take me in to have my bath and change my bandages again. By the time I get back in bed, Arsenio Hall is already on and I fall asleep while he interviews Wesley Snipes.

My buddies Adam and Jake just sent me a cool present. It's a gigantic ace of spades, about as big as a movie poster, that they must have gotten from a magic shop. They sent a card with it that says, To the one true god, the Ace of Spades. Get better soon, Jake and Adam. That's cool.

Mom and Dad ask me what it means. "It's hard to explain," I say, "it's just a joke." They look confused, but they let it drop.

Dawn, the physical therapist, is here and she says I'm going to stand today. She says, "I'll help, but you're going to stand." It's been almost two months since I walked and I can barely even sit up in a chair. But she seems determined, so I decide not to argue with her. She gets some nurses to come and move me from my bed to the blue chair. I'm starting to get nervous.

Dawn puts the brake on the chair and lowers my legs so my Ace-bandaged feet are hovering above the ground. I've never really looked at the floors in this place. They're a weird olive color and they're shiny. Dawn squats in front of me and tells me to scoot forward in the chair so I can get my feet on the ground.

I say, "How do I do that?" I'm not being difficult. I really don't know how to.

She says, "Lean your weight to the left and push your

right hip forward." I do what she says and it kind of works. My right leg is a little closer to the floor. "Now do the same with your left leg." I try, but my body is stiffer on that side or something.

I say, "I'm trying, but it's hard," and my voice sounds really whiny and babyish, even to me.

I think she can tell that if she yells at me, I might start to cry, so she says quietly, "Okay, just do your best and I'll help. Lift your arms up as high as you can." I do it, but the bands are so tight it's hard to lift them very high. She leans forward and slips her arms under mine and puts her hands on my hip bones.

I say, "Be careful, I've got some open spots back there."

She says, "I know," and sounds kind of annoyed when she says it.

She's really strong, stronger than she looks, and she picks me up and slides me forward in one quick movement to the edge of the chair so that my feet are really on the floor. "How does that feel?"

"Cold." I look down. My toes are uncovered, and for some reason the toenail on my big right toe is completely black. Also, I can only feel the floor with my left foot.

"Are you ready?"

"No."

She waits about ten seconds and asks me again. "Are you ready?"

"Okay," I say, but my voice is shaking.

"I'll count to three and then we'll stand up together.

One, two, three." She pulls me up by the hips and I put my weight on my feet and I'm standing. She's still holding on to me, keeping me from falling over, but I'm actually standing.

The floor is so much farther away than I remember it.

"Look at me. Don't look at the floor. Look at me."

It reminds me of the time my family and I went to the top of the World Trade Center and I looked down and got so dizzy.

"Take a step toward me."

I remember this. I remember how this is done. It's done by putting the weight on one foot and moving the other foot forward. It's basic. Simple to do. With one foot on the ground at all times and the other one moving very gently across the floor to match the first one.

"You're doing great. Nice and easy."

I remember this very clearly. Walking. I remember doing this my whole life. Although it might not look like it.

"Okay, let's turn around and go back to the chair now."

Turning, okay, turning is done by placing the right foot at an angle and then moving the left so that it's at the same angle as the right and then moving the right again at an angle and again following with the left. "The chair's just a few steps away. Can you make it?"

"Yes." I can make it, from here to there, to the chair, which is actually quite a bit farther than it looks. The blueness of it, that's probably what makes it look so far away, that and the fact that everything tends to be farther than it first appears.

"You made it. Okay, I'll help you sit down."

She puts her arms around my waist and lowers me into the chair, slowly. I've never really noticed how gentle she is when she wants to be.

Mom and Dad are shocked when they walk into my room and see me sitting in the chair already. I smile and say, "Good morning, Mr. and Mrs. Runyon. Welcome to my lair," in my best Dracula impression. I know that it wasn't very funny, but they laugh enough to make me feel good about myself. Mom comes over and gives me a kiss on top of my head and I bend my elbow so I can kind of get my arm around her. She hugs me back, gently, like she's afraid I'm going to break. Her eyes are wet when she pulls away and she looks like she's going to cry.

I say, "Mom, you don't have to cry." I probably sound a little more annoyed than I mean to, but she's already crying and trying to stop herself at the same time.

Dad leans down for a hug, but he doesn't cry. He just looks happy.

I say, "Mom, you really don't have to cry. It's okay."

"I know. I know. I'm just crying a little bit out of happiness." The last word cracks and she can barely get the last syllable out. She's smiling with her lips turned down and her eyes tipped up to keep the tears from rolling out.

I say, "You don't look happy." My voice did that thing again where it sounded more annoyed than I really am.

"I am. I am happy. It's just that . . ."

"What?" She's really starting to annoy me now. She should be happy.

"I just didn't know if I was going to be able to hug you again." And the tears all pour out in a stream down her cheeks. My dad goes over and puts his hand on the back of her neck and whispers something in her ear. She pulls an old tissue out of her purse and starts wiping away the tears and laughing at herself. "I'm sorry. I'm okay. I feel better."

"Hey, Mom"—I decide to cheer her up—"guess who walked today?"

"What?"

"I walked today. With Dawn."

They both look at me like they've never seen me before and then like they've known me all my life. And now they're both smiling and crying, and I've never seen them look so proud of me.

They've got me walking every day now. Today Mom and Dad are both here to watch me. I walk with Dad and Dawn out into the hallway, one on each side so they can catch me if I fall. I thought for sure there'd be some nurses in the hallway, but nobody is here, so I yell for them to come out and see me. Janice, Mary, Amy, and Calvin all come. They clap and make a big deal out of it and Amy gets the Polaroid camera and takes a picture. They hand it to me, and when I'm back in bed, I look at it, and I can't believe how skinny I look, with nothing but bones in my arms.

It's early, but I'm out of bed and sitting in the blue chair, drinking a second carton of milk and waiting for Mom. She's bringing her brother, Tom, because he and his family are in town for a few days.

After a few minutes my stomach starts rumbling from all the milk I drank. It sounds like someone is opening an ancient tomb. God, that's loud. Mom and Uncle Tom walk in just as I let out an enormous fart. Mom smiles, pretends not to notice, and gives me a kiss on the forehead. Tom's not sure whether to kiss me or shake my hand, so he leans over and pats me gently on the forehead. It's probably the only part of my body that looks normal.

They pull up some chairs and start talking about everyone in the family and how they all wish me well and how they're so sad they can't be here all the time.

I let out another fart that starts out high and tight and goes lower and lower until there's no sound at all, just air.

I say, "Excuse me."

Mom and Tom keep talking. Tom tells some stories about his kids, Jared, Nathan, and Amara. I guess the boys are both playing soccer and Amara is thinking about becoming a ballerina like her mom. Tom says Gayle and Amara might come see me tomorrow, on Easter. That'll be nice. The boys are too busy roughhousing.

Tom starts telling the story about how when he was in college, he got drunk and stole a plate from a fancy restaurant. Just as he gets to the punch line where he's walking out of the restaurant with the plate under his shirt and the maître d' comes up and puts his hand on Tom's shoulder and says, "Excuse me, sir, you forgot your wallet," I let out another huge fart that goes on for at least fifteen seconds.

It goes on so long that Tom starts talking again before it's over. "I'm sorry," I say. This goes on for another ten minutes, him talking, me farting, until I can't take it anymore and ask my mom to have the nurses put me back in bed.

Aunt Gayle is coming today, and she's bringing my cousin Amara, who is maybe four or something. I know Amara loves pink, so I hope she likes my purple bandages that Barbara dyed for me for Easter. God, what if she asks to unwrap them?

Barbara tells me that my aunt and cousin are outside. While they're lifting me out of bed and into the blue chair, I start my little bit about why there's no word in English for female cousin, like cousina, or cousinette, or something.

Barbara is smiling at me. She thinks I'm clever.

"Hi, Gayle," I say, cheerful as can be, and then, "Hi, Amara." I make my voice go up and down, how some people talk to small animals. Gayle leans over and gives me a kiss on the forehead. My mom must have told her to do that. She says, "You look great, Brent." She's from Maryland, so she's got kind of a weird accent.

"Thanks," I say.

"You look really great."

"Thanks."

"Moving around and everything. That's so great."

I'm trying to make eye contact with Amara, who's hiding behind her mom's very long legs.

"Hi, Amara," I say again. This time making my voice sound even funnier.

"She's shy," says Gayle.

"Oh." I don't remember her being shy. I try again.

"Hey, Amara."

She peeks out from behind her mom's knees but doesn't say anything.

"Hey, Amara, how do you like my bandages? We made them purple for Easter. Do you like purple? I know you like pink."

She's still hiding.

"Do you like purple, Amara?"

No response.

"Amara, do you like purple?"

Gayle gets my attention with her eyes and I get the feeling she's trying to distract me. "Brent, you look really great. Really great." Amara mumbles something from behind her mom's legs and Gayle says, "Amara, what do you think of Brent's bandages?"

Amara's still whispering and Gayle leans down to talk to her. "Okay, we can go, but say good-bye to your cousin." Amara looks up and says, "Bye."

Gayle says, "I'm sorry, we're just feeling a little shy. I guess we should go."

"Okay, bye, Amara, thanks for coming. Bye, Gayle, thanks for coming."

"Okay, get well soon, Brent. We're all pulling for you."

They walk down the hallway and around the corner, and Barbara comes out and wheels me back to my room. "How did that go?" she says.

"Fine."

I didn't realize I was such a monster. I don't know why, but I didn't.

Mom's birthday is tomorrow, April 8, and Dad and I are going to have a surprise party for her. We'll decorate the playroom with streamers, and when she comes in the afternoon, we'll have a big party with presents and everything. Dad's going to work on getting some paint and paper to make a sign.

I have these new bandages for my hands. They're called Jobst garments, which are very tight elastic gloves made especially to fit me. They came in a few days ago to measure me for them, but I didn't know what they were doing. They're supposed to keep the scars from getting too thick and also to keep my circulation flowing. Barbara helps me put them on, but they're very tight and it's hard work to get them over my fingers. And now that they're on, I just want to figure out a way to take them off. I think it'll be hard to paint in them.

Dad comes in with the party supplies and starts putting up a canvas on the wall so I can paint it for Mom's party. They let me take off the stupid Jobst garments, and I paint a blue balloon and a red balloon, a yellow one and a green one. Then I dip my brush in the black and paint a big black balloon above the other ones. I paint Happy Birthday in red at the top and To You right below in blue, and I try to make the letter O look like it's a balloon too. And then I paint Love, Brent G. at the very bottom in yellow. I think it's artistic to leave off your last name so nobody really knows who you are. Everybody says it looks great and Carol, the nice social worker, says, "I didn't know you were so talented."

Dad tapes some blue ribbon to the bottom of my balloons so it looks like the strings to the balloons are coming out of the picture. I say, "Looks good, DF."

He says, "DF?"

"Designated Father."

I can tell he doesn't quite know what to make of that, that I called him Designated Father instead of Dad or whatever. It's just something I came up with on the spur of the moment. I hope he doesn't think it means I'm angry at him. That is so stupid. I hope he doesn't tell the stupid psychologist that I called him that and then she'll want to talk to me all about it. God, I hope that doesn't happen.

Mom's coming down the hall. I can hear her footsteps and her talking to the nurses at the nurses' station. They're telling her we're in the playroom, and here she comes. "Surprise!" She actually looks surprised, maybe even shocked. Then she looks so happy.

She's going to hug me. I hope she doesn't start to cry.

"Did you make this sign?"

"Yup. Me. And Dad helped."

"Thank you so much, honey, this is such a wonderful surprise." Dad brings out the cake and the presents and everything and everybody is having such a good time. Mom loves all her presents. Dad didn't tell me what they were going to be.

All the nurses come in and get some cake and ice cream, and Carol gets out the Polaroid and takes a bunch of pictures of Mom and Dad and me. Mom rests her hand on top of mine while Carol's taking the picture and I want to pull my hand away because I'm afraid that it's going to get hurt, but I don't.

Mom tells me over and over again how much she loves the poster and all the presents and everything and how much she loves me.

They're going to cover the holes on my back and butt with skin from my hips and stomach. The good thing about surgery is that it means I don't have to have a burn care for that day. The bad thing is that they're going to have to keep me on my stomach for ten days afterward so that I don't screw up the new skin by lying on it. They say this will be the last big surgery. I might have to have a few more, but they won't be that big of a deal.

Becky's here for my daily stretching. She's got such a great sense of humor and such a nice face. And best of all when she comes to stretch me, she doesn't wear gloves. So it feels like I'm a real person and she's a real person and we're just hanging out.

They haven't let me have anything to eat since midnight and I'm starving. I tried to get Lisa to get me some ice chips, but she refused. Why can't I get a break in this place? The guys in the blue scrubs are here to wheel me down to the OR. I ask them if they know the way, just to be funny, and they say, "Yes, we know the way." And I ask them if they're sure, and they say, yes, they're sure. I think they know I'm joking.

I'm in the OR waiting room. They put a hairnet on me and tell me it'll just be a minute. I think they've already started giving me something because I'm feeling light-headed and tired, but not really good like from the drugs they sometimes give me.

The one thing I have to remember is not to wake up during the surgery. That's all I have to do. If I wake up, I'll be screwed. I'll see all the skin all cut up and stretched and stapled all over me. So, I've got to remember not to wake up this time, not that I've ever woken up before in the middle of a surgery, but really, wouldn't that just be the worst?

They're taking me into the OR, with all the lights and the cold air. So much cold air. Maybe they'll put one of those warm blankets over me. A nurse is putting a warm blanket on me. She's wearing a hairnet, a mask, and glasses and I can barely see her eyes. They're putting the mask over my face and telling me to breathe. I've got to remember to stay awake, no, stay asleep, I have to stay asleep, not awake. They're telling me to breathe deeply. I can do that. I can breathe deeply. It's hard to see with these eyes how they are, they get so heavy and blurry and hard to see with when they make the breathing of the oxygen with the mask, and the breathing and the mask, and the breathing.

I'm waking up, this is bad. I'm supposed to be asleep, maybe if I close my eyes, I can stay asleep while they finish the surgery. Okay, just go back to sleep.

I'm lying on my stomach and I've got the tubes in my mouth, does that mean they're done with the surgery or am I waking up too early again? I'm probably waking up too early. I should go back to sleep.

Mom and Dad are looking at me, smiling, and I'm trying to look at them, but I'm on my stomach, like they said I would be, and I can barely open my eye. The tubes are gone and I'm breathing like I should be, but I just feel so sick all over. I try to tell Mom and Dad that I feel bad, but my throat is so sore and my voice is so hoarse from the tubes they put down there that I can only get out the words, "I feel bad." They say it's the anesthesia wearing off and I'll feel better in a couple of hours. They tell me to go back to sleep.

I close my eye and listen to the sounds around me. The steady beeping is my heart rate, the constant humming is the IV pushing the meds into my bloodstream. There are feet in the hallway outside, tennis shoes by the way they squeak on the linoleum, a sound like a grocery cart, that must be a gurney with a patient going by, so I'm not back in the Burn Unit yet, I'm still downstairs in Recovery. Oh yeah, and I saw a cloth curtain when I opened my eye, so I am in Recovery. I wonder if I should ask Mom to read to me but I don't think I'd be able to pay attention.

I can see a red light and a black light, or no light at all. The red is on my right side and the blackness is on my left and the red light means that my eye is closed and I should try to open it to see what I can see, but it just seems like so much work to open my eye.

I can hear some whispering. That's Dad's voice, what's he whispering? He's got his concerned voice on. Mom says something, but I can't hear any of the words. She's being positive, she's got her positive voice on. I keep my eye closed.

When I was really little, I used to have this brown wallpaper in my room and my bed was pushed right up against the wall and when I was going to sleep I'd stare at the brown wallpaper instead of closing my eyes. Sometimes I'd fall asleep and start dreaming and I'd still see the dark brown wallpaper in my mind, like I was still awake with my eyes open. And sometimes I'd see these olive green silhouettes against the brown background. There was a big one and a medium-sized one and a small one. The big one had a voice like my dad's, deep and gruff, and the medium-sized one had a voice like my mom's, smoother but very serious, and they always started out calm and in hushed voices, but as the dream went on, they got louder and louder and angrier and angrier. There were never any words, just the sounds of their voices. Sometimes the little one would try to interrupt and say something, but then the two bigger ones would just start talking at the same time and the combination of the low gruff voice and the higher serious one would just be too scary and I'd wake up and I'd be staring at the same brown wall I'd been dreaming about, and the voices would still be there.

They must know that I'm awake because they're talking to me, asking if I need anything, if I want to listen to a tape, or watch a movie, or listen to a book. I don't want to do any of that, I just want to go back to sleep.

I'm hungry. I open my eye and see Mom sitting in the chair, reading. She looks up as soon as I do and asks me if I want anything. I say, "Ice."

She scoops a little bit onto a plastic spoon and angles it into my mouth. My mouth was so dry. I love the taste of ice.

Maybe when I get older, I can work in an ice factory, pulling ice out of the lake in the winter and storing it in little log cabins filled with sawdust.

I'm listening to a comedy tape that my mom got me by Billy Crystal and it's got that funny "I hate when that happens" bit. The one where these two guys trade stories about when they hit their tongues with ball-peen hammers over and over again, and then one says, "That really smarts." And the other one says, "I hate when that happens." And the first one says, "I know what you mean."

Stephen and I should do that bit together. We could be funny at that.

Mom's not coming today because she's going to North Carolina with Craig to look at colleges. I'm glad I'm not going with them. I used to hate that. We'd drive for about five hours and then get out and play Nerf football in the quad of some school for forty-five minutes and then get back in the car and go home. I don't even know why they made me go.

There are two kinds of people in this world. People that have to lie on their stomachs for ten days straight and people that don't. And the lucky bastards that don't have to lie on their stomachs for ten motherfucking days are the ones that get to skate through life like they have their own personal Zamboni smoothing the way for them.

People here like to talk to me about Pain Management. They ask me to rate my pain on a scale of one to ten. One being the least painful and ten being the most. I don't think they have a number for some of the pain I'm going through. I don't think they even have a number.

Then they like to tell me if I relax and breathe deeply, then I won't be in as much pain. That's complete bullshit. I'd like to see them breathe deeply and take this pain without drugs. I'm sick of pain.

Anxious, there's a word I hear a lot. They say I get anxious before burn care and anxious before I have my appointments with Dr. Rubinstein. But I don't think they understand the meaning of the word anxious. People get anxious in awkward group situations or before they go to birthday parties. Before burn therapy, I don't get anxious, I get freaked out. Before my meetings with Dr. Rubinstein, I don't get anxious, I get angry because she's going to ask me stupid questions and I don't want to answer any stupid questions.

Dr. Bitchenstein is here to ask me about everything that's ever happened and everything that ever will happen and to try to make me feel worse even though it's not really fucking possible to make me feel worse at this point, unless you were to do something terrible like put me facedown on a bed for ten days and ask me a bunch of questions about things that happened months ago that I don't even remember.

"Brent?" she says in her annoying accented Dr. Ruth voice. "Are you awake?"

"Yes," I say without unclenching my teeth.

"How are you feeling?" How am I feeling. How am I feeling? I'm feeling pretty bad, you bitch.

"Bad," I say.

"I understand," she says, but it's painfully fucking obvious that she understands about as much as I understand Austrian, which is none at all.

"Do you want to talk about it?"

"Uh-uh." This time I don't even open my mouth.

"Are you in a lot of pain?"

"Uh-huh."

"You're not feeling very verbal today. That's all right, I'll leave you alone, but you're going to have to talk to me at some point, Brent."

That's where you're wrong. I don't have to say another word to you if I don't want to. I don't even have to open my mouth.

Dad's here giving me ice chips and not saying much. Every once in a while he tells me about someone I know, or someone he knows, that's doing something great.

He says, "Craiger seems like he's leaning toward George Mason. That'd be good, huh, bud? Real close to home."

"Is he going to live at home?"

"No, he's going to live in the dorms."

"Is he still going out with Valerie?"

"Yup. They're going to the prom in a week."

"Is she nice?"

"She's pretty nice."

"Are they going to get married?"

He laughs, but I wasn't really joking. I guess that's a no. He says, "I brought your mail. Do you want to see it?"

"Sure."

"Here's something from Sue, Roger, and Kellie. They say, 'Get well soon,' and they all signed it. And there's a picture of Kellie here. Do you want to see?"

"Sure." He holds it up. It's a school picture. She's in eighth grade like me, like I was, and she looks happy with a big smile showing both rows of teeth, short blond hair, a blue shirt, and hoop earrings. Her parents were friends with my parents before we were even born, so we kind of grew up together, but we never really got along. She was too stiff and I was too wild. But she doesn't look so bad in that picture. I wonder if I should figure out a way to make her fall in love with me. I mean, she has known me her whole life, so it shouldn't be that hard for her to love me now and maybe she won't care what I look like. Something to think about.

Dad tapes Kellie's picture on the wall. Then he picks up a big manila envelope that's stuffed full. It's from Patty Perry and her fourth-grade class. He reads the note, "'An ancient story from Japan says that a wish is granted for every one hundred origami cranes folded. So here are a hundred origami cranes folded by Mrs. Perry's fourth-grade class. We wish that you'll get better soon.' And then they all signed the note at the bottom." Dad pulls out a string with a crane tied to it and another and another. He keeps pulling them out of the envelope until the string stretches all around the room. He hangs the string over some thumbtacks in the wall, over the quilt my friends at school made with the messages written in bubble paint, over the Aerosmith poster and the pictures of Nanny and Grandpa and my cousins, over the letters from my French class and the Chicago Bulls pennant, over the wall of get well soon letters from God knows who and the Christmas picture of the Humberts, over the Cindy Crawford poster and the signed Magic Johnson T-shirt. The string stops right above the IV that's pumping something into my veins. Dad looks around and says, "You're going to need a bigger room."

When I was in fourth grade, I used to show off and bang my head into different things, like walls and banisters and stuff, just to prove I could take it. It didn't matter to me, the pain always went away eventually. But sometimes, during burn care, the pain feels like it goes on forever—like it's the ocean and I'm crossing it in a rowboat.

So the good part is I don't have to have another major surgery. That's good. The bad part is that I have to lie on my stomach for another four days. Even Becky and Dawn have stopped coming to visit with me, I guess because they can't do any range of motion exercises while I'm on my stomach.

Sometimes Tina still comes in and talks to me about stuff and makes me laugh a little, but she seems busier now. Barbara comes in too, feeds me ice chips and talks to me for a little while, and then goes to see to another patient.

Cheryl, a night nurse who only comes on the weekends, sits with me and brings the TV in close so I can watch my programs and the videos my parents bring me. She has more time because she's only here on the weekend. Once she asked me if I remembered what it was like to be paralyzed, and I asked her what she meant, and she said that when I was first in the hospital, they gave me drugs during burn care that paralyzed me. I told her I didn't have any memory of that. She said I should be grateful that I didn't remember such terrible things, but I don't want to forget anything. I don't care if they are terrible memories. They're mine.

Mom's back from her trip to North Carolina with Craig, and she comes to see me the first chance she gets. She's really happy to see me and she gives me a kiss on my forehead and asks me if I need anything. I say, "Ice." And she goes immediately and gets a cup of ice chips and brings it right back. She has a spoon too and starts giving me little bites while she tells me about her trip and how much she missed me and how she doesn't think Craig thought much of the school but how he started laughing at one point about something I said once when we were all driving together. We passed a big old brick mental hospital on the side of the road with a huge fence made of chicken and razor wire, and I said, "Why do they need a fence? Why can't they just have a sign that says This Is an Invisible Wall."

I'm glad Craig thought that was funny.

I think I hear someone in my room. I can't turn around, so I ask, "Is somebody there?" but nobody says anything.

I keep hearing things, though, like footsteps and the creaking door.

"Who is it?" I ask again, and nobody says anything, again. But there is definitely somebody doing something back there. It's starting to freak me out.

I say again, "Who is it?" I probably sound a little scared. And this time Calvin's voice says, "It's me, Brent."

"Calvin? What are you doing?"

"I was tickling your foot."

"You were? I didn't feel anything."

"Can you feel this?"

"Feel what?"

"This."

"Oh, I think I felt something that time."

"I was pinching you that time."

"You were? I thought I felt something."

"It's just a little nerve damage. Nothing to worry about. It'll probably come back."

The doctors are all here to look at the graft sites and the new skin. Tina has a pair of scissors and she's cutting through the Ace bandages that are wrapped around my chest and legs. I can feel the metal through the bandages working back and forth down my legs. I always worry that she'll cut me with them, but she never has.

She unwraps the layer of gauze slowly, in case I have any sticking, but the grafts haven't leaked very much. I guess that's a good sign, and the gauze comes all the way off. The Xeroform is still a little wet because they just put it on a few hours ago. I can feel the moisture on the backs of my knees where the fire didn't get and the nerves are still working.

The doctors are just talking to each other, not to me. I'm getting pretty cold lying here naked like this.

Tina leans down and whispers, "It's looking really good, Brent, the doctors are very pleased." I'm glad she's here. "Do you want to ask the doctors any questions?"

I think for a second. I can hear them fiddling with their pens and clipboards. Doctors can be so impatient sometimes. "How much longer do I have to lie on my stomach?"

One of them answers, "Oh, let's give it another day to heal, and I'll write in the orders that the patient can be turned for half the day tomorrow, and we'll see where we go from there."

I can hear them start to shuffle through the door, but I have another question. "And when can I walk again?"

"Hmm. I'd like to give the sites a few more days without too much stress, so I'll postpone that decision until next week."

They all leave, but Tina stays behind and says, "That's so great. Only one more day on your stomach." Thank God.

Lisa, my favorite night nurse, is here to check on me. She says, "You should be asleep."

"I can't sleep."

"How come?"

"Too nervous."

"About what?"

"They're going to turn me over tomorrow."

"Why does that make you nervous?"

"I don't know. Just seems like a big deal."

"It is."

"Yeah, but I'm getting kind of comfortable on my stomach. How come I can't just stay on my stomach?"

"I thought you hated being on your stomach."

"I do."

"So what's the problem?"

"I don't know. . . . I'm just nervous."

"I can check your chart and see if the docs wrote any scrips for sleeping meds. Do you want me to do that?"

"Yeah. Could you?"

"All right, I'll be back in a second."

The TV is on, but the sound is off, and the blue lights keep flashing, making weird shadows on the walls with the IVs.

She's back. "Okay, there's no sleeping pills in your chart, but I can give you a Benadryl, that'll put you to sleep. How's that sound?"

"Sounds good."

"Can you sit up to take this pill?"

"I'll try." I arch my back a little, not too much, I don't want to pop my grafts, and take the pill with a swallow of water from a Dixie cup. "Thanks, Lisa."

"Good night, Brent. Sleep well."

When I wake up, it's already daylight. I can hear things

going on outside my door, even though the door is closed. I wonder who the other people on the unit are. I know there's a little kid somewhere because I can hear him screaming. And there's Jimmy, he's the only other teenager around, but he's not in the intensive care section, he's out in the regular unit. Sometimes the nurses tell me about kids who have left the unit, like this one kid who tried to jump on a train while it was moving and got his leg caught in the wheels. They really liked him. He's supposed to come visit sometime, but I haven't seen him yet.

Tina comes in, smiling. She says, "Today's the big day, huh?"

"Yeah."

"Are you ready?"

"Yeah. Who's going to help us?"

"I'll go see who's around." She comes back with Reggie and Janice and starts directing them. "Okay, we're going to turn him over. We'll move him toward the edge of the bed and then roll him slowly over onto his back." They pull the sheet out from under the mattress and they each take a corner. Reggie takes both the corners near my feet and says, "You ready, big man?"

I say, "Yeah."

Tina counts, "One, two, three." And they lift me up in one quick motion and slide me across the bed to the edge where the bars come up and put me down carefully.

"That was fun."

"Ready for the roll, Big Brent?"

"Okay."

Reggie and Tina put their hands flat under my shoulder and hip bone and start lifting me onto my side. I try to help by shifting my weight, but I'm not sure if it does anything. I can feel Janice's hand on the edge of my hip keeping me up but careful not to touch any of the graft sites. All of a sudden, I'm worried about the IV in my arm, and I try to say something, but I can't. I'm going over. So slowly. This is how the *Titanic* must have felt. Maybe I should say that. How would I phrase it? I feel like the *Titanic*. No. I'm just like the *Titanic*. No. Anyway, I'm over.

I forgot what it was like to be on my back. Looking up at the ceiling. Tina brings me a pillow and puts it under my head. When she tilts up my head, I can see part of my chest and it's still got the heart monitors stuck to it. Tina sees them too and says, "What are these still doing here?" and pulls them off quick. "There we go. That's better. It's nice to see your face smiling back at me."

Okay. Here I am, lying on my back again. Mom and Dad will be happy.

I can eat real food again. Dad's filling out my menu for tonight, even though I still have that big nose tube in my face. I'm having some fresh fruit, probably a banana, a container of vanilla pudding, and a carton of two percent milk.

Dad goes out of the room for a minute so Tina can take the catheter out of my penis. It feels sort of weird having a beautiful woman stare at my penis and pull a long plastic tube out of it.

Becky pushes my left arm straight up, like she's trying to hail a taxicab for me, then lets it rest and tells me about her boyfriend, Jeff, who is studying to be an environmental lawyer, whatever that means. I missed Becky when I was on my stomach. She's so strong. She's got a little brother who's a few years older than me and she tells me lots of stories about how she tries to beat him up but that he's getting so big he can overpower her now. I find that hard to believe.

I remember, before I was in the hospital, this movie came out in the theaters called *Pump Up the Volume*, with Christian Slater, about this kid who starts a pirate radio station in his basement, and all the other kids try and figure out who he is. That sounds so awesome. I'll tell my mom to get it from the video store.

Dad's leaving for the afternoon to go to work and Mom is coming in until closing time. In the mornings, she's started tutoring kids that need help with schoolwork. She says she really likes it. She's pretty much quit her job teaching at the elementary school so she can come visit me as much as she wants.

Dad works at George Washington University as an administrator. He takes care of the cafeteria and the bookstore and all of the things that kids buy when they're at college.

He's got all these connections because he deals with Coke and Pepsi and all those people that have a lot of money. I wish we had a lot of money. Then Mom and Dad wouldn't seem so worried all the time.

Mom goes down to the cafeteria to get some food and now I've got this sudden pressing feeling in my belly. Oh wait, I know what this is. I have to pee. I need a nurse. I press the red button.

Okay, here's somebody. Who is this, I've never seen her before. She says, "Can I get you something?"

I'm embarrassed, but I really have to go. I say, "Um. Yeah."

"What?"

"I kind of have to go to the bathroom."

"Okay, number one or number two?"

"Which is number one? Pee?"

"Yes." I can hear in her voice she's a little annoyed.

"Number one, then."

"All right."

She gets a urinal from behind my bed somewhere and hands it to me. It looks like a milk bottle with a big hole in the top.

I look at her and she says, "What?"

"Uh, what do I do with it?"

"You pee into it."

"I know, but I never did it by myself before."

"Okay, do you need a little help?"

"Yes, please."

She pulls down the sheet and there's my penis sitting there between the bandages on my legs. They shaved down there when they took some skin for a graft, so it looks kind of weird.

She puts the urinal between my legs and looks at me. "I'll hold the urinal, you hold your penis."

My right arm is still really stiff, but I can reach down to my penis. I point it where I think the urinal should be. "Is that right?"

"Yes, that's fine. Go ahead."

I just realized, I don't think I can go like this, lying on my back with some strange woman standing over me. I wait. I try to think about waterfalls, and Moses, and the parting of the Red Sea. Nothing's happening.

"Do you still have to go?" she says, sounding more annoyed than ever.

"Yeah."

"Do you want me to turn on a faucet or something?"

"What would that do?"

"I don't know, help you somehow?"

"Okay."

She goes to the sink and turns on both faucets and I try to concentrate on the sound, and it is helping. It's working. Thank God.

Sometimes I think about Megan and about how I liked her so much and then how Stephen liked her so much. And how she's going out with him now, and I hope they're both happy. But sometimes I think about how much I liked her and how much she liked me and how, at the end of last year, she asked me to write in her yearbook and I only wrote three words, Brent. Lumpy. Later. Lumpy is what she called me when I was wearing the dress and the fake boobs in the talent show. And how she was so upset by that because she liked me and she wanted more than three words for her yearbook.

I thought about her all last summer. I couldn't stop thinking about her. But I never asked her out and I never kissed her or felt her up. She's got the nicest boobs, and now Stephen gets to do anything he wants with her, and I sit in here and think about what he's doing to her.

Calvin's here to take me into the bath. But I'm watching Cops, and it's a really good episode. There's this guy who beat up his wife, and the cops are there and the woman is in the other room, crying. The guy is wearing red sweat-pants and no shirt and he's really upset with the cops for coming into his house and messing with him.

Calvin says, "Brent, time to take your bath."

"I know, just let me finish watching this."

The cops are trying to calm him down, but the guy is just getting angrier and angrier. They decide they're going to arrest the guy because there's also a warrant out for him or something, and he starts to put up a fight and tries to climb out the bathroom window, which is about as big as a doggie door, and the cops pull him back in and arrest him.

Calvin looks like he's getting pissed. I forgot he was still here. He says, "Okay, Brent. Time for your bath now."

"Can I just finish watching this episode?" I want to see the next segment. I think there's going to be a gunfight.

"No. You have to take your bath and I have to do my paperwork."

I say, "Well, go do your paperwork now and then come back to take me to my bath. I'll be ready then."

He says, "No. You've got to take your bath now. This is nonnegotiable."

I say, "I don't want to take my bath now."

"You have to."

"No, I don't."

"Yes, you do."

"I'm not going to."

"Yes, you will."

"But I want to watch *Cops*."

"Take your bath, then you can watch as much TV as you want. You can stay up all night watching TV."

I can see Calvin's getting really pissed off and I don't want to make him pissed off. So I say, "Fine. I'll take my bath."

He brings in the gurney and a couple of other nurses and they lift me onto it, being careful about my grafts.

Calvin takes me to the bathroom, gets me all set up, and starts lowering me into the water. As soon as my skin hits the water, I scream, "It stings. It stings so much." And Calvin stops the winch.

110

He says, "Where does it sting?"

"On the new grafts and on my legs. It stings so much. Jesus Christ. Goddamn it, it stings."

"Are you all right?"

"No. I can't go in there—it hurts too much."

"Are you sure?"

"Yes, I'm sure. It hurts too much. Don't do it. Don't make me do it."

"Okay, I'm going to give you a minute to get yourself together and then we'll put you in the bath and get it over with."

"But, Calvin, please, I don't have to take a bath today. Come on, you know I don't have to take a bath today. We could tell them I took a bath and we could get my hair wet and nobody would know the difference."

"Brent . . ."

"Calvin, come on, listen to me, nobody needs to know. Come on, Calvin. Please?"

"Brent, we have to do this. Now take a deep breath and relax. I'm going to lower you into the water." He presses the button and lowers me a little farther into the water.

"Jesus Christ, it hurts it hurts it hurts. Fuck. Fuck. Fuck. This hurts too much. Fucking Jesus Christ this fucking hurts. Oh, fuck God, this fucking hurts."

He lowers me all the way in and the water covers my chest. Everywhere it touches, I sting. It never felt this way before. My nerves must be coming back to life. It's like the bath is filled with salt water.

Finally the sting starts to go away, and I say, "I'm sorry, Calvin. I'm sorry. I didn't mean to swear like that. I didn't mean to yell at you."

He says, "I understand, buddy."

I look up at the ceiling and think, If there is a God, I hope he understands too.

Mom brings in pictures of us at our family reunion last summer. We're all wearing our pink shirts with Runyon Family Reunion printed on them. Why did they have to pick pink? There's me and all my cousins sitting on the deck. Why do I look so sad in all those pictures? I didn't have anything to be sad about. But in every picture I look like I'm about to cry.

I remember, we stayed at a little cottage right on Lake Michigan, and we all stayed up and watched a thunderstorm come across the water. We could see the lightning way in the distance, like flashbulbs in a stadium, and then it got closer and we started to hear the thunder so far away and out of sync with the lightning. And then they just kept getting closer and closer together until the lightning was so bright and the thunder was so loud that no one could really believe it. I wanted to go outside and stand in the rain and have the light and the noise all around me, but my parents wouldn't let me.

The next morning, I woke up early and walked on the beach, listening to my Walkman. Everything was so still, like nothing had ever happened, and I remember how I had the music turned up really loud to help get out my bad feelings, and I started dancing around in the sand with my eyes closed like a crazy person. Just spinning around in circles and falling down, over and over again. I got so exhausted finally that I fell down and just lay there and stared at the sky, which was white and blank. And then all these bad thoughts came into my head and I started thinking about dying.

I got up and started running as fast as I could, faster than I've ever run, all the way down the beach, and I just felt so good and free, and I thought, I've got to remember this. I've got to remember how this feels. If I ever get so sad again that I want to try and kill myself, then I've got to remember how good this feels and that'll help me get through those feelings.

Somehow, I never could remember how good that felt, though. I remember thinking that it felt good and trying to remember, but I never could.

I've been asking my mom about *Pump Up the Volume*, that movie that looks so good with Christian Slater as the pirate DJ, and she says that whenever she goes to the video store, it's already rented. I don't believe her. I ask her about it and she admits that, yes, they have the movie, but she's decided not to rent it.

"Why?" I ask.

"Because . . . we don't think it would be appropriate."

"What do you mean?"

"We've heard that there's some objectionable material."

"What do you mean?"

"There are some things that we don't think you should be watching right now."

"Like what?" This is making me angry.

Her voice is getting really monotone, so I can tell she's getting angry too. "Well, we talked about it, and Dad and I decided that you aren't ready to see some of the things that are in that movie yet."

"Why? What do you mean?"

"Well, there's a boy in the movie who hurts himself."

"How?" So that's it.

"With a gun."

"So?"

"So, Dad and I don't think you should watch movies about that right now. Maybe in a few months when you're feeling better."

"I'm feeling fine."

"Well, Dad and I don't think you're quite ready."

"Well, I am."

"Okay, well, I'll talk to Dad about it again."

"Great," I say in my most sarcastic voice.

One thing I'm really good at is doing impressions of people. I can do Jack Nicholson, and I can do President Bush almost as good as Dana Carvey. I can also do a great impression of my friend Stephen, but my best impressions are probably of my mom and dad.

For my dad, I make my voice low and gruff, I scowl a little bit and try to push my eyebrows together so they wrinkle in the middle like his. Then I flare out my nostrils and clench my teeth. My favorite line to say is, "Goddamn it, Brent." That sounds exactly like him.

For my mom, I open my eyes really wide and flutter my eyelashes. We have the same color eyes, my mom and I, so I just have to make my voice a bit higher. I speak in very even tones, like a teacher (which she is), and I keep my mouth tight and pointed downward. I say, "How are you feeling, honey?"

Dr. Rubinstein is here again to make me talk about things I have no interest in talking to her about. Here we go. Round one.

"Good morning, Brent." God, I hate her voice.

"Good morning." Flat tones. No emotion.

"How are you feeling?"

"Fine."

"That's good. You're feeling better since being turned over?"

"Yes." You can't fool me—you don't care about me.

"And how is the pain?" Don't ask me about pain.

"Hurts."

"You're in a lot of pain?"

You don't care, but since you're asking, I'll tell you. "My back still hurts the worst, but my legs are still hurting a lot in burn care. And the other day, being in

115

the bath stung so much I almost died."

"Yes, I read that in your chart. Calvin said you were very angry that night."

"Yeah."

"Do you want to talk about why you were so angry?"

"No." Why is Calvin ratting me out to Dr. Rubinstein? That's not cool. I look down at my hands. The fabric is so intricate in these Jobst gloves. There are about a thousand little pieces of elastic running through each glove, and there's little holes cut in the end of the fingers and thumb so I can get the tips of my fingers out. I can touch the tips of my fingers to my thumb with every finger on both hands. Becky says that's almost a miracle. People call me the Miracle Man because I'm getting better a lot faster than anybody ever thought I could, but I don't think it's a miracle. I don't think it's fast, either.

"Brent, what are you thinking about?"

They like to tell me how proud they are of me. But I don't think I had anything to do with it. They've got all this medicine and all of these machines and the Six Million Dollar Man skin from Boston that they put on me. It's not like I decided one day to get better and then after that I just started getting better. I wish they'd all stop saying how proud they are of me.

She's gone.

Ever since that day in the bath with Calvin, where everything stung so much, burn care really hasn't been that bad. I mean, it's not like I wake up every morning and say, Hey, guys, when is burn care? I can't wait. But it's nowhere near as bad as it used to be. I guess that's because they covered most of my open spots with skin, that's what made it stop hurting. It's weird I got so used to being in pain all the time, now I'm just uncomfortable.

Mom and Dad have decided to let me watch *Pump Up the Volume*, but they're going to watch it with me. They don't like the part where a kid calls Christian Slater's radio show and talks about how he wants to hurt himself and Christian Slater tries to talk him out of it, but the kid is so sad that he shoots himself in the head. And then everybody gets upset at Christian Slater, except this one girl, who takes her shirt off and has really nice tits. And there's this other part where a popular girl puts all her jewelry into the microwave and turns it on and she explodes her kitchen, and a bunch of stuff catches on fire.

The part with the fire really freaked me out. I felt hot and sick and like I was going to throw up, but then it was over and I started to feel better. I didn't tell Mom and Dad.

These days they like to put me in the blue chair and roll me into the Child Life room. It's fun because I don't have to sit in my stinking room all the time and also because there's much more to do in here.

Today I'm just hanging out watching *Jeopardy* with Mom and Dad. I'm really good at this show, much better than they are. I wonder why that is. In the commercial break, I tell Mom and Dad I have to pee, and they leave the room and I wait for a while before Barbara comes in. She says, "Urine patrol," and I laugh.

She grabs a urinal and I pull up my hospital gown. I'm getting better at this. I can pee with anyone around now. I start to go and she holds the urinal. I can hear by the sound that I really had to go. It sounds like a Super Soaker squirting into a metal bucket. I can hear the urinal filling up.

"You really had to go, didn't you?"

"Uh, yeah."

"Are you almost finished?" She sounds a little nervous.

"Not really."

"Well, you're filling up this urinal pretty fast."

"I am?"

"Yeah. Can you hold it a second?"

"I'll try." I squeeze down and I feel the pee start to stop. It feels like the emergency brake on a runaway train. Finally the pee stops and Barbara looks around. There's no toilet in this room, only a sink, and she dumps the urinal in one big gush down the sink and puts it back between my legs.

"That was exciting," I say.

"Yeah, but you can't tell anyone I did that."

"Okay, it'll be our secret." She smiles at me.

It has been decided by someone, I'm not sure who, maybe

my mother, that I should start wearing clothes. No more sitting around in Ace bandages and nasty hospital gowns. My mom went shopping for loose-fitting shirts that I can get over my head and extra large pants with elastic waistbands, the kind that weight lifters and football players wear, with the funny prints on them. Dad got me a Michigan State basketball jersey.

Becky comes in wearing a green dress and holding a pair of scissors. She says she's going to give me a haircut. Since my last skin graft, when they shaved my head and took my skin off, my hair has grown a lot, way too long on the sides and shaggy up on top. I think that all the vitamins they're always giving me are making it grow faster than ever. My fingernails too are getting really long and thick. They're about four times as thick as they used to be.

She presses the button that makes me sit upright in bed, comes behind me, and starts cutting.

I say, "It must be getting warm outside."

She says, "It's hot."

"Yeah?"

"Really hot."

"What's today?"

"May fourth."

"Wow."

"What?"

"I was just thinking, it's been . . . one, two, three . . . three months since I came here."

"Long time."

"Yeah."

"You should go outside soon."

"What? No way. I can't."

"Yes, you can."

"What about my skin—they said I have to be careful of my skin in sunlight."

"We'll get you some sunblock, a hat, and a wheelchair, and we'll wheel you out there. How does that sound?"

"Sounds good."

"What about your dog? Don't you have a dog?"

"Yeah. Her name is Rusty."

"Rusty Runyon? Good name."

"Yeah. My brother named her. I wanted Cinnamon."

"Cute."

"Why is that cute?"

"Just is. How old is she?"

"We got her when I was eight."

"Getting old."

"No, she's not."

"You should get your parents to bring her to the hospital and you can go out in a wheelchair to meet her."

"That sounds good."

"I'm full of good ideas."

She goes to the bathroom, gets a mirror, and holds it up for me. My hair looks better. I try not to look at my face.

I'm lying here thinking about that red-haired girl on the

cruise we went on for Nanny and Grandpa's fiftieth anniversary, where we went to Disney World and the Bahamas. Her name was Krissy, I think that was her name. We were watching a movie in the movie theater, it was *Working Girl*, and she leaned over and whispered, "If we were on a date right now, what would you do?"

She was sixteen, and I was thirteen, and I don't think I'd even hit puberty yet. No, I definitely hadn't. And I didn't really know what I would do if we were on a date.

She did, though. She put her hand on the inside of my thigh and started rubbing it up and down. It sort of surprised me, but I put my hand on her thigh too and rubbed it up and down. She was wearing these tight jean shorts, and I kept rubbing up and down her whole leg because I wanted to touch her actual skin and not just the jeans. Then she put her hand on top of my penis, outside my pants, and I put my hand on her where I thought her vagina should be. She sort of giggled and said, "It's lower."

I tried to giggle too, but I was getting light-headed, and I could barely pay attention to what was going on in the movie. And then she unzipped my pants a little and stuck her hand inside. She didn't really touch anything, just put her hand inside. I tried to figure out how to unbutton her jeans and unzip them too, but they were so tight I couldn't get the zipper to go down. And then she just stopped. I don't know why, she just did. I kept trying to get her pants off, but then she leaned over to me and whispered, in a really mean voice, "Stop," and I stopped. I never saw her again after that.

I have to pee. I press the call button. Janice comes in and grabs the urinal and pulls down the sheet and I put my penis in the hole. She looks down for a second, then away, then back again and says, "Are you feeling all right?"

"Yeah."

"You sure?"

"Yeah. Why?"

"Your penis looks a little swollen."

"What?"

"It just looks bigger than it normally does."

"You sure?" I look down. "It looks the same to me."

"No, it's definitely swollen. Maybe I should have one of the doctors come in and look at it."

"Okay. If you want."

She looks like she's thinking for a second and then like she realizes something and says, "Oh no, okay, I don't think that's necessary. Are you done?"

"Yeah."

"Shake it off."

I do. She pours the urine in the toilet, flushes, and leaves.

Mom and Dad have been visiting different rehab hospitals for when I leave here. There's a hospital in Delaware that they think I would like. It's called duPont and it sounds pretty cool. They've got a bowling alley and a huge exercise room. The only problem is that it's three hours away from all my friends here at Children's.

Sometimes they force-feed me that Metamucil stuff, which is so disgusting I can hardly believe it. It's like drinking the silt from the bottom of a stream. And then what's worse is that they bring out the bedpan and make me arch my back and put it under my butt so that only my shoulders and my feet are touching the bed. The stupid bedpan is so hard and cold, I always ask if they can get a padded one, but nobody listens to me about stuff like that. It's so gross and then somebody else has to come and wipe my butt. I hate being in my body.

The worst thing about being burned isn't how much it hurts, it's how much it itches. I didn't think anything could be worse than the pain, but now I've got this itching feeling all over my chest, down my arms, and in my hands. It feels just like the time I was playing in the bamboo outside my neighbor's house and a bunch of big carpenter ants started crawling up my legs and all of a sudden I felt like my body was covered with them, even though I knew there were only a few on my legs, and I had to go home and take a shower and try to get the feeling off of me.

I keep thinking about it. I was in the bathroom and I had the gas can and the matches and I sat on the toilet. That's when I should've realized how stupid I was being. That's when I should've stopped it.

But I stood in the bathroom and put the bathrobe on, and it was wet and heavy, and I could have taken it off and gone back outside to play basketball with Craig and said, You won't believe what I almost did. And he would've known what to do. He would've gotten me help and made sure Mom and Dad weren't mad at me. I should've done that.

I could have just lit a little part of me on fire, like my arm or something, just to see how much it hurt, and if it hurt too much, I could've stopped. And it definitely would have hurt, so I definitely would have stopped and then I could have still come in here and met all these people and then gone back to school in only like a week.

But I didn't stop. I lit the match and I put it against my wrist. And maybe if I'd just realized when the fire was going up my wrist to my arm but before it caught the whole bathrobe on fire, maybe then I could have turned on the shower and stopped the whole thing. I should have done that.

I wish, I wish, I wish, I wish, I wish, I wish, I wish, I wish, I wish. I wish I'd stopped. But I didn't.

They're moving me out of Intensive Care and into the main part of the unit tomorrow. There's an extra room out there and I'm not "intensive" enough for them anymore. But I like it here. It's quiet, except for the little kid who screams during burn care. Sometimes I walk by his room and try to see what he looks like. Most of the time, the curtains are drawn so I can't see, but sometimes they're open a little and I see his baby arms all wrapped up in gauze. He got too close to the barbecue and touched the pretty red coals.

One time, when I was little, I was sitting up front in the old Datsun we used to have and Mom went into a store to buy something and left me in the car by myself. I pushed in the cigarette lighter because it looked like something you should push in, and then after a while it popped back out. And I took it out and held it in my hand. The inside was a pretty color of orange and it was shaped in a spiral like my fingerprint, and I wanted to touch my fingerprint to it because they were such a perfect match. And I did. I pushed my thumb right into the orange cigarette lighter and it was either hot or cold, I couldn't tell which at first, and then it was hot, really, really hot, and I screamed and dropped the cigarette lighter and opened the door with my other hand. It was winter and there was a pile of snow right outside the car and I stuck my thumb into the snow. I remember there was a sizzling sound, and some smoke, or maybe I'm just imagining that. But I do remember how much it hurt. When it was in the snow, it felt okay, not too hot, but every time I pulled it out to look at it,

Mom wheels me out of the elevator into a huge atrium that goes up about forty or fifty feet. "There's the gift shop right there, and the chapel, and the information desk, where you have to sign in when you come to visit." I can tell Mom is nervous because her voice is shaking just a little bit.

The last time I saw Rusty she was standing on the stairs with Craig. I wonder if she remembers what I looked like when I came out of that bathroom. She probably doesn't. She probably doesn't remember any of that because dogs don't really have memories, I don't think. I never saw a dog look so scared.

We go out some sliding doors and all of a sudden we're outside. It's incredibly sunny out here and humid and there's a bunch of doctors and nurses taking cigarette breaks. Mom wheels me down to the end of the sidewalk and stops. She puts the brake on.

"I'll go get Rusty, okay, honey?"

"Yeah, okay."

The thing about being outside that you forget is what it smells like. I sort of remember the feeling and the humidity, but the smells, like flowers and car exhaust, I'd forgotten all of that.

Here comes Rusty, she looks tired and confused. Mom brings her up to me and makes her sit right next to the wheelchair, and I reach my hand down to her head. Oh God, her fur is so soft, her ears, especially, are so soft. It still feels like puppy fur.

She's so sleepy, she can barely sit up, but Mom's holding

her on a short leash with one hand and holding her up with the other.

I wish I could lie down in the grass with her and let her kiss my face and jump all over me.

I keep my hand on her head for a long time until she seems like she's almost asleep. After a while, Mom says, "Honey, I should probably take her home."

I say, "Yeah." She takes Rusty back to the car and then wheels me back into the hospital.

So I'm moving. Moving out of the Intensive Care Unit. I know this sounds weird, but it makes me kind of sad. I don't know, I guess I just like the people in here and I like my room and I'm used to everything.

Janice, Rachel, and my mom are moving everything out. All the cards and posters and gifts and everything. All the signed stuff from Magic, the workout suit, the T-shirts, and the hats. And the giant poster of Michael Jordan, that's very cool. All the stuff from people I don't know, like the Hard Rock Cafe T-shirts from all over the world. The Louisville Slugger baseball bat with my name burned into it. The guitar Nanny and Grandpa sent. And the quilt that my friends from school sent. And the Get Well Soon balloon. That was the first thing I got.

My new room is pretty nice, with a TV and everything, of course. There's a lot more noise. Lots more people walking by, peeking in the windows. It doesn't bother me that people look in, that's what I do when I walk by other people's rooms too, but Mom pulls the curtain anyway and starts decorating.

Mom moves my bed against the side wall instead of against the back wall, where it used to be. This is so I can see the TV and also so I can look outside my room and see who's going by.

Mom puts up all my cards and pictures. This room could use some more posters. In my room at home, I've got these two great door-sized posters, both of the same girl in the same skimpy underwear, but one is taken from the back and one is taken from the front. She's so sexy.

I should ask my parents to get those posters for me so I can put them up in my room here. Right now, I've got this Cindy Crawford bathing suit poster that my friend Chris gave me, but that's it, and Mom hasn't put it up yet.

I sit on the bed and watch Mom putting up all the cards and pictures. I say, "What about Cindy Crawford?"

"Um. Let's see."

"How about on that wall?" I point to the white space right under the TV.

"Um. Yeah, we could do that."

"Why not?"

"Oh, I don't know. Wouldn't it look nice here?" Mom points to the bottom of the wall under a bunch of medical stuff.

"No. I can't see it there."

"Oh. Okay. How about here?"

"There? On the back of the door? Then I can only see it when the door is closed."

"What's so bad about that?"

"I want to see it all the time."

"Okay. How about here?"

"In the closet?"

"Then you could see it when you want, and if somebody else comes into the room, then they won't have to see it if they don't want to."

"Why wouldn't they want to see it?"

"Oh, I don't know, it could be kind of offensive to some people."

"Like who?"

"I don't know."

"You?"

"Well, not to me, but to women in general."

"Women in general meaning who?"

"Some of the nurses."

"Who?"

"I don't know. Maybe it's not in good taste to be putting up posters in the middle of a hospital."

"But it's my room."

"But it's in the middle of a hospital."

"But it's my room."

She puts on her more serious, teacherly voice. "But, Brent, you have to understand that your room is in a much more visible place now."

"I know that."

"And you're going to have to adapt a little to your new surroundings."

"Yeah, so?"

"So, it would be nice if there weren't pictures of half-naked women on the walls when the doctors come into the room."

"The doctors don't care. They probably like it."

"All right, then for the nurses."

"The nurses don't care either."

"How do you know? Have you asked them?"

"No, but I will." I press the call button on my remote control and Janice comes back into the room. She's so hot, she could be on one of these posters if she wanted to be.

"Yes?" She says it like she's my own personal maid.

"Janice, do you care if I put up this poster of Cindy Crawford in the bathing suit?"

"No, I don't care. It's your room."

"Ha! Thank you very much, Janice, you're dismissed." She does a little half turn, curtsies, and walks out.

"See?"

"Fine."

Mom keeps putting up the cards and pictures, and I sit back down on the bed, watching her. Then Janice comes back in with Rachel and the Polaroid camera. Janice lies on the bed like a Playboy bunny and Rachel stands behind her like she's on *The Price Is Right*. Mom takes their picture.

They giggle and say, "Now we're your poster girls."

They have no idea.

It's night. I make sure the curtain is closed before I get into bed so no one can see. And I've got the control for my bed so I can put my back up a little.

I pull my sheet down and my gown up and look at my penis. There it is. I wonder if it still works.

My hand feels different than it used to. But my penis feels about the same. Maybe a little bit out of practice. Maybe like it hasn't done this in a while.

God, my arm is getting tired already. It used to move so freely. Got to keep working on my range of motion and strength exercises so I can do this better.

Maybe I should think about someone. Megan. No, I don't even remember what she looks like. No. Maybe one of the nurses, yeah, okay, what if one of the nurses came in and, who would it be, maybe Tina, no, she wouldn't, maybe Barb, that's silly. Janice. If Janice came in and saw what I was doing, maybe she'd come over to me and she'd put her hand where my hand is and she'd lean over so I could smell her perfume and put my hand under her shirt and I'd touch her breast under the bra and I could rub my thumb up against her nipple. Oh God. Oh God. Oh God.

Barbara is here to watch *Ben-Hur* with me. It's that one about Charlton Heston on the chariots, but it's not *The Ten Commandments*. I tried to watch *Ben-Hur* on TV during Easter, but I fell asleep. Barbara said she'd get the video and we'd watch it together sometime. So, today's the day.

She starts the movie and we start watching the previews, and my skin starts to itch. Like seriously itch. Like all over my body, insects burrowing up through the dermis kind of itch. Everyone always said it would feel this way, but I didn't know what they meant. I always thought itches were kind of annoying, but this is a weird pain deep down under the skin, like a buzzing inside my body.

Barbara gives me some Benadryl and says that'll help quiet the itching. She starts the movie.

There's the MGM lion and some music. God, these credits are taking a long time. I'm just going to rest my eyes for a little while until the movie starts.

I wake up and it's dark again. The movie is gone. I don't remember anything about it. I wonder if it was on the whole time while I was sleeping. Barbara, *Ben-Hur*, and Benadryl. I'm going back to sleep.

I've got one more surgery scheduled. No big deal, just a little patch-and-cover job on those few little holes I've still got on my back and butt, but I won't have to lie on my stomach afterward, thank God. After that, about two weeks and I'm out of here. Heading up north to that rehab hospital my parents visited in Delaware. The one with the pool and the basketball court and the bowling alley.

That'll be good. I'll be happy to go. Make new friends. Try new things.

The only thing is, I don't want to leave. I don't want to

go anywhere. I could do rehab here, with all my friends. Don't make me leave.

Fuck it, it's fucking useless.

Dr. Rubinstein sends Mom into my room to talk about the stuff I don't want to talk about. The other suicide attempts and stuff.

I don't want to tell Mom that stuff. I don't want to upset her.

And I'm different now. I don't do those things. I'm sorry. I was making mistakes. I didn't know what I was doing and I couldn't stop.

But Mom is here and she looks like she's ready to talk. If I just say it, then maybe I'll be able to stop feeling so bad inside.

So I'll say it. What will I say? I'll say, Hey, Mom, guess who tried to kill themselves a bunch of other times besides the one you know about? That's right, me. Hey, Mom, remember the Band-Aids on my wrist? Well, I didn't really scrape it on my locker. I cut it with a knife that I kept under my bed.

And remember all the black clothes, well, I liked black because it reminded me of death.

And you know the furnace in the basement, I thought about pouring gasoline in there and blowing up the whole house. And remember the time I got caught stealing supplies from Mrs. Loftus, the algebra teacher, well, that night I lay in bed, dressed up in my best suit, and sliced my wrists open. And you know how I got the book on how to make knots? It was so I could tie a noose and hang myself from the closet pole.

And a lot of the time I used to spend in my room alone, I was writing my will so you'd know who to give all of my stuff to.

I can't say any of this. I can't say any of this. So I say, "Mom?"

"Yes, honey."

"When I . . . when I tried . . . to hurt myself, before . . ."

"Yes, honey."

"That wasn't the first time that I tried to do something like that."

She doesn't look surprised, but she's starting to cry. She puts her hand on top of mine. "I know, honey. I figured it wasn't the first time."

"You did?"

"Yes, honey, I'm sorry I didn't know you were so sad." She's crying hard now, and I'm crying too. "I didn't know, honey, I didn't know you were so sad."

"I know. I'm sorry, Mom."

"It's okay, honey. It's okay. We didn't know you were so sad."

We cry together some more.

"Brenny?" she says. "About a week before your accident, we got into a fight at the dinner table and you stormed up to your room, and I remember, I said, 'Where are you going?' and you said, I think I heard you say, 'I'm going to set myself on fire.' Do you remember that?"

I think about it. "I don't think I said that. I mean, I might have, but I didn't mean it."

She's crying harder now. "Okay, okay, because I thought you'd said that, and I just wish I'd been there to try and help you, and I wish I'd been there, and I just wish I'd known you were so sad." She can hardly get the words out, she's crying so hard.

"It's okay, Mom. It's okay. You didn't know. I didn't tell you."

She sniffs hard, and all of a sudden, the tears stop. "But if you ever get that sad again, you have to promise to tell someone so they can help you."

"Yes. Okay. I'll tell someone."

"And know that we love you so much and we don't ever want to lose you."

"I know. I know."

So the last surgery is today. I wish they'd stop talking to me about it. Just do it and get it over with and stop talking to me about skin and mesh and graft sites and scarlet and Silvadene and morphine and bacitracin and Eucerin and total body surface area burned and antimicrobial and cultural epithelial autograft and range of motion and all of that shit. Just do it and shut the fuck up about it. Please.

I'm awake. This is the first time I've been completely covered in skin since I got in here.

When I'm better, Tina and I are going to go out of the hospital together. We've got it all set up. We're going to Ben & Jerry's to get some ice cream and then to the movies to see *What About Bob?* which I've seen commercials for on TV, and it looks really funny. Bill Murray and Richard Dreyfuss. They're so funny.

I was in fourth grade the first time I heard the word suicide. I remember exactly where I was, I was walking down the hall in my elementary school, and I was talking to my friend Chris B., this kid who had cystic fibrosis and was always pale and skinny. He said, "Maybe I'll commit suicide." I don't remember what he was talking about or why he said that, but that's what he said.

I said, "What does that mean?"

"You know, kill myself."

That was the first time I'd heard the word, and I just kept

thinking, Why would someone want to kill himself? Why would anyone do that? I couldn't stop thinking about it and it got inside my head and started squirming around in there like a worm in the dirt, and then it seemed to disappear. But when it came back four years later, it was so big and so powerful, and it seemed like it ate up my whole brain and it was the only thing I could think about.

I just keep wondering, What if I'd never heard that word? I wonder what would've happened.

Dawn's taking me down to the cafeteria for a little exercise. She says if I can walk all the way there, then she'll buy me a Coke, but she's bringing the wheelchair just in case I get tired.

I can do pretty well getting around, but my right foot is still kind of hard to walk on. Dawn says it's because when I had to lie on my stomach for ten days, the muscles contracted and that's why I can't stretch out my toe anymore. She's designing a special strap that I can wear to stretch my toe while I walk. That'll be cool.

It's a long walk, so I entertain Dawn with stories. I tell her about the time I was in the cafeteria at Kilmer, my junior high school, and everybody was supposed to clean up all the trash before we could be dismissed, and the janitor came up to me and told me to pick up this fork that was on the floor. I said, "It's not mine," but he didn't care, he just told me to pick it up and don't talk back. Anyway, by the end of lunch I still hadn't picked it up and he came back to check on me and the fork. I saw him coming and I put my foot down over the fork. He said, "Where's that fork?" And I was like, "I threw it away." And he said, "I didn't see you." And I said, "Well, I did." And he said, "Scoot back your chair." And I did, but I kept my foot over the fork and slid it back at the same time. He said, "Lift up your foot." And I did, but I lifted up the one without the fork under it. And he goes, "No. The other foot." So I did, and I got three days of eating lunch in the Box, the room for in-school suspension.

Dawn says I'm a good storyteller. And now she has to buy me a Coke. I made it.

Reggie, the tall skinny black guy who used to help me out of bed, says that when I leave here, I'm going to forget all about him. That's not true. That is so not true. First of all, the people here are my best friends in the entire world and they love me for who I am and they don't care about anything I did before, they just love me. Reggie bet me that I won't invite him to my high school graduation. I said, "Reggie, that's only four years away, of course I'll keep in touch with you, man." He said, "We'll see." He's so wrong.

There's less than a week left here at Children's. Less than a week. The twelfth of June, that's next Wednesday. Then Mom and Dad are going to drive me up to duPont.

Mom asked me if I wanted to make a trip home before

they take me to Delaware, and I had to say that I didn't really want to. I think she was disappointed because she knows that I'm going out to the movies and ice cream with Tina.

I told her I didn't want to come home yet because I didn't feel like I was ready, which is partially true, but also partially untrue. I don't know, I just can't really imagine going back there with the bathroom, and my old room and all that stuff, and the neighbors outside welcoming me back home. No, I don't want to do that.

Dad asked me if I thought I'd ever want to come home, and I had to lie and say, "Sure, sure I will. Of course I will. I just need a little more time to get better." The truth is that I don't know when I'll be ready to go home again.

They're having a telethon downstairs in the atrium for the benefit of Children's Hospital. Rosemarie, one of the social workers, asked my parents and me if we wanted to be featured on it. I said yes.

But then I thought about it, and I didn't want to walk all the way down there and stand up under the lights and have someone shove a microphone in my face and ask me what happened. So, anyway, Mom and Dad have gone downstairs to do it by themselves. I'm staying in bed and watching it on TV.

It's pretty boring actually, the whole TV show thing. They just keep talking in circles about how important the hospital is, and then they tell you how much money they've raised, and how important everything is, and how much money they've raised.

But there's Mom and Dad, oh God, they look nervous. That's so funny. Dad's so stiff and Mom looks like she's going to faint. The woman's asking them something. I turn it up.

"Your son's name is . . ."

"Our son's name is Brent and he's a burn patient up on the Burn Ward."

"And how long has Brent been a patient here?"

"About four months."

"And how has his care been?"

"It's been absolutely tremendous."

God, this is cool. I wonder if anyone I know is watching this.

"And how did Brent get burned?"

Oh shit.

"Brent was burned in an accidental house fire a few months ago."

"And how is he doing?"

"He's just doing great. He was burned over eighty-five percent of his body and he's had numerous skin-grafting procedures and he's doing so great now and he's going to be released from the hospital next week."

An accidental house fire. Right. Okay. Okay. We can say that. We don't have to tell anyone what really happened. An accidental house fire. Why did they lie? I mean, I don't blame them, but did they have to? But I'm glad they didn't say the truth. I don't know.

"That's great. Thanks very much, Mr. and Mrs. Runyon, for talking with us today."

Oh God, I have this sudden tightness, this sticking feeling in my chest like I've been breathing Krazy Glue.

This strange woman with a tackle box is knocking on my door. She comes over next to my bed and starts talking to me. She says she's a representative from a cosmetics company and she helps people like me, who've suffered severe injuries to their face, overcome their self-consciousness and go on to lead happy and healthier lives. She says that with just a little bit of base, chosen especially to match my particular skin tone, something between Light Olive and Lady Fair, I'll look as good as new.

She has this little girl with her who's been burned by some hot oil or something, and she shows me how good she looks. She looks fine, and she's smiling a lot. The woman also has the little girl's parents with her, and they tell me how the girl's self-confidence has already started to increase. She feels so much better about herself.

The woman gives me a big smile. She's pretty in the way mannequins are pretty. She asks if I'd like to try a free sample. I say, "No." She asks if I'm sure because the products can really make a difference in your self-confidence and make social situations that much easier. I say, "No." She asks if I am sure. I say, "Yes."

I'm not going to cover anything up. This is me.

Becky and Dawn and I are making a video today for the people up at duPont, describing all the things we've been doing in OT and PT so they know what my limits are.

Here we go. Becky says, "Hi, my name is Rebecca Bernhardt and I'm an OT here at Children's National Medical Center. This is Brent Runyon. Say hi, Brent."

"Hi." I give a little wave.

"Brent is a fourteen-year-old patient who has received second- and third-degree burns to over eighty-five percent of his body, of partial and full thickness."

She's not going to say how I got burned, is she? God, that would be terrible. She wouldn't do that.

"As you can see, Brent has been wearing pressure garments on his head, torso, and hands. At this time, Brent has trouble with the range of motion and strength needed to put on his garments, but he's done well getting them off, with just a little help."

Becky's voice sounds tight and nervous. She seems like a different person.

"Brent, why don't you show everybody how you can take your garments off."

I'm wearing a Magic Johnson T-shirt and a loose pair of shorts, with some red, white, and blue boxers on underneath, and all of a sudden, I realize I look like an idiot.

"I can't," I say.

"Yes, you can. Just start with your shirt like we've

practiced." My shoulders are up near my ears and all my muscles and my skin feel really tight, but I can reach up with my hands and grab the shirt at my shoulders and pull it slowly over my head. The shirt gets stuck with my head in it and the lights are dim and I can't see the camera anymore. This is nice in here. I could live like this.

Becky pulls the shirt the rest of the way over my head and keeps talking about my range of motion and about how the scar tissue over my joints restricts me. She explains that the scar tissue forms these things called bands, which are really like thick rubber bands, that make it really hard to move my arms and hands normally. She helps me unzip my Jobst garments and takes off the jacket.

I look down at myself. My skin is so purple. So gross. I look like I'm made of raspberries. God. I'm so disgusting. I can't do this anymore. Let's stop for a while. Let's just stop.

"Becky, can we stop?"

She's ignoring me. I can tell she's not going to stop, no matter what I do. I feel sad and sick and tired inside, and I'm crying, I don't want to be crying, but I am. I just can't do this anymore. I just can't go on doing this anymore. I just want it to stop. Please stop. Please.

She goes on for another twenty minutes, and I still can't stop crying. The people in Delaware are going to think I'm a baby.

Tonight's the big night. The big date night with Tina. Our night on the town. She's picking me up at six, and we're going to Ben & Jerry's, then we're going to the movies.

I've got my outfit all picked out. I'll be wearing my black Hard Rock Cafe London T-shirt. There was some concern that black would be too hot, but it's my favorite color, or it used to be, I'm not sure if it still is, and we're going to be inside for the whole time anyway.

My pants are those loose stretchy pants that you see on weight lifters and football players, not that I'm like those guys. They're just comfortable for me to wear, and also, they cover up the bandages on my legs.

Shoes. That's complicated, my feet are still too sensitive for anything too nice. I guess I could wear tennis shoes, but they might scrape against my skin and open up another hole, and then I'd have to stay in the hospital for three more months. I'll wear the shoes Magic Johnson sent me in the mail. Yeah, those have to be lucky anyway. I have to wear my stinking Jobst garments on my arms and chest. The part for my chest slips on like a jacket, but there are zippers that go up the arms, and when I'm all zipped in, I feel like I'm being swallowed by a boa constrictor. I'm not wearing my gloves tonight, they say my hands will be okay without them, but having the jacket on without the gloves makes all the blood push into my hands and they itch. I try to shake the itch out of them, but it doesn't really work. At least I already have my gloves off in case I get to feel her up or something.

I also have to wear the stinking face mask made out of the Jobst material, that's supposed to flatten out the scars on my face. Besides the fact that it sucks that I have to wear a stinking mask the first time I go outside, it really sucks that it makes my hair stick up. I put on my Lakers cap. That's better.

Tina's here. It's time to go, but Mom and Dad want to take a couple of pictures. One of me and Tina together outside my room, like we're going to the prom or something, and one of Calvin leaning down to tie my shoes for me because I'm not flexible enough to do that yet.

So, here we go. On our way. We're taking a wheelchair just in case, and since we're taking it, I might as well ride in it, at least to the car. "To save your strength," says Tina. Hmm, save my strength for what?

At the elevators, I look around at the signs, trying to think of something funny to say. "Spina bifida, that sounds like some sort of Greek food."

Tina doesn't laugh. She says, "You wouldn't say that if you knew what it was."

Okay, parking garage, please. The elevator drops fast and I feel my stomach go into my throat. Being in an elevator in a wheelchair makes that feeling twice as bad.

Here we are in the garage. I've never been down here before. God, it's hot. It's like a hundred and twenty degrees down here.

"What kind of car do you have?"

"Mazda."

"Miata?"

"No, I wish. There it is."

"Oh, it's nice."

"Yeah."

Tina wheels me up to the passenger side and opens the door for me.

I can get myself in the car, but Tina puts her hand on my back anyway. I think she's a little nervous or something, she doesn't quite seem like herself.

She puts the wheelchair in the trunk and I look around for something to talk about. There's a bunch of tapes. I guess we can talk about music. There she is. Sweet Tina.

She starts the car and pops a tape in the stereo. It's rap. That's okay—I like rap.

I say, "Who's this?"

"Tribe Called Quest."

"What?"

"A Tribe Called Quest."

"Oh, I thought you said, 'A Tribe Called Quest.'"

"I did."

"Oh."

We're pulling out of the parking garage. It's hot. I should roll down my window. That's a little better. Oh, look, the flowers are blooming. God, it's so humid and the air is so thick, but I'm outside and I can smell the cherry blossoms.

I forgot what this was like, being in a car, with the wind in my face. Tina rolls down her window and turns up the music.

She says, "I can't wait to see this movie."

"I know. Bill Murray is so funny."

"I love *Ghostbusters*."

"Me too."

We're out here and we're driving around and we're going to get ice cream at Ben & Jerry's, just like we planned, and then we're going to the movies. God, I'm lucky.

I look over at Tina. The sun is on her face. Her hair is coming out of her ponytail. I should reach over and push it behind her ear. No, I shouldn't do that. I shouldn't do that.

Ben & Jerry's is a little ice cream shop right on the corner. Tina finds a parking space right away and pulls in. Okay, here we go, the moment of truth, as they say. Out in the real world.

"Do you want the wheelchair or are you okay to walk?"

"I'm okay to walk."

"Sure?"

"Yeah."

I'm opening the door and it's just a matter of pulling myself onto my feet with the door and the side of the car. I can do this. Okay, here we go. That's good. Now we're walking. Tina puts her hand on my back and steadies me. She's so sweet. It's easier once I get going.

She opens the door for me and we go inside. It's so much cooler in here. And the smell, I've never smelled anything so good. It's like waffles and syrup or something.

Okay, the first problem is that I look like a total freak right now. People are looking at me and trying to figure out what happened to me and why I'm so burned up. I'll just keep looking out the window and pretend that I'm looking at something across the street.

We sit at a table next to the window and Tina goes up and gets a menu. I'm still looking out the window. God, my back is starting to itch. I try and scratch it by rubbing against the bench.

"So, Brent, they've got this sundae, which is enormous. It's got twenty scoops of ice cream, ten scoops of chopped nuts, brownies, cookies, M&M's, and whipped cream. How does that sound?"

"We're really going to get that?"

"You want to?"

"Can we? We can't eat it all."

"We'll order it now, come back after the movie, and take it back to the Unit for an ice cream party afterward."

"Oh God, that sounds great. Twenty scoops."

"Yeah." She's laughing. This is fun.

"So what should we get?"

"I don't know. Twenty scoops is a lot. Let's just get one of everything."

I laugh and say, "Okay, but a few extra of New York Super Fudge Chunk."

"Yeah, that's my favorite too." We have a lot in common.

I think I see the people behind the counter looking over every couple of seconds to see what's wrong with my face. They're whispering too. What are they saying? I can't hear them, but they're definitely talking about me. They keep talking and looking back over to try and see what's wrong with my face and why I'm wearing these weird clothes. I shouldn't have worn these clothes, I just realized that they look really stupid, and I shouldn't be wearing a Lakers hat because nobody around here likes the stinking Lakers anyway. God, I'm an idiot. A stupid burned-up idiot with a big purple face and a bunch of bandages on under his clothes. I hate myself.

Wait, Tina just said something. "What?"

"Do you like Chocolate Chip Cookie Dough?"

"Oh yeah."

"What were you thinking about?"

"Um . . . I was thinking about the movie and how funny it's going to be."

"You were?"

"Yeah."

"Okay, I'll put the order in."

"Yeah, okay."

Tina's talking with the guy behind the counter. He's older than me. Like in college or something. I bet he's thinking about her breasts. He's probably going to ask her out. And she'll say yes. He just looked at me. Looked right at me and I didn't have a chance to turn away first. He looked right at me and saw all the big purple scars and these bandages and I couldn't do anything.

I hope he doesn't ask Tina what happened to me.

Here she comes. "Are you ready to go?"

"Yup."

"How are you feeling?"

My face is purple and everyone is staring at me and I itch all over like I've got bugs crawling under my skin. "Pretty good."

We go back outside and get in the car. Maybe we should just go back to the hospital. No, we shouldn't. We shouldn't. We should go to the movie. Bill Murray and Richard Dreyfuss. I just hope I'll be able to sit in the seat for the whole time. I think Tina is worried about that too because when we get to the mall and park the car, she asks me if I want to bring an extra cushion so I can sit on it.

I say, "No thanks."

"It's going to be a long walk from here to the movie theater. Do you think you're up to it?"

"Sure. No problem." How long a walk? I hope I don't fall down and faint in front of everybody.

I've never been to this mall before. It's huge, with glass ceilings and big holes cut in the floor so you can look down at the shops below.

Last year, before everything, when I used to go to the mall near my house, I would stand next to the open balconies and look down. I used to wonder what it would be like to fall. Would I be scared or would I just relax and enjoy the view as I fell? Would I feel it when I hit the ground or would my neck just snap against the floor? I used to like that feeling, of being right on the edge, ready to let gravity do all the work, but now I don't even like looking at the holes in the floor.

Here we are at the movie theater. I should pay for the tickets. No, I don't have any money. Okay, Tina can pay, just this once, but next time I'll be the man. She hands me the tickets to give to the usher. All right, I can do this.

The usher is Indian, and I can see him looking at me as I walk. He's looking at my face. He's looking at my hands. He's going to say something. I can tell he's going to say something. He's going to ask me. He better not ask me. If he asks me, Tina, you tell him. Tell him I got hurt in a house fire, and if he asks what started the fire, say electricity. Say that.

He takes the tickets out of my hand and looks at me again. Don't say anything. Don't say anything.

"Theater four is on your right. Enjoy the show."

What? Oh, okay, he didn't ask me anything. He didn't say anything. "Where do you want to sit?"

"I like the aisle."

"Back here?"

"Yeah. This is good."

Laura and I sat in the back of the theater the only time we ever went on a date. We saw *Ski Patrol* and I spent the whole time trying to put my hand up her denim skirt, but I never got farther than halfway up her thigh.

I look at Tina's jean shorts. No, it's never gonna happen. Just enjoy the show.

The lights are going down. Here we go. Oh God, Bill Murray is so funny. He's walking along the street and he looks like he's afraid to touch anything. He's holding the door open with a handkerchief. I wish I was that funny.

Richard Dreyfuss is a doctor who is going on vacation with his family and Bill Murray wants to come too so he can be cured by the great doctor. The only good thing about leaving Children's is that I'll never have to see Dr. Rubinstein again.

Now Bill Murray's shown up at the vacation spot where Richard Dreyfuss is. Okay, here we go, here comes the comedy. Here comes the funny stuff. I don't know, I'm not really laughing. I'm sure it'll start to be funny in a few minutes, though.

Dreyfuss is trying to get Bill Murray to go back home, but he won't. And he's trying again, but he won't. And he's trying again, but he still won't.

Now Dreyfuss is kind of going crazy, he can't stand it anymore, and he's going to get Bill Murray to go home no matter what. He's tying Bill up, and he's pouring something on him. What is that? Oh God. That's not gasoline, is it? Don't be gasoline. Don't be gasoline. Don't put gasoline on him. That's not funny. This is a comedy. Don't put gasoline on him. Please don't burn him. That's not funny. Please don't. Don't burn him. Maybe I should close my eyes. I shouldn't watch this. We should have seen a different movie.

I feel sick. This is the worst. The absolute worst movie I've ever seen in my life.

Oh, now the house is blowing up. It's on fire. Everything is on fire. I didn't want to see a movie about fire. I wanted to see a funny movie. This is terrible. Tina shifts in her seat like she's uncomfortable. I wonder what she's thinking.

Finally it's over. Thank God. Thank God, it's over.

"What did you think of the movie?" asks Tina.

"It was good. How'd you like it?"

"I liked it."

"Good."

"Let's go pick up our ice cream."

"Yeah."

Back in the car and we're driving. I look down at my Hard Rock Cafe T-shirt.

I say, "Hey, Tina, did I ever tell you about the time when I got lost in D.C. by myself?"

"I don't think so."

"It was my brother's birthday and we were all supposed to go into D.C. to go to the Hard Rock Cafe for a celebration. We took the Metro in and we were supposed to meet my dad there, 'cause he works in the city, you know. I remember I was mad at my mom and my brother and I just wanted to be alone, so I walked up to the very end of the track, up where all the electrical equipment is, like the fuse boxes and all this other stuff.

"And I started thinking about how if I wanted to blow up the Metro station, a good place to put a bomb would be right there on the power supply. It would probably blow the whole thing up." She's not going to think this is weird, is she? I should laugh to make the story sound less scary. I laugh, but she doesn't, she's just listening.

"Anyway, while I was up there, the train came, and I didn't hear it, and my mom and brother got on, but I didn't.

"So, I got on the next one and rode it all the way into D.C."

"Yeah?"

"And so"—I'm laughing again, and I think I hear Tina chuckle too—"I walked all the way across D.C. trying to find the Hard Rock Cafe. All the way from Foggy Bottom to Metro Center, which is like four miles, and I still couldn't find it. I did find the Louis Farrakhan rally, though. And the funniest part is that just when I gave up and got back on the Metro to go home, I was within one block of the Hard Rock Cafe."

"I bet your parents were worried."

"Yeah, they totally freaked out. I thought I was just doing what anybody else would do."

She shakes her head and looks at me out of the corner of her eye. We're back at Ben & Jerry's. Tina says I should just wait in the car while she goes and gets the Vermonster, then we'll go back to the Burn Unit and share it with everyone else. Sounds good.

Here she is. She opens the door and puts a giant bucket in my lap. "Doesn't it look good?" says Tina.

It looks like the best thing in the world.

"We'd better hurry back before it melts."

"Yeah, let's go home," I say.

"Home?"

"I mean the Unit."

That's weird. I wonder why I said that. I'm glad there aren't any psychologists here. They're always trying to make it seem like when you say something, that you actually mean it, instead of it just being a mistake.

Here we are. I can't wait to go and tell everybody about how good it smelled in the ice cream place and how fun it was to sit in the movie theater. I'll tell them I really liked the movie, but I'm not going to say anything about the fire part.

I'm kind of tired and we have to take the wheelchair up with us anyway, so I sit in it and Tina wheels me over to the elevator. It's so quiet and peaceful in here after eight o'clock, when visiting hours are over. We're in the elevator alone, Tina and I. I should say something about how grateful I am and about how I'm so happy that she was the one that took me out into the world. I want to thank her for everything she's done for me. For all the times she helped me when I was hurting. I want to tell her about how much she meant to me even before I could talk and how she made me feel better just by looking at me.

"Tina?"

"Yes, Brent."

"Thank you."

"You're welcome." I don't think she knows what I'm thanking her for.

"Thank you for everything."

"You're welcome."

We've got family therapy today. Dr. Rubinstein thinks it's important that we get together as a family and talk about the effect my hospitalization has had on everyone. So we're meeting in her office at two, which is in three minutes.

Mom is wheeling me down and Dad and Craig are going to meet us there. I can't wait to get back upstairs and eat some more of the Vermonster. A lot of the ice cream has melted and now it's just a big mush, but it's still good. I'm going to eat it for breakfast, lunch, and dinner from now on.

Here we are. Dr. Rubinstein's office reminds me of her, small and cold, with lots of diplomas on the wall. She says hello to me and my mom and points to where Mom should put me and the wheelchair, right in the middle between three other chairs.

Dad and Craig come in. They both look a little nervous, but they say hi and try to act like they want to be here. Everybody is very serious. I can tell right away, this is not going to be fun.

Dr. Rubinstein starts. God, I hate her voice. "Thank you all for coming, and I'm glad that you were willing to sit down together and discuss what has happened in your family in the last few months. I think it is vital that you as a family express your feelings to each other and begin the healing process."

Mom is smiling with her head tilted sideways. Dad looks gruff and uncomfortable. Craig is looking straight at Dr. Rubinstein. He looks so angry.

She's still talking. "Let's begin with you, Brent. Why don't you tell your family about how you were feeling before your accident."

What? I can't even believe she just said that to me. What did she say? I'm not going to answer that. I don't even know what she's talking about.

I look down at my hands. My hands. My hands.

Look how the fabric of the Jobst garment is like a layer of skin on top of my skin, the color of my skin, but it's elastic. Elastic and fantastic.

It's interesting that my hands only got burnt up to the first knuckle. And the fire didn't get to my palms. I must have been making fists. Let's see, if I make a fist, it almost perfectly covers the part of my fingers that isn't burned. That's very interesting. There's also the little circle of normal skin on my right elbow. I wonder how that got there.

And my armpits, those are normal, and most of my stomach, and the insides of my thighs, and my penis. I must have curled up like a potato bug after I lit the match.

"Brent, what are you thinking about?"

"Nothing."

"Nothing?"

"Nope." I wonder if they can hear it in my voice, what I was actually thinking about.

"Do you want to say anything to your family?"

"Not especially. Not right now, thanks."

"How are you feeling?"

"Great, how are you?" Everyone loves sarcasm.

"I'm fine, Brent. Your parents and your brother want to know what was happening with you before your accident."

"So?"

"Do you have anything you'd like to tell them about that?"

"No." If you ask a stupid question, you'll get a stupid answer.

"Do you think there's anything they should know?"

"No."

"What were you thinking about? What was making you so unhappy in those days?"

"I don't remember." That's true. I don't remember. I don't remember anything about myself back then.

"You don't remember?"

"No."

"Why do you think that you don't remember?"

"I don't know." I really don't know.

Mom says, "We'll love you no matter what, honey."

"I know."

"We want to know whatever you want to tell us."

"Okay."

"Do you want to think about it for a few minutes?"

"Sure." I'll think about it. And I'll think about how my fingernails got so thick when I was on all those vitamins and how now, since I've been off them, they've gone back to normal thickness, so that there's a ledge on my fingernails. What's the word for that stuff at the end of your nails? Cuticle. Cuticle. I have cute cuticles. That's funny. I'll remember that.

"Brent?" That's my mom's voice, but I'm not going to look up.

"Yes."

"Have you thought of anything you want to tell us?"

"No."

"It's been five minutes."

"No, it hasn't. It's been more like one minute."

"No, honey, it's been five."

"Well, what time did you ask me?"

"Twelve-thirty-five."

"And what time is it now?"

"Twelve-forty."

"So that's five minutes."

"I know it is, honey."

"But you said it was ten minutes."

"No, I didn't, honey, I said five."

"Well, if you said five, then you would have been right, but you said ten."

"I didn't say ten, honey, I said five." I can hear her getting annoyed at me, but I can tell she doesn't want to yell.

"Goddamn it, Brent!" Oh God, I forgot my dad could yell like that. He sounds like a lion when he yells like that. I'm not going to look at him. I'm not going to say anything.

"Brent! Answer the question!" He's calmed down a little. I think he remembered where he was.

No one can make me say anything. No one can make me talk. I think I'd do well in one of those prison camps where they tie you down and torture you. I can't imagine that they could come up with anything more painful than this. I think it would be kind of relaxing, actually.

"Well," Dr. Idiotstein says in Idiot, the native language of Idiots from the island of Idioticus, "our time is up for today, but I'd like to thank you all for coming and I think that we've made some progress today." If that's progress, I'd like to see regress, or egress, which means exit. Remember what P. T. Barnum said, This way to the egress. That's where I'm going.

Mom pushes me back to my room. We're silent the whole way.

Last day. Last night. Last night in the Burn Unit. We're going to have a party so that everyone can come and say good-bye, all my friends that I've made over the last four months. It's June 11th, and I was admitted on February 4th. God. I don't know, I got so used to everything and everyone, it seems like my home here now. I know this sounds crazy, but I don't really want to leave, I really don't. I don't understand why I can't just stay and live here with the nurses and do my rehab here.

So, here we go, the party's all ready. They made a poster that says GOOD LUCK, BRENT. All the letters look like they're made of balloons. It's kind of like the poster I made for Mom on her birthday, but this one is a lot better.

There's ice cream and cake and everyone is here and they're all smiling at me. I don't know how to thank them all. I can't thank them enough. I can't say thank you enough times.

I don't know how to tell them all how much they mean to me. Becky: helped me learn how to use my arms again. Dawn: taught me how to walk. Dr. Rudolph: put my skin back together. Barbara: cleaned my wounds and called me Gorgeous. Lisa: helped me go to sleep at night. And Tina. Tina, you did everything for me. You held my hand and you told me I was going to be all right and made me laugh and took me outside the hospital and made me feel normal.

Mom has little presents, wrapped in bags with tissue paper coming out the top, for Lisa, Barbara, and Tina, my primary nurses. I feel like I should say something.

"You guys, uh, I just wanted to say thanks for helping me, you know, get better. I just wanted to thank you for everything. And everything." The words aren't good enough. They're all smiling at me. "So, here you go. I just wanted to say thank you. So, thanks."

They all open them at the same time. They all got the same thing, a little plastic Snoopy dressed up like a nurse with a hypodermic needle. It's perfect. No, it's not. It's dumb. It's so dumb, I can't believe it. It doesn't say what I wanted it to say. It doesn't say, I could never have gotten better without you. It doesn't say anything.

They all say thank you and give me big hugs. Mom gets the Polaroid from the nurses' station and gets us all together. Lisa kisses my left cheek. Barbara kisses my right cheek. Tina kisses the top of my head. I close my eyes, pucker my lips, and kiss the air.

Mom is saying something to Dad. The car is slowing down. I open my eyes. We are driving past a huge stone wall that has to be ten feet tall. There's something on top of it. What is that? Is that broken glass? It's got broken glass on the top of the wall. They're taking me to a fucking prison or something.

"What is that broken glass supposed to do?"

"What?"

"There's broken glass on the top of the wall."

"Oh, I didn't notice it."

"You didn't? How could you not notice a bunch of broken glass on the top of a huge stone wall?"

"I don't know."

"You don't know? Well, why is it there?"

"I'm sure it's just to keep people out."

"What? Keep who out?"

"I don't know."

"Jesus, you're taking me to a prison."

"We're not taking you to a prison."

"It looks like a prison. Are there Nazis in a tower somewhere?"

"Brent, it's not that kind of place. It's nice. It has a bowling alley."

"Great. Does the bowling alley have armed guards too?"

We park the car and get out. It's hot here. Really hot and really humid. This place better be air-conditioned. Oh good, okay, it's air-conditioned. There's the cafeteria, I wonder what kind of Jell-O they have. Probably just green and red. I hope they put whipped cream on it.

We wait for the elevator.

My parents told me there's another burned kid here. He's eight, and he was at school when a senator's plane crashed into a helicopter above his school and he got covered in flaming jet fuel. Compared to me, I mean, compared to the way I got burned, it's like the complete opposite.

Okay, here we are, this is it, this is the new place. For one thing, it's much bigger than the Burn Ward at Children's. And for another thing, Children's has lots of fun stuff on the walls, like cartoon characters and that cute bear with the stethoscope, and it's got green carpet. But this place is awful. It's just white walls and gray linoleum.

Dad introduces himself to the woman behind the nurses' station. God, I hope he doesn't flirt with her.

"Hello, I'm Don Runyon, this is my wife, Lin, and my son Brent. Brent's going to be staying here." I feel like I'm checking into a hotel.

"Hello, Mr. Runyon, we've been expecting you. This is Brent? Hi, Brent, I'm Rose. I'll be your nurse." The words she says are fine, but the way she says them is a little harsh, like she's angry inside and just barely keeping it in, but maybe that's because she's a smoker.

She shows us into my room, which is right next to the nurses' station, and leaves us alone so Mom and Dad can say good-bye.

The room is okay. It's got a TV and windows and at least I don't have a roommate, I was nervous about that. I sit on the bed and start looking for the remote control. Wait, maybe I should say good-bye to Mom and Dad first.

"What do you think, Brenner?"

"It's okay." Actually, the bed isn't as nice as the one I had at Children's, but it's all right. I wonder how many channels we get here.

Mom's already put all my clothes in the drawers and Dad's opened the drapes to let some light in. Mom brought the signed Magic Johnson picture and the Get Well Soon balloon. They both come over and sit on the bed with me, one on each side.

Mom says, "We're going to go, honey."

"Okay."

"Are you going to be okay?"

"Yeah."

She's starting to cry.

"We love you and we're so proud of you. We're going to miss you so much."

"Me too."

"And we'll be back in a few days to see you, okay?"

"Yeah, okay."

"And we'll call you tonight."

"Okay."

"Okay."

Dad says, "We love you, Brenner." He slips a couple of folded twenties into my hand. "Don't tell your mother."

We all laugh and they both kiss and hug me one last time on their way out the door. I can tell Mom is going to break down in about fifteen seconds, probably Dad too.

"Bye, honey. We love you."

"I love you too."

"Bye, Brenner."

They're gone. I turn on the TV and start flipping through the channels. Someone's knocking.

"Come in." It's Rose. "Hi."

"Hello, Brent."

"What's going on?" I hope I don't sound as nervous as I feel.

"Well, I'm going to get you all set up and then Dr. Cawley is going to come in and do a complete physical. How's that sound?"

"Fine."

"Good because you don't have a choice." I'm not sure if I should laugh or what. "First, we have to get you undressed."

"Okay."

"Can you do it yourself, or do you need my help?"

"Um, I can get my shirt and shorts off, but I need help with my Jobst garments."

"Is that what those things are called?"

"Yeah."

"And what do they do?" Shouldn't she know that?

"I guess they keep my scars from swelling up, and they keep my circulation going."

"Like support stockings."

"I guess."

"The kind old ladies wear."

"Yeah. I guess."

"Okay, show me what I need to do." I pull my shirt over my head and throw it on the bed. I look down at my chest with the Jobst jacket on. And just for a second, I think that it's my actual skin.

"I need you to unzip my arms." There's a zipper that runs all the way from the back of my wrist to the top of my shoulder, and it's too hard for me to unzip.

"You can't do it yourself?"

"No."

"You sure?"

"Yes." There's something about her I don't like.

She unzips the arms and my skinny purple arms start showing through the space.

"Oh my, you really did a number on yourself, didn't you?"

"Yeah."

"You set yourself on fire." I can't tell if it's a question or a statement.

"Yeah."

"Why'd you do that?"

God, I can't believe she's asking me that. "Um . . . I don't know."

"What do you mean, you don't know? You did it, didn't you?"

"Yeah."

"So?" She's got my jacket off now and I'm just wearing my Jobst gloves, my shorts, and a bunch of Ace bandages on my legs. "Take your shorts off."

"Okay." I pull down my shorts, but I'm kind of embarrassed by my Stars-and-Stripes boxers. I wonder if I should get another pair of those glow-in-the-dark boxers. No, I don't think I want them.

"So, why did you set yourself on fire?" She's unwrapping my legs now.

Not this again. "I don't remember."

"You don't remember?"

"No."

"Did your penis get burned?"

God. "No."

"Lucky guy."

"Yeah."

"Were you trying to kill yourself?"

"Yeah."

"You were?"

"Yes."

"Why?"

"I told you, I don't remember." I wish she would shut up already.

"Well, don't try anything like that here, or you'll have to deal with me."

"Okay."

"How do you get these gloves off?"

"Um, usually they grab them around the wrists and pull them straight off, you know, kind of turning them inside out."

She grabs the glove around my wrist and pulls. She pulls it so hard that my whole arm comes with it and my hand lands right on her breast.

"Sorry."

"And don't try anything like that again either."

"I'm sorry, it was an accident."

"Sure it was."

"It was."

"The other burned kid tried the same thing his first day. Lie down, the doctor will be here in a minute."

I lie down and look up at the ceiling. I hope the doctor's nicer than Rose. I've never met anyone who's so mean the first time you meet them. Usually people at least pretend to be nice, even if deep inside they're really mean.

When I was little, my brother and I would lie on our backs and imagine what it would be like to walk on the ceiling. We'd have to walk around the chandelier and step over the doorways. It always seemed so cozy to live on the ceiling, up where nobody could bother you.

Here's the doctor, come to inspect me. He's tall and blond. "Hi, Brent, I'm Dr. Cawley. How are you doing today?"

"Fine."

"How was your drive up from D.C.?"

"Fine."

"Good. Well, what we're going to do here is a complete physical. We're going to check you inside and out and make sure everything's working all right. How's that sound?"

"Fine."

"Do you have anything you want to talk about before we begin?"

"Like what?"

"Physical complaints. Concerns. Questions."

"I itch all over my body all the time and my big right toe is screwed up."

"Okay, we can give you medication for the itching. What's wrong with the toe?"

"It got screwed up when I had to lie on my stomach and now it's hard to walk."

"Okay, we'll take a look at that a little later on. Hold on, let me go get Rose." Great. She comes in carrying a notebook and a pen.

He says, "Okay, Brent, if you could step up on that scale, please. I'm just going to take a few measurements."

I get up off the bed and stand on the big doctor's scale.

"Height is one hundred fifty-nine point five centimeters."

What is that in inches?

"Weight is, let's see . . ." He moves the little weight to

the right with his index finger. "Fifty-two point six kilograms."

I'm trying to get down to fifty-two point four, but Weight Watchers isn't working for me. That's funny. Should I say that?

He takes my head in his hands and tilts it. "Scalp is clear. Facial features are slightly asymmetrical, with burns to both sides of the face. Ear canals are clear. Tympanic membrane is gray with a good light reflex." I've always said my tympanic membrane had a good light reflex, really, always said that.

He's shining a flashlight in my eyes. "Pupils react directly and consensually to light. Look to the right. Look to the left. Extraocular eye movements are intact. Acuity is grossly intact."

Grossly intact. Is that good or bad? I wonder.

"Nasal membranes are pink and noninflamed. Open wide." He sticks a tongue depressor in my mouth. "Gag is strong. Say ah. Soft palate rises symmetrically. Tongue protrusion is midline."

Fantastic.

I'm beginning to feel like one of the dead people they cut up in that movie *Gross Anatomy*.

His hands are around my neck. "No lymphadenopathy." Now he's using the stethoscope on me. "Breathe deeply. Chest is clear bilaterally, with decreased audibility in the right base. Chest wall excursion is equal bilaterally. Respiratory rate is twelve. There is no stridor. No retractions."

This is getting old. He asks me to stand up, sit down, roll over, stand up again, stand on one leg, then the other leg, touch my toes, touch my fingers to my thumb, push down on his hand, touch my head, and on and on and on. I think he can tell I'm getting sick of this because he says, "Only a few more things."

He asks me to lie down again and starts touching different parts of my body first with his finger and then with a pin to see if I can feel it. I'm pretty good at figuring out where he's touching me, especially in the arms and back, but my legs aren't so good. They told me at Children's that I had lost some feeling in my arms and legs and that was normal, but I can't feel anything at all in my right foot and through most of my right leg. Sometimes I can feel a light pressure when he pushes down on the thick scars, like someone's touching me through a wet suit.

"Okay, Brent, we just have a few more tests and then we'll be all done."

"Okay."

"I'm going to say five words and then you repeat them back to me. Crust. Tree. Ball. Scissors. Footprint."

"Crust. Tree. Ball. Scissors. Footprint." I've always been good at stuff like this.

"Good. Now count upward from seven by sevens. Okay, you understand?"

"I think so. Seven, fourteen, twenty-one, twenty-eight, thirty-five, forty-two, forty-nine, fifty-six, sixty-three, seventy, seventy-seven, eighty-four, ninety-one, ninety-eight.

Want me to keep going?"

"No, that's fine. What's four times five?"

"Twenty."

"Eight times six?"

"Forty-eight."

"Okay, great. That's it. You're done. You can relax. Hope you enjoy your time here at duPont. I'll be checking in on you from time to time."

"Okay."

"Someone will be in later to show you around and to bring you dinner."

"Okay." They leave and shut the door and all of a sudden I feel like having them come back in and do more tests on me. It's not that I really want more tests, I just don't want to be alone in here. This room, this whole place, it all seems so, I don't know, empty, or not empty exactly, but hollow.

I turn on the TV. News, no, too boring. Golf, definitely too boring. Some science-fiction show? Oh, *Quantum Leap*, I've heard about this show. It's the one about the guy that goes back in time to help people who've had problems and he fixes them and then goes somewhere else. This looks good. I'll watch this.

I wonder if it's real, I mean, I wonder if there is someone out there who's figured out how to travel in time and who goes back and fixes people's mistakes that they've made. Someone who could jump into your body just when you were about to make the biggest mistake of your life and keep you from doing it. That would be great. That would be amazing. I wish that was true.

There's someone in my doorway. She says her name is Lisa and she's going to be my nurse for the next couple of hours. "First things first," she says. "Let's get you in the shower."

"It's been a long time since I've taken a shower," I say. I'm not going to tell her about the last time I was in the shower, I think it would freak her out. "I'm not sure I can do it."

"Well, we've got a shower chair if you want to try that."

"That sounds good." She leaves the room to go find the shower chair and I look down at my body. I'm still uncovered from the physical, only wearing my red-white-and-blue boxers. At Children's, I got really used to people seeing me naked, I didn't care who it was, Tina, Lisa, Barbara, even Reggie and Calvin, but here I feel a little self-conscious.

She's back with what looks like a plastic lawn chair. She goes and puts it in the shower, which is connected to my room, and then comes back to get me. "Can you walk, or do you need some help?"

"Well, the circulation in my legs isn't so great when I don't have the bandages on, so maybe a little help."

Lisa brings over a wheelchair to get me into the bathroom and then helps me into the shower chair.

Everything is going smoothly enough. Just as she's about to turn on the shower, she stops and asks, "Want to take off your boxers? You don't have to if you don't want to."

"Oh no, I will." I scoot up in the chair and push them off my butt and down to my ankles and then I kick them off and catch them in the air. She laughs.

"Ready?"

"Yup." The hair down there is still growing back from when they shaved it for the graft sites. My penis looks small too, probably because it's so cold.

The shower is so nice and warm, but not too warm, and it feels so good falling down on my head, like warm rain. I close my eyes, suck some of the water into my mouth, and spit it against the wall, like I used to.

I wonder if they painted the bathroom at home. Did they get a new shower curtain? Did they cover everything up? God, I hope so.

"What are you thinking about?"

"Oh, nothing, just enjoying the shower."

"Is it too warm? Too cold?"

"No, it's just right, like the Three Bears." She smiles. She sort of looks like Ellen Barkin, the actress in that sexy movie *Sea of Love*.

When I'm done, she takes me out of the shower and back into my room. I lie on my back while she wraps my legs in new Ace bandages and helps me into my Jobst garments.

Lisa says she'll come back a little later with some dinner and I say that sounds good, even though I sort of wish she'd stay.

"Do you need anything?"

"No thanks." I hope she didn't hear my voice shake when I said that.

I watch *Entertainment Tonight* and part of *Current Affair*, and Lisa comes back with some dinner, chicken potpie, a carton of whole milk, and a container of vanilla pudding. It tastes almost exactly the same as the crappy food at Children's. At least some things stay the same.

Lisa says that I'm going to be on a schedule here and that I'm going to be responsible for going to the places I need to go and for making sure I get there on time. She's got a chart of all the day's activities on the door. I've got a lot to do. Every morning I get up and have a massage, that sounds good, then I have occupational therapy until ten, then physical therapy until noon, then lunch, and then school from one to four. On Tuesdays and Thursdays, I have a therapy session for one hour. That'll be fun. Lisa says someone will come to my room in the morning to get me up and take me to my first appointment and she says I should try and get some sleep because I have such a big day tomorrow. I just hope the night goes fast because I know that if I can get to tomorrow, I'll start to feel better.

There's a woman standing over me. She's got crazy red hair, like Medusa, and long Lee press-on fingernails that she keeps poking me with.

"Wake up. Wake up. It's time for your pills."

"What?"

"It's time for your pills."

"But it's not morning."

"I know. It's time for your pills."

"What?"

"Your pills. For itching. You're supposed to take them at midnight."

"What?"

"Wake up and take your damn pills." Oh God, she's mean. Her name tag says her name is Laurie. "I'm your night nurse. Now take your damn pills."

She picks up two little gray pills between her fingernails. When the nails touch my hand, I get chills from my toes to my scalp. I take the pills quickly and roll back over and try to go to sleep. She's like Freddy Krueger with those things. Going to give me nightmares.

More knocking but now it's light, is it morning? I think it's morning. "Come in."

"Hi, Brent."

"Hi." It's Rose.

"Get up and get moving. Time for your first day."

"Okay."

"Get up. Get up. Get up."

"Okay. Okay. Okay."

"Let's get you in the shower."

"I took a shower yesterday."

"Well, you stink and you need another one."

I can't tell if she's kidding or not. I think she's not

kidding. She's already unwrapping my bandages and taking off my clothes.

"So how'd you sleep?"

"Not very well."

"Why not?"

"People kept coming in."

"Oh, poor baby, you're in the hospital. That's what people in the hospital do." She's not a very sympathetic person.

The shower does feel pretty good. It's waking me up and I start singing a little tune I heard on the radio yesterday.

"'Imagine there's no heaven. It's easy if you try. No hell below us, above us only sky.'"

"Don't say that."

"What?"

"Don't say, 'Imagine there's no heaven.' That's sacrilege."

"No, it's not, it's just a song."

"No, it's not. It's sacrilege. Keep it to yourself. How'd you like it if there was no heaven?"

"Fine with me."

"Oh, fine with you, huh?"

"Yeah."

"How'd you like it if you'd died and found out there was no heaven?"

I don't know what to say to that. I never thought about it.

She says, "Oh, never mind. Get out of there."

I get into some shorts and a shirt, but I leave off my Jobst garments and bandages because I'm going to get a massage. Maybe it'll be a bunch of hot chicks rubbing me down.

Rose puts me in a wheelchair and takes me out to the elevator and down to the basement. She brings me into a little room with a massage table and leaves me there.

"Don't get into any trouble."

"Okay, bye, Rose." She's a strange person.

There's nothing in here to look at, just blank walls, some drawers, and a few chairs. I guess I'll just sit here and wait. The door opens behind me. "Hey, are you Brent? I'm Gina. I'm going to be your massage therapist." She's young, like twenty, and she's cute and short with a little blond crew cut.

"Hi."

"So, we've got to get you out of those clothes and onto this table. How do you want to do that?"

"Um. I can get undressed. But then can you help me onto the table?"

"Sure." After I'm up on the table, she gives me a little towel to cover up with and she gets out a tongue depressor and uses it to dab the Eucerin cream, like cold cream cheese, all over my disgusting purple legs.

"Hey, Gina?"

"Yeah, Brent."

"Do you have to wear those rubber gloves the whole time?"

"Um, I guess not. Why?"

"I just hate the feeling of them on my skin. Is there any

way you can do it with just your hands? That's how they did it at my old hospital."

"Well, I don't see any open spots on your legs, so I guess it'll be okay." I like her already. She takes off the gloves and starts rubbing the cream into my feet and ankles. "Tell me if I push too hard. I'm just trying to get the cream into your scars to soften them up a little."

It doesn't hurt, this rubdown thing, but it doesn't exactly feel very good either. I was hoping it would be a little more, I don't know, sexy.

"Brent."

"Gina."

"You like music?"

"Sure."

"Do you mind if I turn on the radio?"

"No. Go ahead." She's got a little boom box that she switches on and it's Extreme right in the middle of "More Than Words."

"Hey, this is nice, I just lie here and listen to music while you give me a massage?"

"Yup. You're living the good life now, buddy."

"I like your haircut."

"Thanks, I just got it cut for a part in this play I'm doing."

"Cool. What play?"

"Peter Pan."

"Wow. Are you Peter?"

"Yup."

"That's awesome."

"Yeah, I get to fly around the stage and everything."

"That sounds so cool. I'd love to try that."

She's worked her way up to my thighs now, and when she works this one heavy scar on my left leg, her fingers move up and down the inside of my thigh. I hope I don't get an erection. Well, I'm definitely getting an erection, but I hope she doesn't see it. I wonder if she's thinking about that, about my dick, I mean. I wonder if she's thinking about how she'd like to reach up and play with my balls under the towel. Oh God, that would feel good.

Oh shit. I just glanced down and the towel is standing straight up between my legs. I hope she doesn't notice. How embarrassing. What did my friends used to say? Think about baseball and boners are gone? Okay, Wade Boggs is up to bat, and there are two out in the ninth inning, and the Red Sox are behind by a run. Oh and there's a guy on first base. Ellis Burks. That was cool when we met him at the baseball card convention. Was he Rookie of the Year? I can't remember. Okay, that's better, I think it's starting to go down now.

Gina asks me to roll over and does the back of my legs. When she rubs the really heavy bands on my shoulders and legs, they hurt. She has to rub the cream in to keep the scars from getting too rigid.

There's the one that stretches all the way from the inside of my ankle, up my whole leg, through my crotch, and all the way down the other leg. That makes it hard to spread my legs too far apart. Then there's the one that's over my shoulders, especially my right shoulder, that keeps me from raising my hand much farther than the top of my head. It feels like if Gina plucked the bands with her fingers, she could play a song. Hopefully, if we keep doing this, the bands will loosen up and I'll be able to move around better.

Gina's done and it's time to get dressed again. "So, Gina, do we get to do this every day?"

"Yup."

"Good." Looking at her again as she's wrapping up my legs, she really is a cutie.

Gina gets me all dressed and back in the wheelchair. I've got OT next, so we've got to go up to the fourth floor. She rolls me down the hall and into a big open room. There's all sorts of workout equipment, massage tables, a little girl lying on top of a huge red ball, a boy in a wheelchair who's tipped over onto his back, a big tall black guy with a metal ring around his head and posts connected down to his shoulders.

"Brent, this is Jodi. Jodi, this is Brent. Have a good time, Brent. I'll see you tomorrow."

"Bye, Gina."

"Hi, Brent, how ya doin'?" She's got a big toothy smile.

"Fine, how are you?"

"I'm great. Are you ready to do some work?" There's something about her that reminds me of a children's television host.

"Sure."

"Great! Let's get you into one of the back rooms and see where you're at."

She rolls me by a bunch of other people in wheelchairs. I wonder if they can tell that I'm not one of them, that I don't belong in this wheelchair, that I'm just lazy.

Jodi takes me into a room and closes the door behind us. It's much, much quieter in here, and one whole wall is just mirrors, like an interrogation room on one of those cop shows. I wonder if there's anybody behind those mirrors watching me. Probably. There's probably a whole team of psychologists and psychiatrists behind those mirrors with big notebooks and cameras trying to figure out what's going on inside my head. I'm not going to say anything while I'm in here.

"Brent, I'm going to check your range of motion and then we're going to go outside and test your strength."

I don't say anything. I bet they're getting frustrated back there. I bet they're wondering if I know that they're there. Yes, I know you're there. You shouldn't put me in a room with mirrors on the walls and expect me not to know you're back there watching me. I'm not stupid.

Jodi's stretching me, checking my passive motion, and I'm staring right at the mirror. You're all trying to figure out what went wrong inside my head. Fucking idiots. You'll never crack the code that's inside my head. You'll never get into my castle. You'll never even get past the gate.

"Brent, what are you thinking about?"

"What?"

185

"What are you thinking about? You were making some strange faces there for a second."

"Oh, nothing."

"Really? Okay, we're all done in here. Let's go out into the main room. So, what are some of your goals while you're here?"

"Um, what do you mean?"

"Well, what can't you do now that you want to be able to do when you leave?"

I can think of one thing, but I'm not sure I should tell her. Should I tell her? Okay, shit. "Well, one thing is, I've got this chance to meet Magic Johnson in a couple of months, and it might turn out that he wants to play some basketball. So, I'd like to be able to play basketball. You know, like jump and stuff."

"Oh yeah? That's a great goal. We can definitely work toward that. I'd also like to work on getting some better range of motion in your arms, especially your right side."

"Yeah."

"Yeah. And we'll also work on strengthening. How's that sound?"

"Good."

"Great."

God, I can't wait to get back to my room and watch TV.

Lunch is okay. Turkey sandwich and a carton of milk. I'm watching *The Price Is Right*. Isn't it funny how nobody can spin the wheel just hard enough to get exactly a dollar? It must be hard to judge how hard to pull on that thing. Jesus, somebody else is knocking at my door. Who is this guy? He must be a psychologist. He's got a beard and corduroys and one of those sports jackets with the patches on his elbows, the only thing he's missing is a pipe. He looks like Donald Sutherland. As if Donald Sutherland were playing Freud in a TV movie of the week.

"Brent, hi, I'm Doug Foust. How's it going?"

"Fine." Was he watching me through the mirror?

"Good. I just came by to introduce myself. I'm a psychologist."

"No kidding."

"Is it that obvious?"

"Yes."

He laughs. "Well, yes, I'm a psychologist and I'll be working with you here."

"Okay." What am I supposed to call him? Doug? Dr. Foust?

He pulls up a chair to the edge of my bed and sits backward in it, like the Fonz would. "So, how's it going so far?"

"I'm tired."

"Oh yeah? They working you hard?"

"Yeah."

"That's what they get paid for."

"Yeah."

"Well, I don't want to talk about anything serious today."

"Okay."

"But we've got regular appointments on Tuesdays and Thursdays to talk."

"Great." Can he hear the sarcasm?

"I just wanted to find out which would be more comfortable for you, to meet here in your room or downstairs in my office."

"I don't know. My room, I guess."

"Okay. So I'll meet you here, Tuesdays and Thursdays at two."

"Okay."

"Great. Nice to meet you."

"Nice to meet you too." I'm not sure why, but I kind of like this guy.

After Dr. Foust leaves, Rose takes me upstairs to the school. It's on the fourth floor, but it's not really a school at all. It's just a little room with a bunch of computers and some kids in wheelchairs. One girl has her face pressed right up against the screen even though the letters are as big as her head. She must be blind or something.

The teacher comes over to introduce himself. "Hi, Brent, I'm Tom Sicoli. I'm the teacher at duPont. Welcome to our humble classroom."

"Thanks."

"Have a seat here at this table next to Elaine. Elaine, this is Brent. Brent, this is Elaine."

"Hi."

"Hello." Wow, she's beautiful. She's about my age, maybe

a little older, with dark hair and big beautiful eyes. The most amazing thing is that she doesn't seem to have anything wrong with her. She's not in a wheelchair. She doesn't have any artificial limbs that I can see. The only thing I can see is a small scar right in the middle of her forehead about as big as a quarter. I sit down next to her.

I say, "So what are you in for?"

"What?" She looks at me as if I'm speaking Latin.

"What are you in for?"

"What?"

"Why are you here?"

"Where?"

"Here."

"Where am I?" What's wrong with this girl?

"At duPont."

"Where is that?"

"Here."

"Where?" God, I feel like I'm in an Abbott and Costello routine.

"Why are you here at the hospital?"

"I'm in a hospital?"

"Yes, you didn't know that?"

"No. Oh, wait, yes, I did."

"So, why are you here?"

"To get better?"

"Okay. What are you getting better from?" This girl is really frustrating.

"I was in a car accident and I hit my head." Boy, did you ever.

189

"How are you two getting along?" It's Tom.

I say, "Fine."

She says, "What?"

"So, Brent," says Tom, "we're going to go through a couple of tests to see where to place you in relation to your grade."

"Okay."

"You were in eighth grade, correct?"

"Yes."

"All right, I'll get the proper tests and be back in a moment." Elaine looks at me again and smiles.

Tom comes back with a bunch of forms and sits down next to me. He explains that he's going to say some words and I have to write them down. I guess it's a kind of spelling test. I'm okay at spelling, but it's not my best subject. Spelling and handwriting, those have always been my weak areas. Everything else I've always been pretty good at, at least until last year.

My parents worked something out with the school system so that I only have to finish two subjects to be able to pass eighth grade. Science and English. That's it. Even though those were the classes I was having so much trouble with before, I don't think it should be that hard.

When we finish with the tests, Tom gives me a copy of *Tom Sawyer* and says my homework is to read the first ten pages by tomorrow.

"Ten pages?"

"Yes."

"I can't read ten pages in one night."

"Try."

"Okay." I'm not going to tell him I already read it when I was in fourth grade. Ha ha, joke's on him.

When I get back to my room, there's a pile of mail on my bed. That's cool—it's only my second day and already I'm getting mail. There's a letter from my mom, which means she must have sent it before we even left to come up here. That's just like her. Something from the McCannells, our family friends. And a big manila envelope from Carolyn, a girl from Kilmer. I wonder how she got this address? My mom must have given it to her.

I open the envelope and pull out the Joyce Kilmer Intermediate School yearbook for 1991. Cool. Pictures of all my friends. Here's a bunch of girls all dressed in fluffy, flower-print dresses and smiling really big with makeup on, the caption says, Julie, Jenny G., Jenny S., Jenny S., Allison, and Angie in a limo after the dance. The eighth-grade dance. I totally missed it.

Here's another picture, another bunch of friends at a fancy restaurant all dressed up in suits and ties under a huge oil painting of naked people and lions. The caption says, Evan, Ryan, Kate, and Kevin at Clyde's after the dance. Everyone looks so much older than I remember. They look like high school kids.

I bet they all went out and got laid after the dance. They probably got drunk and had a big orgy in a fancy hotel room. That's what they probably did. And I missed it. I missed everything.

Here's everyone's school pictures. There's Patrick. Kimberly. Kevin. Brian and Greg. There's Stephen. There's me. Right next to each other, just like we should be. Robie and Runyon, one of the great comedy teams in the history of Kilmer Intermediate. He looks a little funny. Not that I look that great, all dressed up in my black button-down shirt, buttoned right to the top. My hair is just a little too long, and my smile isn't right. It's like I raised my eyebrows a little too soon and made myself look surprised. Idiot.

But look at all that skin, look at all that smooth tan skin all down my neck. How it just folds smoothly over my chin and down my throat, just one color all the way around. No big purple spots or anything.

Turn the page. Awards for Best Looking: Ryan and Moira. Yeah, that's about right. Most Athletic: Patrick and Deanna. Deanna's not athletic. Most Academic: Leah and that kid from GT English. Fucking dork. Best All-Around: Moira and Ryan again. Best Sense of Humor: Megan and Stephen. Most Likely to Be Remembered: Maya, because she's so smart and sassy and doesn't take anything off anyone, and me.

Me. Most Likely to Be Remembered: me. Most Likely to Be Remembered for All the Wrong Reasons: me. God.

I close the book and put it in the bottom drawer.

Today Jodi is showing me the rest of the hospital. They really do have a bowling alley. Also, there's a huge gym with a basketball court. I think it actually could be pretty cool here, you know, if I got to do whatever I wanted and didn't have to work on my strength and stupid range of motion all the time.

I live in the spinal injury section of the hospital, me and all the kids in wheelchairs. Some of them can push the wheelchairs by themselves, others have those motorized wheelchairs, and a few can walk with a cane. There's a black guy, who's at least six feet, who can walk without a cane or anything, but he's the guy that has the big black metal ring around his forehead and the posts that go down to his shoulders. That big metal ring is actually screwed into his skull. I saw the screws going right into his skull. It's so gross.

Rose, the nurse, told me that he was a gangbanger from Philadelphia and that he broke his neck falling out of a car during a drive-by.

The other section of the hospital is the head injury section. That's where people like Elaine who were smashed in the head go to get better. So, between the cripples on the one side and the idiots on the other, I feel like I'm the only normal person in this place.

They say I can't have dinner in my room anymore. I have to go down to the cafeteria with everybody else. It's just like junior high school down here. Everybody that can walk gets a tray and stands in line waiting for the meat loaf. The food smells bad. Especially the corn.

The desserts look okay. Some kind of chocolate cake or Jell-O in a cup with whipped cream on top. I'm going to try the Jell-O.

They have fountain soda. Yes. That's awesome.

I sit with a bunch of people from the Unit, but nobody says anything. I keep looking up right when Lisa puts a big spoonful of corn in a paralyzed girl's mouth. It's so disgusting. Can't she chew with her mouth closed? Maybe not, I guess.

Dinner's over. One of the nurses announces that we're having a little get-together on the Unit. Everybody is meeting in the common area to have soda together.

I'm the only one standing, except for the nurses, and that must be the other burned kid, Harry. He's just a little guy. Oh God, his face got all melted away, and a bunch of his hair is just scar tissue, and the fingers of his hand are melted together so it looks like a claw. Jesus, what a freak. It makes me feel sick to look at him.

I have a song in my head. It's "Man in the Mirror."

Why is that song in my head? I don't even like Michael Jackson. Wasn't he on fire once? Yeah, with the Pepsi commercial that caught his head on fire. I wonder if that's why he looks so weird.

Lisa wants to introduce me to a couple of people. She

takes me over to a blond girl in a motorized wheelchair. She's the one who was eating corn before.

"Brent, this is Chelsea. Chelsea, this is Brent."

"Hi, Chelsea." I put my hand out to shake.

"Hi, Brent." I forgot she probably can't move her arms. Wait, no, she's moving her arm a little. She's lifting up her hand. Wow, she's giving me five.

"Nice to meet you, Chelsea."

"Nice to meet you." I wiggle my fingers under her hand like the cool kids do at school, and she giggles a little. I wonder if she can really feel that. Hey, she's not so bad when she's not eating.

There's another kid right next to me. He's got red hair and he looks a little older than me, like maybe seventeen. He's in the middle of telling the story of how he wound up in the wheelchair.

Lisa whispers, "That's Ben. He crashed his motorcycle."

"Well, it was raining out and, stupid me, I decided to take out my dad's bike, a real sweet Honda 150 cc. Anyway, about two miles away from my house, I took this turn too fast, went straight off the road and headfirst into an oak tree. Snap." He sounds like it happened to someone else.

A chubby nurse standing next to him with a name tag that says Mary says, "So what are you, a C4?"

"Yup. C4." I wonder what that means.

The other burned kid, Harry, pipes up, so I don't have to, "What's C4?"

Mary answers him, "Fourth cervical vertebra, honey. It

means he broke the fourth bone in his spinal column."

"Oh, did it hurt?" asks Harry.

"Not really. I mean, I don't really remember any pain, just the feeling of the rain coming down on my face."

God, I hope this isn't one of those "I'll show you mine, you show me yours" contests. Because I'm not about to tell any of these people what happened to me. Screw that.

Lisa introduces me to the big black guy with the metal ring around his head. The gangbanger. "Brent, this is Latroy. Latroy, this is Brent."

"Nice to meet you."

"Nice to meet you too." He seems nice enough. Not as scary as he seemed from a distance. Anyway, he probably can't hurt me with his neck broken like that.

Lisa says, "Have you met Harry yet?"

"No." And I don't want to.

"Well, let's introduce you two." She takes me over to him.

"Harry, I want you to meet someone."

"Why?"

"Because he's very nice and I think you'll like him."

"Fine."

"Harry, this is Brent. Brent, this is Harry." We don't shake hands. I don't want to touch his hand.

"Hi, Harry."

"Hi, yourself." What? "Lisa," he says, "I hate this. I want to go back to my room."

"Okay, Harry. You can go back to your room."

"Good." This kid is a little brat. But now that he said that, I'm really tired too.

"Lisa, I'm really tired. Can I go back to my room too?"

"Sure. Thanks for coming out."

"Okay."

I sit in bed and watch TV. Sometimes I think I'd be happy if I could just lie in bed and watch TV all the time. That's the way it used to be at Children's. God, that was so great. I miss those guys.

Phone's ringing. They gave me this weird little phone when I checked in that just sits on the dresser. I guess I'll answer it.

"Hello?"

"Brenner?" It's Mom.

"Yeah?"

"Hey, bud. How's it going?"

"Good."

"What are you doing?"

"Watching TV."

"How's the hospital?"

"It's fine."

Dad picks up the other phone. He says, "Hey, Brenner. How's it going, budder?"

I laugh. Dad's funny sometimes. "It's good. What are you guys doing?"

Mom says, "Well, it's Craiger's graduation today, and we

just wanted to call and say hi and say that we miss you. And that we really wish you were here with us. Nanny and Grandpa are here too. Wait, I'll put Nanny on. Here's Nanny."

"Hello, Brent."

"Hi, Nanny."

"Hello, sweetheart. Just wanted to say a quick hello and that we miss you down here. We're just so pleased you're doing so well and can't wait till we see you again."

"Okay, Nanny. Thanks."

"Love you, dear."

"Love you too, Nanny."

"Here's Grandpa."

"Hey, champ." Grandpa's got the most recognizable voice. It's so deep and gravelly. When you sit in a room with him, you can actually feel it through the furniture.

"Hey, Grandpa."

"Good to hear you're doing so well up there, but we miss you down here. So keep getting better."

"Okay, Grandpa. I will."

"Okay, love you, buddy."

"Love you too, Grandpa."

"I'll get Craig."

When I was little and we'd go down to Florida to visit Nanny and Grandpa, I'd sit down by the pool with him in the plastic chairs and listen to his voice through his chest. He had that big old scar on his belly from where he got his gallbladder out. It was so big and smooth and it looked like an oak leaf. I liked to put my hand on it and feel the outline.

Craig's on the phone. He says, "Hey."

"Hey."

"What's up?"

"Nothing. What's up with you?"

"Nothing. Just this graduation thing."

"Yeah. Congratulations."

"Thanks. What are you doing?"

"Nothing. Watching TV."

"Oh. Okay. I'll let you go, then."

"Okay. Bye."

"Bye."

We both hang up.

Dr. Doug Foust is here to see me, just like he said he would be. That's one thing about psychologists—they're consistent. I sit in my bed and he pulls a chair up close.

He says, "So, how's it going here?"

"Okay."

"Good. What have you been up to?" He's got this way about him that makes it seem like he doesn't really care what I say, but I feel like he's listening hard.

"Nothing, just school, OT, and PT."

"How's that?"

"Fine."

"Good. Any complaints?"

"No."

He looks over at my guitar sitting up against the wall.

"Do you play?"

"I tried to learn, but it's out of tune, like seriously out of tune."

"Want me to tune it?"

"Sure, can you?"

"No problem." He picks it up, turns the things at the top, and plucks a few strings. It sounds much better in his hands than it does in mine.

I say, "Do you know any Beatles tunes?" Dad bought me a Beatles tape last weekend.

"Yeah. I know the early stuff, but the later stuff is much harder. They got into a lot of difficult tunings and strange chords."

"And strange drugs."

He laughs. "Yeah. So, had any thoughts of suicide lately?"

"Um . . . no."

"No feelings of taking your own life?"

"Nope."

"Why not?" Did he just ask me why not?

"What?"

"Why not? Why haven't you thought about killing your-self?"

"I don't know. I just haven't."

"You could have, you've had plenty of opportunities." I don't understand, does he want me to try and kill myself?

"Like what?"

"Lots of drugs in the hospital. Lots of windows."

"Oh. I guess I just never thought about it."

"I find that hard to believe." Now he's starting to piss me off.

"Well, it's true."

"Okay. Great." He hands me back my guitar. "So, I'll see you Thursday?"

"Okay. Bye." Maybe it's weird that I never think about suicide anymore, but I don't know. You only get to live for such a short time anyway. It doesn't make sense to kill yourself.

Mom and Dad are here for the weekend. They got me some presents. A Beatles tape and one of those Hypercolor shirts that changes color when your body temperature changes. It's purple when you're cool and pink when you're hot. I put it on over my Jobst garments, they sign me out, and we walk out into the parking lot.

It's so hot out here, my shirt has already turned completely pink. I can't believe how hot it is. It must be like a hundred and twenty degrees. I wish I could sweat, but I don't have very many pores because of the burns and the graft sites. I can feel the sweat making a traffic jam in my body, trying to find a place to get out, but it can only get out of my forehead and armpits.

We get in the car and turn on the air-conditioning full blast. My shirt starts to turn back to purple.

We pop in the tape and listen to the good Beatles songs.

There are places I remember
All my life, though some have changed
Some forever, not for better
Some have gone, and some remain.

Dad says, "Isn't it beautiful here, Brent?"

"What?"

"Beautiful here."

"Yeah. It's hot, though."

"Sure is."

We drive into the main part of town, looking for something to do. It's so hot outside. I can feel it coming through the window even though it's closed. My itching is getting bad.

Dad stops the car in front of a shoe store. He says, "Want to go check out some shoes?"

"Not really."

Mom says, "Jodi said you needed some new shoes to work out in."

"Oh. Can you get them?"

Mom gets out of the car and goes into the shoe store. I wish they could air-condition this whole town. They could put it in a bubble and pump some cool air in, and then we could have a good time.

Mom comes back with a pair of sneakers that look okay. The heat comes in again when she opens the door and my shirt turns pink again. All this heat, all this humidity, is making me have a sick feeling, like kind of dizzy. It makes me want to go back to the hospital and take a bath in ice water.

Dad says, "So, what else do you want to do?"

"I don't know. What else is there?"

"A movie?"

"Okay. *New Jack City?*"

"No. We're not going to see that."

"Why?"

"We're just not."

"That sucks."

Mom says, "How about *Teenage Mutant Ninja Turtles?* Craig saw it and he said it was really good."

"No thanks."

"Then what do you want to do?"

"I don't know. Go back to the hospital?"

"Okay. We can do that."

At least back inside the hospital it's cool, that's one good thing.

They're moving me. I've only been here for a week and they're moving me in with a roommate down the hall. This fucking sucks. I was in Children's for like four months and had my own room, and now I have to fucking share a room with another person. They're putting me in with Latroy, that big black guy with the ring halo on his head.

We're both lying in our beds after dinner watching our TVs. I'm watching *Quantum Leap*, and he's watching I don't know what.

Mary, the chubby nurse, comes into the room. She's Latroy's primary nurse. "Hey, guys."

I say, "Hey, Mary."

Latroy doesn't say anything.

She says, "Hey, Latroy, time to take your shower, buddy."

He doesn't say anything.

"Hey, buddy, time to take your shower."

He's still not saying anything.

"Hello in there."

"I don't want to." Oh, this could be interesting.

"Well, you don't have a choice."

"Well, I don't want to."

"Sorry, buddy, you're taking a shower."

"No, I'm not."

"Yes, you are."

"No, I am not." This is getting a little scary.

"Latroy, get your ass up and into that shower."

"Forget it."

"What did you say?" Maybe I should leave.

"Forget it."

"Get up."

"No."

"Get up!"

"No!"

"Get your ass up!" Mary's only about an inch away from his face now.

"Fuck you."

"Move your ass or I'll move it for you."

"Fuck you." Jesus.

Mary grabs the steel rods that connect his halo to his

shoulders, pulls hard, and drags him by his head out the door and into the bathroom. I guess he's in the shower now. He didn't even try to fight back, even though he's about a foot taller than she is. God, I thought she was going to pull the screws right out of his forehead.

At night, they make me wear these splints to stretch the bands in my shoulders. They're called airplane splints because they make my arms stick out like the wings of an airplane. And also a mouthpiece that fits between my lips and stretches them lengthwise because the scars on my face pull my mouth down a little and they're trying to stretch it back to normal. They also made me a clear plastic mask molded especially for my face that's designed to flatten out the scars on my cheeks. I don't wear that at night, though, only in the day. I feel like a cyborg. "He's more machine than man now." That's how I feel. No joke. Just like a frigging cyborg that doesn't have a mind of his own.

Every night, in the middle of the night, that freaky nurse, Laurie, comes in and gives me pills with her creepy extra long fake nails. I get a shiver up my whole body when I see those things. I try to take my pills without opening my eyes.

I'm in a car. I'm driving a station wagon and I'm going up to the top of a waterfall because I've got to get rid of these bodies. I killed them. I killed these people and now I've got to get rid of these bodies that are in the way back. I don't remember it. I don't remember why I did it, but I know I did it. I killed them. I killed them. I'm so sorry. I'm so sorry. I wish I could take it back. I wish I hadn't killed them, but I did, and I wish I didn't, but I did. They're so dead, so pale, and I have to throw them over the waterfall and they'll fall over and no one will ever see them again.

"Wake up. Wake up, Brent."

What? What? What do you mean?

"Wake up, Brent, it's just a bad dream." No, it's not. It's not a bad dream. I can feel it. It's all over me. I can feel it.

"Brent, it's okay, you're just having a bad dream." I open my eyes, it's Celeste, and she's rubbing my stomach. Maybe I should ask her if she'll help me get rid of the bodies. No, don't ask her. She won't understand. No one will understand.

"It's okay, honey, you were just dreaming." But I wasn't, I wasn't dreaming. It was real. I killed people and I was getting rid of the bodies on top of a waterfall, and I feel, I really feel like I killed someone. I feel so awful.

"You were just dreaming." I don't know. I guess I was dreaming. Something about some bodies and a cliff. Throwing a body over a cliff or something.

"It's okay, honey. You were just dreaming."

"Was I dreaming?"

"Yes, you were just dreaming. It's okay. It's okay." Is she right? Maybe she is right, but I still have this guilty feeling all over me, like oil on one of those birds in Alaska. I feel so terrible, so sorry.

Jodi is taking me down to the bowling alley in the basement. This'll be fun. It's just like the White House in here, with the gym and the bowling alley. The only thing we need is the movie theater and a bunch of jellybeans.

I still feel bad after that dream. Even after I woke up this morning. Even after I took a shower and got my rubdown. I feel like I want to run as fast as I can, like I want to run right out of my skin.

It's just a little bowling alley, three lanes with a ball return and a bunch of balls. Not like in the real world.

"So, Brent, let's start you out with a ten-pound ball."

"Okay." Ten pounds is a lot heavier than it sounds, I can hardly lift it with two hands, let alone one. "So, what should I do?"

"Just roll it toward the pins."

"With both hands?"

"If you want." I stand at the line and look down the lane to the pins. God, they're far away.

"Is this regulation?"

"Yup."

"I'm not sure I can get it that far."

"Try."

"Okay." I put the ball down on the lane and push it forward with both hands. It's hard to bend down that far because the skin around my shoulders is so tight. The ball just rolls right into the gutter and slowly down the lane. It's going to take about five minutes to get all the way to the pins. "That sucked."

"Good first try. Go again."

I go back to the rack and pick up another ball. This time an eight-pounder. At least now I can hold it with one hand, barely, but my fingers are too big to put in the holes. This time when I roll it, the ball goes a little farther but goes in the gutter about halfway down the lane.

"Better. Go again."

"What should I do different?"

"Give it a little more oomph."

"Okay." I find another eight-pounder, this one with bigger holes, and head back to the line. I'm sure I can get at least one pin this time. At least one. I bend over and roll the ball with my right hand. My right elbow doesn't straighten all the way, so the ball drops down on the floor and bounces a couple of times on its way down the lane. It's going down the middle, though. Right down the middle. Now it's moving left. Come on, baby, come on. Get one. Get one. "Yes! I got one!"

"Good one." Jodi gives me a high five on my way back to the ball return. "Way to go, kid." I make a fist and pump it one time in the air, just like Jordan when he won the NBA finals. I'm the man.

Dad is coming up on Friday. Mom and Craig will be here

on Saturday. It was his birthday the other day, the twenty-sixth of June. He turned eighteen. I wonder if they had a big party with all of our family friends. I wonder if anyone asked about me.

I wonder if we'll ever be friends, my brother and I. Ever since we were little kids, we always fought, but now I kind of wish I could talk to him. Or even, I don't know, just hang out and be friends. I know that sounds stupid, but I think about that sometimes.

I wonder what would've happened if I'd told him what I was going to do. Would he have stopped me? Or just said, That sucks, and kept shooting baskets? No, I think he would've tried to stop me, but to be honest, it was too late. I would've found some way to do it.

Dad's here. I'm happy to see him. He takes me across the street to the Ronald McDonald House, where he's staying. It's pretty nice. It kind of feels like a bed-and-breakfast because it's real quiet and there's a lot of old furniture, but there's also fun stuff like in a real hotel, like a TV and a VCR and a Ping-Pong table.

Dad says, "Want to play Ping-Pong?"

"Okay."

I used to be good at this. I wonder how I'll do now. My friend Jake and I used to play in his basement a lot. We'd crank up *Appetite for Destruction* or the new Poison album and hit the ball around. He was a lot better than I was, though.

Dad gets the ball and hits me a nice soft lob. He's taking it easy on me. I can't quite get my arm high enough to smash it, so I hit him back another high lob.

He says, "Good, Brenner." I give him a look. What does he think, I'm a fucking baby?

He hits another soft lob, right at me, and this time I smash it. Fuck. Right into the net.

I serve and he volleys to my forehand. Big mistake. I swing and hit it hard right at him. It hits the table and then bounces off his beer belly. I'm loosening up a little.

He says, "Whoa, Brenner. Take it easy, budder."

"My point. Serve."

He gives me another softie and I smash that one too. I say, "Serve."

Another lob. Another smash. "Serve."

I can tell he doesn't like where this is going, but screw it, I don't want to play like a first grader. He's still smiling, but I can tell something just changed. He's gritting his teeth now.

This time he hits a hard serve right to my backhand, and I miss it completely.

"Shoot."

"You okay?"

"Yeah."

He serves again and this time I hit the ball, but it goes right into the net.

"Your serve, Brenner."

I give him one of those heavy spinning serves, where it's impossible to see where it's going. He whiffs it.

His weakness is that he doesn't have a forehand. I can tell because every time I hit it on that side, he turns his body around so he can hit it backhand.

I say, "Do you still play racquetball all the time?" He used to always be out playing racquetball after work. He even played with that old guy who used to coach the Celtics, Red Auerbach. Yeah, I think that was it.

"Yup. I still play with Julius during lunch."

"Isn't he really good?"

He laughs. "Yup, but, Brenner"—talking in his voice where it sounds really gruff—"last week I played him, and I slaughtered him, budder." He moves the paddle through the air like he's a swashbuckler.

"He must have been sick." We both laugh.

After a while we go into the TV room and pop in a video that they have there. It's called *Goodfellas* and it's about gangsters and their lives. Although it seems to be more about cooking than it is about gangsters.

Dad and I both fall asleep when the gangsters are in jail talking about how to slice garlic. We wake up and the TV just has static. He drives me back to the hospital. That was nice, though, just sitting together like normal people watching a movie.

Mom and Craig are here. I promised I'd take them on a tour, so I show them the basement, where the bowling alley and the gym are, and all the different areas of the hospital. Mom says I'm walking a lot better. I wonder what Craig thinks, he hasn't seen me in weeks, but he doesn't say anything one way or another. That's the thing about my brother—it's hard to tell what he's thinking. It's like he's got a few extra layers between him and the rest of the world. It's funny because when we were kids, he was always the more sensitive one. Whenever we said good-bye to our grandparents, Craig would cry. I asked him why and he just said, "What if they die before we see them again?" I never understood that. We should be happy when we see them, not sad. I wonder if that's why it's so hard to see what he's feeling because he tries to cover everything up.

Before everything, I used to do this thing when I was upset—I used to take all my feelings and push them down inside me. It was like they were garbage and I was compacting it to get more in. I felt like I could keep pushing all my feelings down into my socks and I wouldn't have to worry about them. I don't think I do that anymore.

We have family therapy today with Doug Foust in the recreation room, which is just a little room in the corner with a bunch of windows and a piano. Doug says he wants to give us all the opportunity to talk to each other and say what we've been feeling. He asks Mom to start. That's a bad idea because Mom is just going to start crying.

She says, "Well, it's been real, real hard." She's crying. "Sorry. It's been real, real hard, saying good-bye to Brent. Not having him around so we can see him every day. That's been hard." She wipes the tears with the palm of her hand and Doug hands her a box of tissues. I hate it when she cries, it makes me feel so guilty. "And it's also been hard, you know, getting ready to send Craiger off to college. And I know he's gonna be close, but that's gonna be hard too." She has this habit of talking like a baby when she's really upset. I hate that.

Dr. Foust says, "Thank you, Lin. Don, what would you like to say?"

"Well . . ." When Dad talks in a group, he puts on his business voice and sounds like he's giving a presentation. I hate that too. "Well, I, all of us, really, have had a really hard time the last few months, adjusting and adapting to the new challenges and making sure the things that have to be done are getting done. But on the other hand, I think this has brought us together, made us stronger, and we've had a lot of support from our family and friends, and that has been great. We appreciate it all." Who is he talking to?

"Thank you, Don. Craig, what would you like to say?"

"Um . . . well, I don't know. I don't really have anything to say. It's been pretty hard, you know, for me, to watch what's been going on at home. You know, to watch Mom and Dad sort of fall apart at the end of the day. That's been tough. I think that's been the hardest because that's what I see all the time, you know?

"And at first, I think that sort of made me really angry at Brent. Just to watch all the pain that Mom and Dad are in, and I know that Brent was in pain too, but it was hard to watch what Mom and Dad were going through at the end of every day. So that made me really angry."

He stops for a few seconds. What the hell is he doing talking? Jesus. He says, "It's just because I was home. Because I was the first one to see him. I mean, because I was there and I saw him walk out of the bathroom, and the look on his face, and how all this black smoke came out from behind him." Craig stops talking. I can't tell if he's angry or he wants to cry.

"Brent, what do you have to say about that?"

"Nothing."

"Nothing?"

"No."

"Don't you have any response to what your family said?"

It's the Fourth of July. Mom and Dad and Craig want to go watch the fireworks somewhere. I don't know. I always used to love the Fourth of July. I loved going down to the Washington Mall and watching the fireworks around the monument. It looked like the stem and the fireworks were the flowers.

This year, I don't even want to hold a sparkler. I'm sure one of the sparks will catch my Jobst stockings on fire and go right up my arm and over my back and down the other arm and down my legs. And I'll be rolling on the ground trying to put it out and I'll never be able to put it out. I'll just burn and burn and burn.

It's weird because I used to be such a pyromaniac. When I was eight, my brother and my cousin called me Firebuggie. It was summer and we wanted to dig a tunnel in the backyard, like in *The Great Escape*. Craig and Reune did most of the heavy digging and it was my job to get light so they could work. They gave me a book of matches and told me to give them some light. That was my favorite part, when I got to light the matches. It gave me a little thrill every time I did it. My heart would start racing and then I'd flick my wrist and the flame would come out of nowhere. I loved the little explosion, the ignition and the smell, and the way it blossomed and then wilted into almost nothing and started to grow again. I loved the layers, the blue, the red, the orange, and the little seed of black in the middle. I used to hold it in my hand and watch the flame burn down the match until it just about touched my fingers, and then I'd blow it out. We spent our whole vacation digging in the backyard, making that tunnel.

We watch the fireworks on TV at the Ronald McDonald House, and then they all drive me back to the hospital. They're leaving tomorrow. I'm going to miss them.

I'm going to Dr. Doug Foust's office today for our appointment instead of him coming to my room. It's down on the ground floor.

His office is strange. I sit down in an easy chair and right across from me are two puppets. One is a little kid with blond hair and a funny kind of *Sesame Street* smile. The other is a puppet that looks exactly like Dr. Foust, with the beard and the corduroy and everything. I say, "What are those for?"

"The puppets?"

"Yeah."

"For people who find it easier to talk through a puppet than through themselves."

"Weird."

"Do you want to try them?"

"Me? No way."

"Okay. Well, Brent, I wanted to talk to you about something."

"Okay." I hate it when people do that, tell you they're about to tell you something. It makes me nervous.

"I'm going to be taking a job at another hospital in a few

weeks, and that means that I'm not going to be able to be your therapist anymore."

"What?"

"Yeah. I'm sorry that it worked out like this, I liked working with you and talking to you. I wish we could have kept it up."

"Me too. So who am I going to be talking to now?"

"Well, it'll actually be two people."

"Two people?"

"Yes. Dr. Sheslow, who's worked here for a long time, and Mark Miles, who's just finishing up his residency."

"What does that mean? He's a student?"

"Well, yes, he's just finishing up his studies to become a full-time doctor."

"Are you kidding me? What am I, a fucking classroom? That's fucking stupid."

"No, you're not a classroom. It's just the way it works at this hospital."

"That's fucking stupid. I don't want that."

"I know, but—"

"Give me a fucking break. Jesus. Why do I have to have two psychologists hanging around giving me a hard time? Isn't one of you assholes enough?"

"Well, normally I would agree with you, but in your case—"

"What? I'm so fucking crazy that I need two of you dickheads making my life difficult? Fuck you." I get up and slam the door behind me and head up to my room. Fuck those guys. I can't believe this. Just when I was starting to like him, he picks up and gets another job. Dickhead.

Foust is here with the new doctors. Give me a fucking break. Look at these guys—they look like the Marx Brothers of psychologists. All three of them have facial hair and lab coats on with their names on them.

Foust starts talking. "Well, Brent, I just wanted to introduce you to your new doctors. This is David Sheslow, and this is Mark Miles." The Sheslow character is skinny with a mustache. Miles is fat with a mustache. They both look like dickheads.

"Hello, Brent. I'm David Sheslow." He reaches out to shake my hand. His hands are sweaty. Gross.

"Hi."

"Hi, Brent. Mark Miles." He's got really fat hands. Sick.

"Hi."

"We're both very excited about working with you."

"Great." Smell the sarcasm.

"Dr. Foust has told us a lot about you, but we're anxious to get to know you on our own." What, are these guys such idiots that they share a brain too?

"Well, it's nice to meet you. We'll see you in our office on Thursday. It's right next to Dr. Foust's."

"Okay. Bye." Jesus.

Jodi and I are the only people in the gym. I wonder why nobody else ever uses this place, maybe because they're all in wheelchairs. She gets me a tennis racket and a ball and I start hitting it against the wall. The scars around my shoulder are so stiff. I can't really get my arm high enough to hit it very well. I keep hitting it too high up on the wall and it bounces over my head. This sucks.

I hate it when I try and do stuff that I used to be able to do and then I can't do it anymore. It's depressing.

Every time I open my mouth to say what I'm feeling, something stops me and I have to make sure I'm not going to say anything stupid. It makes me crazy. And then, once I've figured out what I'm going to say, I have to go over it, over and over again, just to see if what I'm feeling is right. And then I have to figure out how to say it. Like, if I want to say, I feel sad, do I say, I feel sad, or, I feel so sad, or, Sad I do feel, or what? How about, Feeling sad am I. How about, I'm the saddest boy in the world.

Sometimes, when I'm feeling something really strongly, the next thing I know I'm singing some song that's almost exactly what I feel, and I don't even know I'm doing it.

Every day I wake up and take the wheelchair down to see Gina and get my massage. Then I go see Jodi and then Viki, the physical therapist. After that's lunch. Then school. And on Tuesday and Thursday, I have to see the therapists.

I like having a routine.

More fun with dickhead therapists. I guess they thought better of having me talk to both of them at the same time, so Mark Miles is talking to me by himself.

"Hi, Brent."

"Hi."

"How's it going?"

"Fine." Dickhead.

"How are you feeling?"

"I told you, fine."

"Okay. So, let's talk about your feelings before the accident. Had you been feeling suicidal for long before the accident?" An accident? Is this a trap?

"Hmm." This is the oldest trick in the book. I just pretend I'm thinking about the question and start looking around for other things to think about. This guy's got nothing on me. I sing quietly to myself. "'Let me take you down, 'cause I'm going to Strawberry Fields.'"

"What are you singing?"

"'Strawberry Fields Forever.' The Beatles. Heard of them?"

"Sure. I grew up with them."

"Yeah, they're good. Do you know, 'For the benefit of Mr. Kite there will be a show tonight on trampoline'?"

"Yup, and, 'I've got news for you all, the Walrus was Paul.'"

"No, it wasn't, it was John."

"No, it's from a song, 'the Walrus was Paul.'"

"What?"

"Never mind, have you thought about my question?"

"No, what was the question?"

"Had you been feeling suicidal long before your accident?" Accident?

"Um, I don't know, let me think about it."

"Okay."

Now I mumble to myself, "Well, you see, I could have, but actually, what I was thinking was . . . since he was bothering me . . . I didn't behave . . . the correct procedure . . . nevertheless . . . irregardless."

"Brent? What are you saying?"

"Oh, I'm just mumbling to myself."

"Do you hear voices in your head?"

"Sure, who doesn't?"

"Voices distinct from your own?"

"Yes."

"Really?"

"I guess so. I mean, some of them sound like me, and others sound like different people."

"Like who?"

"I don't know. Just like other people."

"Are you bullshitting me?"

"No. You asked me a question and I answered you."

"I think you're trying to avoid my questions."

"That's interesting. I'll think about that." This guy is a complete fucking tool. I could run him in circles all day long and he'd never even know he was spinning.

"Brent?"

"Yes."

"Do you have any intention of answering my question?"

"Which one?"

"The first one."

"Which was that?"

"How long had you been feeling suicidal before your accident?"

"Oh, I don't know, let me think about it."

We're having a family therapy session in my room. Mom and Dad are here. Dr. Foust is here. Dr. Dickhead and Dr. Prickhead are here. After this therapy session, I have a weekend pass to go home for the first time.

Foust starts, "It's nice to see you all again. Mr. and Mrs. Runyon, as you know, I'm leaving the hospital, and today is my last official day on Brent's case. Dr. Sheslow and Dr. Miles have already seen Brent a couple of times, and I just wanted the opportunity to introduce you to them and to wish you all well on the road to recovery. I know it'll be difficult, but I'm sure you'll all make it through. It's been a pleasure working with all of you."

My parents thank him and he gets up and leaves the room. That's it. I guess he's gone. Now it's just me and them.

Dr. Sheslow nods at my mom and dad and they start talking. "Brent," says my mom, "we've been in contact with your new doctors and we've been talking about what it means to be going home. We all understand that it's a big step for you, and we want you to be as happy and as comfortable as possible. . . ."

Now my dad starts talking. "Brent, we talked with the doctors and we all agreed that before you came home, we should look through your room and make sure everything is safe."

"We found some things in your room, honey, that we need to ask you about." God, I hope they didn't find the porno.

"What?"

Mom says, "We need to know what some of the things in your room are."

"You searched my room?"

She nods.

"Why the fuck did you do that?"

"We talked to the doctors and decided that it was necessary."

"What?"

Dad says, "Brent, we found a knife under your bed."

"So?"

"And a piece of paper with the word Death written on it."

"So?"

Now Mom starts again. "And we talked to some of your friends at school, honey, about the religion that you created. The Ace of Spades, I think it's called."

"So?"

"And we need to know, honey. Brent, are you involved with the occult?"

"What?"

Dad says, "Are you involved with the occult?"

"What's that?"

Mom says, "The occult. Witchcraft and Satan worship. We need to know if you were involved with those sorts of things."

"What?"

"We know you were worshiping the Ace of Spades and some of your friends said you were into devil worship, and we need to know what you were involved in."

"This is stupid. What are you talking about?"

Dad says, "Brent, just tell us."

"I don't know what to tell you."

Mom says, "Tell us what you were doing."

"I don't know what you're talking about!"

"Tell us, honey."

"We need to know."

"I don't know!"

"Tell us!"

"I don't know what to tell you. You're asking me all the wrong questions."

Mom yells, "What are the right questions?"

Jesus, who do these people think I am? Some kind of Satan worshiper? Jesus, leave me alone. I can't help myself, I'm crying, I'm crying. I can't keep it in, they're asking me all the wrong questions. They know nothing about me. Nothing at all.

I'm standing in the closet with my head in the shirts. I

can't stop crying. I can't stop.

"You're asking me all the wrong questions. You're asking me all the wrong questions." Why don't they love me? Why don't they take care of me? Why don't they act like I'm their son? The tears are all over my face and I can taste them in my mouth, like salt water, but I can't stop crying. I can't stop crying. I can't believe how little they know me.

Finally they stop asking me questions, and I go back to my bed and lie down.

> Help, I need somebody,
> Help, not just anybody,
> Help, you know I need someone, help.

The doctors are gone. Mom and Dad are the only ones here. I'm still crying. I wonder if they still love me. I wonder if they still want me to come home.

"Brenner."

I can't say anything.

"Do you still want to come home this weekend?"

Yes, yes, I do, yes. "Sure."

"Okay, let's get your things together and get out of here."

"Okay."

My bag is already packed and we're out the door. I pass by Mark Miles in the hallway. I can't believe they did that to me right before I go home for the first time.

"Have a good weekend, Brent."

"Fuck you," I say under my breath, "go fuck yourself."

I wonder who I'll see when I go home. Mom told me that everyone knows I'm coming home, but she told them not to bother me too much because I'll be tired.

I can't wait to see Rusty. Jumping up and kissing my face.

We pass a sign that says Washington, D.C. I never thought I'd be happy to see one of those. God, it's kind of hot in here. It's just so weirdly hot all of a sudden. The sun is coming in my window. That must be why I'm feeling so hot. That must be why.

The doctors said if I get my scars in the sunlight, they'll turn purple and stay that way. I put the sun visor down and lean into the middle of the car. Christ, you know, it's not like I can get out of the sun. I mean, it's daytime. I close my eyes and look at the orange light through my eyelids.

Next exit, Falls Church. Falls Church. Slow down. There's the overpass my friends and I used to walk over on our way to the ball field. My house is just down that road. I always wanted to climb out from the overpass and stand on that exit sign with the lights shining up in my face and the cars rushing under my feet and smoke a cigarette.

We're getting off the exit. We're turning right. When we first moved here, I thought it was False Church.

There's the bike trail that goes all the way to D.C. There's the pool I used to swim in during the summer. Oh, here's my favorite part, the dip in the road that makes your stomach go up into your mouth. I'm glad Dad's driving because he always goes faster than Mom. There's where I went to elementary school. Shrevewood Elementary. I played Nerf football right there, every day during recess. I was a pretty good wide receiver. Not great, but I was pretty good. I kind of wish I'd played real football.

God, I remember the time the elementary school was having a contest where you had to guess how many jellybeans were in this giant jar. And if you guessed it, you would win a deluxe Lego set. And Craig decided to break into the school and count the jellybeans so he could win the prize. He really did get into the school. He just couldn't break into the case with the jellybeans. He must have set off an alarm because I remember hearing the sirens from our yard. And then the cops brought him home.

There's the house. God, there it is. It looks exactly the same. With the basketball hoop outside and the split rail fence with chicken wire all the way around so the dog can't get out. The cream-colored aluminum siding and the carport and the bay window and the brick. There's the front door. That's the door they wheeled me out of. That's not the door we usually use. We usually go through the carport.

Dad undoes the latch of the big wooden gate for me and opens it. Just a few steps up to the door. Rusty's jumping on the other side of the glass. Mom cuts in front of me and grabs her by the collar so she doesn't scratch me.

Rusty, Rusty! She wants me to pet her belly. Oh, I love to rub your belly, Rusty. You're a cute dog. Yes, you are. Yes, you are.

Rusty keeps getting up off the floor and running around

the house like a crazy dog and then coming back and lying on the floor in front of me, just like she used to when we'd come home from vacation.

I was lying over there on the rug when the fireman came to get me. I was lying right there.

There's the microwave. I saw my reflection in the microwave. Mom leads me downstairs to the family room so I can watch TV. They got a new La-Z-Boy, much nicer than the old one. In the old days, only Dad was allowed to sit in it, but now it's all mine. Mom brings me a Snickers ice cream bar that is so fucking good I can hardly believe it and a glass of milk to drink while I sit here and watch TV.

Isn't it weird how you can live in a place and never notice the specific smell that it has, and then you go away and come back and you notice that the smell is really strong? That's what I noticed when I came in. It smells like spaghetti and meat sauce, and wet dog, and chicken potpie, and Mom's perfume.

God, this is fun. This is so much nicer than I ever thought it would be. It's so nice to be home. It's so nice to be home.

It's nighttime. Mom and Dad went to bed about an hour ago. They asked if I wanted help going to bed, but I said no. I can do it. I've been sitting in this chair for about six hours, and I think it's just about time to go upstairs to bed. The only thing is, I'm kind of not sure about going back up there, I mean, when I think about it. I guess I just can't think about it.

I used to sit here, in this exact spot, and watch that show *Twin Peaks* and get really scared because the evil spirit Bob, this really creepy-looking guy with long greasy hair and crazy eyes, would take over people's bodies and make them do things that they would never otherwise do. He was the one who took over Laura Palmer's dad and made him kill her.

When I'd go up to my room after watching that show, sometimes I'd see Bob crouching on the other side of the window, getting ready to come get me. I really could see him. He'd be right there, with just his eyes peeking over the ledge, and then I'd imagine him opening the door and running after me, like an animal. I'd get in bed and hide under my covers. I'd get so scared.

Sometimes I still think about Bob, and to be honest, I'm still a little scared when I think about him staring over the window ledge at me.

I turn off the TV with the remote and stand up out of the La-Z-Boy. I'm like Grandma trying to get out of this thing. Shit, how do you get the footrest to go down? Oh, I just had to push the handle.

Seven steps up to the main level and then turn right and seven more steps to my room. Is this carpet new? It looks like a different carpet. When Jake used to sleep over, we'd pile all the couch cushions at the bottom of the stairs and jump off the top step onto the pile. That was fun until somebody hit their head on the ceiling.

Okay, I'm at the top of the stairs. I'm there. I don't even have to look in the bathroom. I don't even have to glance in there. Eyes on the ground. Shit, my hands are shaking. They shouldn't be shaking. Okay, there it is. There's the bathroom. I'm not going to look. Oh shit, I looked. Wait, it doesn't look that weird, though. It doesn't. There's nothing black or burnt. And there's a new shower curtain. That's good. I'm glad there's nothing weird in there. I mean, I didn't really expect that there would be, but I sort of expected that there would be. It's kind of weird that there's nothing weird. I'm just going to go into my room and close the door now.

Okay. This feels better. This is nice, being back in my room. Someone's obviously been coming in to clean up the place, but all my posters are still up. There are my favorites, the two posters of the same blond in the little pink top and panties, one taken from the front and one from the back. She's so beautiful. I feel like I can almost slip my hand inside her shirt.

I used to sit in here and put my headphones on and listen at full blast. I'd jump around the room, moving my mouth to the words and making faces like I was screaming them, but I wouldn't make a sound. Sometimes Mom and Dad would yell at me for jumping so much.

The twin beds are still pushed together, the way that I left them. Craig used to sleep in that one. I've got the same black bedspreads my mom got me back when my favorite color was black and I wanted to paint the whole room black.

One cool thing about this room is the closet. I've got this little cubbyhole in my closet, hidden behind one of the sliding doors. When I was younger, my friends and I would use it as a hiding place during hide-and-seek, but when I got older, I used to sit in there and think about how terrible my life was.

The bathroom is right there. Right there, through that wall. That's where it was. That's where it happened.

The thing about being here, the strange thing about being here, is that I hardly ever think about what happened. I mean, I'm sleeping in the room right next to where everything happened, but I'm not even thinking about it.

Like, right now, I'm not thinking about what it was like going in there and what the gasoline smelled like and what the fire felt like. You would think I would be thinking about those things, but I'm not.

Maybe I did it because I hit my head when I was six. Or maybe because my parents named me Brent, which sounds like burnt. Or maybe because of all the school stuff. Or maybe I was just depressed.

Mom and Dad said I could use their bathroom while I'm home, and at first I said that I didn't want to because I'm not a baby, but then I thought about it, and I thought it was a good idea.

Their room is right across the hall from mine, and their bathroom isn't too much farther.

But I'm not going to take a shower now. I'll take a shower when I get up. I just have to go to sleep first.

I get under the covers. I can't really remember why I wanted to paint my whole room black.

There's too much to think about. Too much to think about, at night, here in this room.

A car comes down the street and the headlights show up on the wall across the room. The light moves down the wall toward my head and disappears again. I wonder where light goes when it's not here. I mean, I know that darkness is the absence of light, but where does the light go when it's not here? And how do you know if it'll ever come back?

I wake up and it's already ten-thirty. I can't believe I slept this late. I get up and walk across the hall to my parents' room. I can hear them downstairs making breakfast. Coffee cake. I love that. I love being able to smell breakfast when I wake up.

I unzip my Jobst garments and wiggle out of my gloves. I turn on the shower and sit on the toilet while I wait for the water to get warm. This scar on my left thigh is still so thick. I can't feel anything through it. It feels like the skin of that dead shark we found in Florida a couple of years ago, except that it's not cold and it doesn't smell as bad.

Actually, my thigh kind of looks like a shark took a bite out of me right there. I wonder if that's what I should say when people ask me about it.

Hey, kid, what happened to you?

Shark attack.

Oh shit. Where did that happen?

At home, in my bathroom.

I get into the shower. I like my parents' bathroom, it smells so much like them, with all the shell-shaped soaps and the Pert Plus shampoo. Smells like home.

They've also got one of those fancy showerheads that lets you adjust the water to different speeds to massage your neck. I suck the water into my mouth and spit it out again.

I get out of the shower. The whole room is completely filled with steam. I can't even see myself in the mirror. I write, I love you Mom and Dad, on the mirror with my finger.

I wrap a towel around my waist and walk out into their bedroom. I wonder if I should ask for a new bathrobe for Christmas.

I open the bedroom door and yell downstairs, "Hey, Mom! I'm ready!" Did that sound mean? I didn't mean it to sound that way.

She comes right up the stairs. I don't know what this is going to be like. We agreed that she'd help me with this, but it's not exactly her area of expertise.

I lie facedown on their bed and wait for her to get her act together. She gets the jar of Eucerin cream from the bathroom and sets it next to my leg. She says, "So, honey, what am I supposed to do?"

"Just put some cream on the back of my legs and rub it in."

"Like this?" She dabs the tiniest little bit on my calf. It's cold. "Is that too cold?"

"No. It doesn't matter."

"I can try and warm it up on my hands first."

"No, it doesn't matter. I'm used to it."

She rubs a little into my calf with the palm of her hand, like she's spreading suntan lotion.

"Not like that."

"Like how, then?"

"Harder. It's supposed to be a massage."

"Like this?" She uses her thumbs this time and pushes a little on my calf.

"Harder." She tries again, but she's not really getting the point. "Mom, you can do it harder."

"I know, but I don't want to hurt you."

"You can't hurt me, Mom."

"Okay." I can tell she's getting frustrated, but I don't really know what to do about it. She's not doing it right.

"Mom, like this." I show her how to hold her hands so her thumbs have a lot of strength. "It's supposed to be hard. Like that."

She tries again, but she's still not getting it. I guess it doesn't really matter. At least I'm getting some cream on my skin, so it won't be dry.

When she's done with my legs and back, I sit up and ask her to get my clean Jobst garments from my room. She's never done this before either, and I think it's going to be harder than the cream.

She says, "What do you want me to do?"

"Just hold them so I can get my foot into it." She sits down on the floor and holds the foot open. I just realized these are like the pajamas I used to wear with the feet. Except these don't have toes and they're skintight and they have zippers up the outside.

I get one foot in and pull the elastic up. Now the other foot. My skin is so sticky from the cream it's hard to get my feet in.

She says, "What do I do now?"

"Zip them up." She tries to get ahold of the zipper, but because the foot's not on exactly right, it starts to twist. "You're getting the zipper turned."

"Sorry." She tries to smile.

"It's okay." I guess it's understandable because she's never done this before, but she has no idea what she's doing.

Finally I'm dressed and I go downstairs to have some breakfast.

Right in the middle of my coffee cake, Mom calls from upstairs, "Brent?" Oh shit. Her voice sounds sharp, like it does when I'm in trouble.

What did I do? "Yeah."

"Did you write that on the bathroom mirror?" Who else would have written it?

"Yeah."

"That was so sweet, honey. That was so sweet." She's crying. "Did you show Dad?"

"No." Why would I show Dad? It was supposed to be a surprise.

"Honey? Don, come and look at what Brent wrote on the mirror."

"Okay, I'm coming." Dad runs up the stairs and I walk behind him.

Now he's standing in the bathroom, staring at the mirror. He's hugging Mom. He's crying.

"Brenner, that was so nice. Thank you." He can't really get the words out.

Mom says, "It's so nice to have you home." She's crying even harder.

"We love you so much, honey."

"We love you so much."

They're both hugging me, but I didn't want this. I wanted to do something nice, but I didn't want all those tears. God, that's the last time I do something like that.

After breakfast, Dad comes back into the kitchen and says, "Brenner, what do you want to do today?"

"I don't know."

"Want to go outside?"

"Not really?"

"Want to go to a movie?"

That could be fun, except I don't want to see anyone. "No thanks."

"Rent a video?"

Well, I could do that. I bet it wouldn't be that big of a deal to do that. "Sure."

We get in the car and drive over.

"Do you want to go in, Brenner, or do you want to tell me what you want?"

"No, I'll go in." I reach up and unstrap my face mask. It sort of suctions to my face and makes a popping sound when I take it off. Must be because it's so hot and I'm sweating a little out of my forehead. I open the car door and put my legs out. Shit, I wish I wasn't wearing shorts because now everybody can see my Jobst garments and the big zipper going up the side.

I'm stiff from being in the car. I stretch my back and get a couple of good cracks out of it. That's better. I stand up and get a head rush. I hope I don't pass out. No, I'm cool. I'm cool.

I'm glad I'm not wearing my face mask. I think people would stare at me if I was. This shouldn't be too big of a deal. Just walking into a video store, but God, I just thought of something—what if I see someone I know? That would be terrible. Then I'd have to talk to them.

They changed this place all around. The new releases used to be over there on the right, but now they're on the back wall. And now comedy is where classics were.

Don't see anyone I know.

Do I know that little kid? Oh. No, he's staring at my face. Don't look at me, kid. Don't look at me. Stop it. I move farther down the aisle. I can feel him looking at me, even though I can only see him out of the corner of my eye.

Stop it. Stop it. Okay, he's not going to stop. I've got to find a movie and get out of here. A comedy, definitely a comedy. How about *Kindergarten Cop*, with Arnold Schwarzenegger.

"You ready, Brenner?"

"Yeah."

"What'd you get?"

"Uh, *Kindergarten Cop*. It's a comedy."

"What's it rated?"

"Oh, I don't know, PG, I think."

"Okay. Let's go."

Dad gives the guy the card and the money, and I stare at the carpet and my shoes. Hurry, hurry, hurry, let's get out of here. Let's get out of here before someone says something. Come on, come on, come on. Why is it taking so long?

Okay, here I go. I'm at the door. I'm outside. I'm back in the car. Thank God. I did it.

This really is the life. I sit in the chair and watch movies. Mom and Dad get me whatever I want. They wait on me like I'm the king of England and all I have to do is sit here and relax.

I should have a little bell that I can ring in case I need an ice cream sandwich or I need them to put in the next video. I'm just going to sit here all day and watch movies and no one is going to bother me.

All this time I didn't want to come home because I was so worried about how it would feel, and now I'm home and I don't want to leave. I don't want to go back to the hospital tomorrow.

Lying here in my bed feels so much the same. I feel like I'm lying here going to sleep back before everything went bad.

It's hard to go to sleep when you're thinking about everything. I always had trouble going to sleep, even when I was a little kid. I couldn't stop thinking about the things I'd said during the day. All the stupid faces I'd made and the dumb jokes I'd made. And then when I got older, I started thinking about really bad stuff. I used to think about killing different people. Like one time, after my brother beat me up, I told my friends I was going to go down into his room in the middle of the night and kill him with this knife I kept under my bed. I really thought I was going to do it. I could picture it so easily. Slipping into his room. Putting the knife in his chest.

I also used to think about going down into the basement and opening up the furnace and pouring a whole bunch of gasoline in the furnace and then leaving, and when somebody turned on the furnace, the whole house would explode.

I'm glad I didn't do that. I'm glad I didn't do anything like that to anybody else. I only killed myself. That's one good thing.

Mom is driving back to the hospital. It's hard to think of things to talk about, so I turn on the radio and listen to music. Mom can never understand the lyrics to the music. She says she's a visual learner, but that's really no excuse for how bad she is at understanding them. For years she thought that song "Shake, Rattle, and Roll" was actually called "Shake Marilyn Monroe."

I say, "Let's play a game."

"Okay."

"We'll put on the radio and the first one to guess the name of the song wins."

"Okay, but you know I'm no good at this."

"I know, but let's do it anyway."

"Okay."

I turn the channel until I find what sounds like an oldies station, just to give her a little advantage.

She should know this first one. Easily.

> *Ooh, I bet you're wonderin' how I knew*
> *'bout your plans to make me blue.*

She should know this. This is the song she sang at our school Christmas party when she and all her teacher friends dressed up in black trash bags and sunglasses and pretended they were raisins. God, that was so embarrassing. Why did she do that?

She says, "Wait, I know this. I know this."

"Do you know it?"

> *I'm just about to lose my mind. Honey, honey. Yeah.*

She says, "I do know it. Shoot, what is it?"

I say, "'Heard It Through the Grapevine.'"

"Darn."

We wait for the next song. Some other Motown-sounding thing.

> *People say I'm the life of the party*
> *'cause I tell a joke or two.*

She says, "I think I know this one. Is it 'Tears of a Clown'?"

I say, "Wait. No. It's 'Tracks of My Tears.'"

"Shoot. This isn't fair."

"How is it not fair? This is all your music. It's practically the entire *Big Chill* sound track."

She smiles. "I'll get the next one."

"Yeah, right."

What's this one? Some acoustic thing.

> *If I could save time in a bottle.*

She says, "Jim Croce, 'Time in a Bottle.' Yay, I got one."

Shit, a song she actually knew.

She says, "I beat you. I beat you." She's really rubbing it in.

"Mom, just because you know the lyrics to one song in the entire world that I don't know doesn't mean you're some all-star lyricologist or something."

She stops talking. I can tell I hurt her feelings. Fuck, why am I always being mean to my parents?

It's so depressing to be back at the hospital. Latroy is leaving. His mom and brother are here taking all his stuff out. I just lie in my bed and watch them. I wonder if I'll ever be discharged.

His mom takes down a picture he has on his bedside table of a girl that he used to go out with. I wonder where she is.

Mary, the nurse that got into a fight with Latroy that one time, comes in. She gives him a big hug and then tries to kiss him through his halo. She has a hard time figuring out how to get her head through the bars. She finally does and gives him a little kiss on the cheek.

Ben and I are going upstairs to the school together to do some work. He's the guy that broke his neck in the motorcycle accident.

Ben's gotten really good at the whole wheelchair thing. He can do a wheelie and hold it forever. I can do one too, but I'm not as good as he is.

We get in the elevator, press our button, and wait for the doors to close. Just as they start to close, one of the janitors runs down the hall, yelling, "Hold that elevator or I'll break your neck."

I press the doors open button and he gets in.

"Thanks," he says.

Ben looks up at the guy from his wheelchair and says, "You know, you should really watch what you say around here."

The guy says, "What?"

"Watch what you say about breaking people's necks. It's a sensitive subject."

"I didn't mean it like that."

"Whatever."

Ben and I get off at the fourth floor and head for the classroom.

"That fucking guy. That fucking guy. I can't believe he said that to me. That fucking guy."

Ben's really upset, but I sort of think he's overreacting.

Mark Motherfucker Miles wants to give me some tests. Tests. I don't know what that means exactly, but I do know that I have to sit in a room about the size of a supply closet and answer his stupid questions. I always thought this room was for the janitors, but there's a sign outside that says Psychological Testing Room. This is going to be fun. What an asshole.

He says, "So, Brent, if you were an animal, what kind of an animal would you be?"

God, what a dumb question. This is like Barbara Walters.

"Um, I don't know."

"Well, don't think about it too much. Give me the first thing that comes to mind." The first thing that comes to mind is that you're a complete asshole.

"Maybe a dolphin."

"A dolphin." He nods and writes something down. "Why?" I don't know why, I just said it so you'd get off my back.

"Um, because they're graceful and they're smart and they seem, I don't know, kind of free or something."

"And what kind of an animal would you hate to be?" Jesus.

"A cow."

"Why?"

"Because they're slow and ugly and just sit around eating grass and throwing it up again."

"Okay. Great. That was just a little warm-up. Next I'm going to show you some cards with some ink stains on them, and you tell me what you think they're pictures of, okay?"

"Okay." We're doing inkblots? I read a book about this once, and it told you how to beat the test. Let's see if I can remember. Oh yeah, all the little inkblots are supposed to look like penises and vaginas, but you're not supposed to notice that, otherwise they'll think you're crazy. He's got his notepad and pen ready.

"What might this be?" It's the one that looks like a

butterfly. I wonder if I should say that or if I should make something else up.

"A butterfly?"

"Okay, where is the butterfly?"

"You mean you want me to tell you?"

"Yes."

"Okay, those are the wings and those are the antennae."

"Okay, how about this one?"

I'm going to say two people playing pat-a-cake.

"Two people playing pat-a-cake."

"Okay. Show me where you see that."

"There's one person, there's the arm, there's the leg. Same on the other side."

"And this one? What might this be?"

This one is weird. It's got two people, like the last one, but they both have penises and breasts, and there's a big red butterfly between them. I'm not saying any of that stuff.

"Looks like a horseshoe crab or a beetle."

"Where?"

"That kind of looks like a horseshoe crab, and these things kind of look like a beetle's pincers."

"Okay, and what might this be?"

Oh Jesus, this one looks like a man with a giant dick and no arms. What a weird picture.

"Looks like a dinosaur with a huge tail. Like a stegosaurus."

"Where?"

"That's the tail. That's the legs. That's the head."

"And what might this be?"

"This one's definitely a bat. Head. Wings. Feet."

"Okay, and what might this be?"

"This doesn't look like anything. Maybe a woman giving someone a hug. Or a boat. Or an animal skin. It doesn't look like anything, really."

"Okay, and what might this be?"

"A woman looking at herself in the mirror, but she doesn't really have a body, so maybe a statue or two statues."

"Okay, and what might this be?"

"Do you have to say that over and over again? It's kind of annoying. Um, this one doesn't look like anything either. Maybe a big black inkblot."

"Okay, see anything else?"

"Nope. Sorry."

"Okay, last one."

It's just a big mess of a bunch of stuff. It kind of looks like a man in the center on fire, but I'm not going to say that. Sea urchin. Pelvis bone. Tangled mess of seaweed. Okay, that's good enough.

"Tangled mess of seaweed."

"Okay, anything else?"

"No."

"Okay, good."

"How'd I do?"

"You did fine. There are no right or wrong answers."

"Yes, there are. I read a book about it once."

"You did?"

"Yeah. I think I passed."

"There are no right or wrong answers."

"Right." Dickhead.

Mark has a bunch more tests for me to do. I have to answer some general knowledge questions first, then do some analogies. Tuna is to fish as grizzly is to _____. It's all pretty easy. After that I get some lunch and then back to the tests.

I don't understand what the point is of giving me all these tests. I mean, like, what exactly are they trying to find out by making me fit some shapes together? Do they want to know if I'm crazy? They should ask me because if they do, I'll tell them I was crazy, but I'm not anymore. I don't know why I was crazy, but I was. They never ask me the right questions.

I've started doing magic. Mom and Dad bought me a book from the gift shop called *The Klutz Guide to Magic* and it's pretty cool. For one thing, you can make a handkerchief disappear into your hand. Another good one is tying a knot in a rope without letting go of either end.

The sleight-of-hand stuff is really hard to do with the Jobst gloves on. I take them off to do some of it, but then the jacket I have to wear pushes all the blood down into my hands and they turn purple and start to itch. It's a real pain in the ass. Plus when I take off my gloves, my hands are really fragile and weak, and when I'm trying to do a trick with a coin, my hands start to shake.

Every morning I wake up, take a shower, get in my wheelchair, and zoom down the hall for my morning massage with Gina. I get this thing going as fast as a motorcycle, it's such a long hallway. I should be in the Special Olympics. But they'd probably find out I can actually walk and kick me out.

When I get to the corner, I grab the left wheel and take the turn so tight, the chair almost tips over.

I love these morning massages with Gina. I love hearing all her funny stories about what's going on backstage at *Peter Pan*. She got her hair cut even shorter and she's really starting to look the part.

When it's all done, she helps me into my Jobst garments and then comes upstairs with me. I like it because she sits in the wheelchair on the way back up and lets me rub her shoulders as I push her around. She's got really strong shoulders. And the skin on the back of her neck is so smooth. I don't know, it makes me feel romantic. I know she doesn't feel anything like that, just by the way she talks, but to me, it's great.

We're standing at the elevator, waiting. I'm rubbing her neck. I'm singing, "'There's something happening here; What it is ain't exactly clear.'"

She says, "You like Buffalo Springfield?"

"Who?"

"Buffalo Springfield. You were just singing their song."

"I was?"

"Yup."

"Hmm. I heard it in the preview for that movie *Born on the Fourth of July*. Did you see that?"

"Nope. Did you?"

"No. I don't know if I want to. I mean, I like Tom Cruise and I think *Top Gun* is probably one of the best movies ever made, but I don't really want to see him in a wheelchair."

"Did you just say you think *Top Gun* is one of the best movies ever made?"

"Yeah."

"You're kidding."

"No. Have you seen it?"

"Sure. It's stupid."

"What?" I'm laughing.

"It's the stupidest movie." She's laughing too.

"The stupidest movie? It's great. Tom Cruise flying F-14s. It's awesome."

"Please."

The elevator's here. God, she's so cool. If I ever get married, it'll be to someone like her.

Jodi and I are playing basketball. Well, trying to play basketball. I don't have the right shoes, and even if I did, I can't get my stupid arms above my head to make the stupid ball go into the basket. The other thing that's hard about basketball is jumping and shooting at the same time. There's no possible way to get my body to jump up and shoot the ball.

I feel like one of those really uncoordinated kids on the team that can't even make a foul shot. I can't even make a layup. I guess playing one-on-one with Magic Johnson is out.

Miles and Sheslow have an appointment with me today. Christ, when are they going to get the message that I'm not going to talk to them?

Miles says, "So, Brent, I want to talk about something different today."

"Yeah. Why are there two of you and only one of me?"

"It's not a competition, Brent."

"Yeah, right."

"Do you believe in God?"

"What?"

"Do you believe in God? It's a simple question."

"Um, let me think about it." This is what I always do. I pretend like I'm going to answer the question and then I start thinking about something else and then fifteen minutes later they ask me again and I say I forgot the question. Works every time.

"Why do you have to think about it?"

"I don't know. It's a hard question."

"Well, do you have any opinions?"

Maybe they're not going to let me get away with it this time. Okay, I could tell them about how I used to wonder if I was Jesus. No, too revealing. I could tell them about the time I made the deal with the devil to be the world's best soccer player. That didn't really work. I could tell them about how I'd put a Ping-Pong ball on the table and stare at it and think, Okay, God, if you really exist, all you have to do is move the Ping-Pong ball and I'll believe in you. I promise, I'll spend the rest of my life devoted to you. I promise. I will. But nothing ever happened.

"I guess I don't really believe in God, like how people normally talk about God."

"What exactly do you mean?"

"I mean, we can't really know about stuff like that, about God or anything like that, until after we're dead. But I think, maybe, it's possible that there is something that exists that is bigger and, kind of, like, around us, but I don't know what that is."

"Interesting."

Why am I talking so much today? It's okay. It's harmless.

"When I was . . . after I was in the . . . when the firemen were there around me, and I was lying on the floor looking up at them, I don't know how to explain this, but their eyes were kind of glowing. Like there was a light inside their eyes."

"Yes."

"And when my mom came, I remember her eyes, which I've looked at all my life, and they were so green, like emeralds. They were so full of light and, like, love. I don't know, I can't explain it."

"So, what does that make you think about God?"

"I think that maybe, if human beings have souls, that maybe their souls are in their eyes. That maybe that's what the color is. Their souls."

"Well, they say the eyes are the windows to the soul."

"No, that's not what I mean. I mean, the actual color is kind of like your spirit, like your soul. And the black space, maybe the black space is the tunnel that people talk about when they die. Do you know what I mean? Like when you die, you go into the eyes of the person you're looking at and walk through their eyes and, at the other end, that's where heaven is."

"That's interesting. So you think that when people die they walk through the eyes of others? Almost like a Native American right of passage?"

"No, not like that." Goddamn it, why did I start talking to these guys? I'm talking about something, and they try to make it about something else. I hate these guys.

"Well, let's talk about something else."

"Fine. Great. I'd love to talk about something else. What else would you like to talk about?"

Mark gets this look in his eye like he's pissed. He probably doesn't like my tone of voice. I've never seen him look like that. "Let's talk about why you feel the need to be so scarcastic."

Did he just say what I think he said? Scarcastic?

"What?"

"Why do you feel you have to be so sarcastic?"

"That's not what you said."

"What did I say?"

I look over at Sheslow. "Did you hear what he said?"

Sheslow says, "He said sarcastic." Oh right, he's going to back up his friend there. What the fuck, I know what I heard. Fucker.

Jodi and I are bowling. It's always hard to find a ball that will work for me. Most of the balls are too heavy, and the light ones don't have big enough holes.

So most of the time I wind up throwing gutter balls, but today, maybe they waxed the lanes or something, but my balls are rolling really well.

I get in position. Relax. Focus on the arrows, not the dots. Visualize. Visualize. Without my Jobst glove on, my hand is starting to itch, but it's not bad yet. Here we go. Come on, baby. Come on. Come back, baby, come back. Yes, strike.

I pump my fist and Jodi gives me a high five. She says, "Great job, kid. Was that your first strike?"

"Yup. And I'm not a kid."

"Well, excuse me, you're a bowling machine."

One thing about Jodi, she's always exaggerating her voice and her facial features to make it seem like we're really having fun. I wish she'd chill out.

Next frame. Relax. Visualize. Be the ball.

Another strike. I'm fucking awesome.

"Wow, Brent, you've really got it going on today."

Jesus, if there's one thing I can't stand, it's older people trying to talk like they're not old.

Okay, tenth frame. Last chance. If I get this, I'm definitely going to break one hundred. Focus. Use the hand. Follow through. Come on. Come on. Come back. Yes. Another strike. Yes. Yes. Yes.

Maybe I should be a professional bowler.

They're finally discharging me from this fucking place. Lisa just told me. I've been in here for almost three months. Three months?

My parents and the doctors are talking about where I should go next. It seems like a choice between a mental hospital or high school. I don't know which one sounds better, but nobody is asking me anyway.

Tom, the teacher, wants me to do some reading comprehension, but I don't feel like it.

He says, "Are you planning on doing any work today?"

"Not really."

"Are you going to do anything productive?"

"Not if I can help it."

"Okay."

I think Tom understands there's nothing he can do to get me to do any work. He says, "So, Brent, what are you going to do when you're discharged?"

"Um, I don't know, go home, I guess."

"And then?"

"I don't know, high school eventually, but probably not yet. We're going to have a tutor come to our house for a while. And be doing some outpatient therapy."

"That sounds good."

Yeah, that sounds good.

When I go home, this is how it's going to work. I'll go into Children's twice a week for physical therapy. The rest of the time Mom will do my cream massages at home, and I'll work with a physical therapist from the school district. So before I get discharged, they have to make a video so my mom and the person from the school district will know what they're doing.

I remember when we did this video thing at Children's, God, that was terrible. I started crying right in the middle. Whatever I do this time, I'm not going to cry. No crying.

Jodi's got the camera. The thing I hate about being on camera is how it makes me feel like I can see myself from the outside. Before, I used to like that feeling. I used to always ham it up for the cameras. Make funny faces and do little jokes. People always said I took a good picture.

Jodi tells me to go over to the weights and do my pulley exercises, that's where I grab on to a handle with a rope and a weight at the other end and pull down over and over again. Jodi says, "Are you ready?"

"Sure."

"Okay, I'm going to press record."

"Okay. Action."

"This is Brent. He's a fourteen-year-old, um, teenager who was burned in February following a gasoline, uh, fire and was burned over eighty-five percent of his body. He spent several months in an acute care hospital and has been here at the duPont Institute for three months doing an intensive rehab program to restore his arm range of motion, for scar management, and to restore range of motion in his legs and his knees. Right now, what you're watching Brent do is his upper-extremity range-of-motion exercise program, where he's lifting ten pounds of weights, then pushing down. This has helped him restore his elbow range to full. Brent's going to show you a variety of exercises that he's able to do, and note how well he's able to get his arms over his head, because he does have a lot of scar tissue on his shoulders and on his back."

She motions for me to come forward and stretch my arms out wide and do the circles with my arms. I can almost get my arms even with my shoulders.

I look down and notice I'm wearing my Magic Johnson T-shirt that he sent me when I was at Children's.

I say, "Note the signed Magic Johnson T-shirt."

"Magic is a personal friend of Brent's."

I switch to my next exercise, lifting my arms up as high as I can go. My hands can almost reach to the top of my head.

Jodi says, "Note how well Brent can get his arms above his head. When he first came here, this was a major task, as he was not able to get his arms as high as he can now."

My arms are starting to itch because my Jobst garments aren't on.

She asks me to do some more exercises. Touching my hands in front and behind my body. Stretching my neck. Opening my mouth really big. She wants to show how the scars pull at my skin and make me look like a freak.

We stop for a while and go into a private room with one of those white sheet dividers for a background. Jodi asks me to take my shirt off and stand in front of the sheet. I don't like to look at myself with my shirt off, but now it's hard not to. I still can't believe how purple my scars are. Not even purple, more like magenta.

Jodi's talking about my skin and my graft sites and how they made my skin in Boston and sent it to me. I should make a joke. A joke would make me feel better.

I say, "I feel like that guy . . ." What guy? I can't remember. I know who I'm thinking of, but I can't remember who he is or what he's called. I feel like that guy who stands naked in front of a white sheet with his purple scars all stretched out for the video camera.

She's still talking. I don't like this.

She's saying something. "And the color is excellent."

The color is excellent. Yeah, right. The color is excellent.

Finally she lets me get the Jobst garments and comes over to help me put them on. "The purpose of wearing an elastic garment over burned skin is to prevent the scars from growing out of control as the skin heals."

"Are they going to know what you're talking about?"

"These are the Jobst garments." She points. I think she's a little annoyed with me.

Finally I've got them all on. They make me feel better, like I've got a protective coating on.

"The last thing Brent puts on, before he's ready to roll, is his mask. It's a clear mask made especially for Brent's face."

I show off the mask like I'm a flight attendant.

Now we're going down to the gym so I can show how good I am at bowling.

A couple of weeks ago, I bowled a one forty-three, but now I can barely hit any pins. All my balls keep going off to the left. Jodi's still yammering on about how much I've improved.

I say, "What am I doing wrong?"

"What are you doing wrong? I think you're rushing."

"Okay."

I look at the camera, hold out my hands, and say in my most sarcastic voice, "I'm usually really, really good. Just not today." That was kind of funny. Maybe I should do more stuff like that.

Jodi's telling me to bend down like I'm picking something up from the floor. I can do it pretty well with my left hand. I can bend over and stretch my trunk and just barely reach the floor. It kind of hurts because the scars are so tight and banded, but I can do it. With my right hand I can't even reach down to my knees.

Jodi says, "Okay, one more. Bowl a strike."

"Okay." Focus. Focus. Visualize the pins falling. Line up to the right. Bend over. Release the ball. Good. It's moving slowly, but it's headed toward the center pin. Keep going. Keep going. Shit. I got eight. I always get an eight when I'm trying for a strike.

Now I have to get naked and lie on the table and let

them rub cream into my skin while they videotape. I get my clothes and Jobst garments off and get up on the table. Gina throws a towel to me so I can cover up my penis.

Viki sets up the camera in the corner, down near my left foot. Everybody seems so tense. I hope they can't see my penis with the camera. I try and adjust the towel so the camera can't see anything.

Viki says, "Okay, you guys, I'm going to start recording. Are you ready?"

Gina says, "Okay."

I say, "Okay." Viki presses record. My heart is beating so fast, just lying here. This sucks.

Viki's saying something about the scars and how they need moisture. God. God. God. Let me out of this fucking place.

Viki's voice sounds nervous. "The hypertrophic scarring in the lower extremities should be rubbed using a lateral motion, applying the Eucerin cream in an even fashion so that Brent's scars are blanched and the scar tissue is made more supple by the cream."

I say, "I feel like Frankenstein." Either no one heard me or no one thought that was funny. Maybe it wasn't funny.

Finally they finish and Viki turns off the camera. I feel like I've been under water for a long time. I leave tomorrow.

I'm gone. No party. No ice cream. No pictures. They didn't do anything special, not like Children's, and I don't even care. I'm just happy to be finally leaving. I'm so happy to be leaving. God. It's September 13th. Friday the 13th. Is that a bad omen?

February, March, April, May, June, July, August. That's more than seven stinking months. Seven months in hospitals, eating hospital food, sleeping in hospital beds, wearing hospital clothes, talking to hospital people. I used to be really nervous about going home, but now I can't wait to be back in my own bed, in my own house, with my dog and my mom and dad. Craig is off at college already.

Oh God, there it is. The carport, the bay window, the aluminum siding, the wooden fence with the chicken wire to keep Rusty in, the wreath on the front door, and Mom and Dad and Rusty and me. It's all here.

They made a Welcome Home sign. That's so nice. And there's Rusty. "Hey, Rusty. Hey, Rusty. Hey, Rusty. Yes, I'm happy to see you too. Yes, I am. Yes, I am."

She's doing that thing she does when she gets excited.

She runs around in circles around the kitchen into the dining room and back through the living room. That's so cute. She's so cute. God, it's nice to be back here.

I go downstairs into the family room. Yes. The comfy chair. I get to sit in the comfy chair. Mom asks if I want anything. "Maybe a Coke and a Snickers ice cream bar."

This is the life. This really is the life. This is, like, what everybody dreams about when they come back home and they try to figure out what they're going to do next.

Chris calls, he says our old soccer coach Darrin wants to take us bowling. I think about saying no, I'm not in the mood, and then I think why the hell not.

I met Chris at the bus stop when we were eight years old, and we've been friends ever since then. We started playing on the same soccer team, and then we started hanging out, playing G.I. Joe and going to each other's birthday parties. He's a nice guy, although he's never been the coolest kid on the block.

They come to pick me up in Darrin's Jeep. For a long time, when he was our soccer coach, he had a red Mustang convertible. That was awesome.

"Hey, guys."

"Hey, Brent. What's up?" Chris shakes my hand.

"Not much. What's up with you?"

"Nothing."

"Cool."

"Hey, Brent." Darrin shakes my hand.

"Hey, so do you want to go?"

"Yeah."

We head out to the Jeep. They leave the front seat for me. God, Chris has gotten tall. He must have grown six inches since I've seen him.

"Chris, you got so tall."

"Yeah."

"How tall are you?"

"Six-two."

"Six-two?"

"Yeah."

"Jesus, you're a giant." The other thing is, now he's cool looking. He's wearing a blue bandanna on his head, I've never seen him do that before, and he kind of carries himself differently, like he's a man now or something.

"Chris, have you been working out?"

"Yeah."

"Yeah?"

"I'm going out for JV soccer so I've got to, you know, bulk up."

"Yeah?"

"Yeah."

"Cool."

"Yeah."

"Do you have a girlfriend?" I'm just asking, kind of as a joke. Chris has never been much of a ladies' man. That was always my department.

"Yeah."

"Yeah?"

"Yup."

"Who? Anybody I know?"

"Did you know Denise? Laura's friend?"

"Yeah, I think I talked to her on the phone once."

"Yeah, her."

"What does she look like?"

"She's pretty. She's got brown hair."

"Does she put out? Do you get it on?"

Darrin laughs. Chris sort of squints. I'm sure the answer is no.

"Well."

"What?"

"We have some fun."

"Yeah?"

"Yeah."

"Like what? Kissing? Second base? Don't tell me you're doing it?"

"No. No. Like second or third."

"What? You're joking."

"No. No. I can't really talk about it, though. You know, you shouldn't kiss and tell."

God, I always kissed and told him everything. I can't believe it. Chris is getting more action than me. I can't believe it. God, he's changed so much, and I'm just, Jesus, I'm just the same.

Chris and Darrin both have their own bowling balls. I can

still only handle an eight-pound ball, and it's hard to find one of those with big enough holes in it. This one is nine pounds with big holes. I'll try it.

I have to take one of my Jobst gloves off to get my hand in the holes. I try to do it so nobody notices. It's always so weird when I take my gloves off because I have them on most of the time, and I start to think that that's what my skin looks like. And then I take them off and I'm always surprised that my fingers are so skinny and the skin is so fragile.

Darrin sets up the electronic scorekeeper. He puts me first, then Chris, and then him. I get my shoes on and walk out into the middle of the lane.

No pressure. No pressure. I don't like the way these shoes feel. They feel all sweaty and they hurt my heel. I pick up my ball with both hands and walk to the line. My arm feels stiff. This is much different than bowling in the hospital. There's so much more noise here. A guy next to me whips one down the lane and the pins clatter everywhere.

I roll my ball down toward the pins and it looks for a second like it's going to hit the headpin, and then it goes off to the right side and knocks down a couple. I look back at Chris and Darrin and they nod.

Chris says, "Go for the headpin."

"I was."

"Oh. Okay."

My second ball goes down the left side and knocks down only one pin.

Chris goes next and gets a strike. How did he get so good?

Darrin gets a strike too. What the hell is going on?

It's my turn again. I get up. The ball feels heavier this time. Chris says, "Just relax."

"Okay."

I let the ball roll and it hits the ten pin and just barely knocks it down. I roll my second ball, but it just drifts right into the gutter. I sit down before it even gets to the pins.

Back home, Mom says, "How'd you do?"

"Okay, I bowled an eighty-two."

"How'd everybody else do?"

"They're good. They bowled up in the hundreds."

"Was it fun?"

"Yeah."

"Was it nice to see Chris?"

"Yeah."

"How'd he do?"

"I told you, a hundred and something."

"Oh."

"Yeah."

"Oh. And was it fun to see him?"

"I told you, it was fun."

"Okay. Did you guys make any more plans?"

"No."

"Do you think you'll see him again soon?"

"I don't know."

"Would you like to?"

"Sure."

"Great, honey, I'm glad you had such a good time."

"Okay. I'm gonna go watch TV."

"Okay. Have fun. Do you need anything?"

"No. Thanks."

When my skin is really itching, I have to get Mom or Dad to rub my back. I lie facedown on the brown corduroy couch and breathe through the cushions while they scratch my back with the palms of their hands. They still can't use their nails because the nails might tear the new skin, so they just use the palms of their hands.

Dad is much better at back scratching, probably because he likes his back scratched so much. He moves his hands really fast all over my back, and it feels great. When Mom does it, she's much more gentle and careful, but the itch is so down deep that she hardly even reaches it.

They're both pretty good at back massages. Dad rubs deep in the muscle and Mom rubs softly.

For back cracking, Dad is the one. I lie on the floor and put my head to the side. Dad and I have figured out that if he puts his hands on the sides of my spinal cord and pushes down hard, we can get a few of the vertebrae to crack. Sometimes he pushes down so hard that it feels like my rib cage is going to snap. Mom gets freaked out when we do that, but when they crack, God, it feels so good, it's like a little drug being released right into my brain.

We're going to meet Magic Johnson today. He's in D.C. doing a basketball camp. I've been waiting for this for so long.

Craig doesn't want to come. I don't know why. He says it's not his thing. I don't care.

I was going to wear my orange warm-up suit he sent me, but it's too small now. I never got to wear it. Not once. I'll just wear my signed T-shirt. That's good enough.

Dad's wearing a Michigan State T-shirt because both Dad and Magic Johnson went to college there. Maybe he thinks that Magic will like that. Dad brought two Magic Johnson official basketballs for Magic to sign. They're pretty cool. He got one for Craig too, even though Craig didn't even want to come. I wonder why he didn't want to come.

Dad parks the car. This must be the place. How do I look? I look stupid. I look really stupid. I'm wearing a Magic Johnson signed T-shirt to go meet Magic Johnson. Why am I doing that?

Dad goes into the building first and sees someone he knows. Dad always knows somebody. There are all these kids running around shooting baskets. Oh my God, there's Magic. He's showing some kid how to shoot.

Dad whispers in my ear, "Brenner, do you still want to play one-on-one with Magic?"

"No."

"You sure?"

"Yeah. I'm sure." God, he's so tall. I've never seen anyone that tall. I didn't realize there were going to be other people here.

This guy leads us up some stairs into a private room. There's some cold cuts and cheese on the table and two giant buckets shaped like Pepsi cans filled with ice and soda.

The guy says, "You can have anything you want. Magic will be up in a few minutes."

My hands are shaking. Why do my hands always shake when I'm nervous? Why am I so nervous? This is no big deal, just meeting my idol. My hero. The guy I've wanted to meet my whole life.

The door opens. There he is. He's so tall and sweaty. I can't think. I can't talk.

He comes right over to us and shakes my dad's hand first. He's smiling just like he does on TV. He says something to Dad about his Michigan State T-shirt.

Magic's looking at me. His hand is out. "Nice to meet you finally."

"Hi. Nice to meet you." His hands are so big. I can't believe it.

Magic leans down to me and says, "Your dad and I both went to Michigan State. I want you to go there too."

"Okay." Why does he want me to go there? Why does he care where I go to college?

Someone takes a picture and we shake hands again. That's it. He's leaving. It's over.

I'm in the basement playing *Super Mario 2*. I'm having trouble getting past the egg guy on level two. It's so cool down here, and there's no sun to make your scars even more purple and disgusting.

My hair is all long and shaggy and stupid looking. I really need it cut, but I don't want to go to one of those beauty salons because what if they start asking me questions? I asked Mom to call Craig and see if he'd cut my hair this weekend.

"Brent?" Mom calls from the top of the stairs.

"What?"

"Craig's on the phone."

"Tell him I'm playing *Super Mario 2*."

"All right."

God, every time I get to the egg guy, he jumps on top of me and kills me. Maybe if I use the princess, I'll have a better chance of killing him because she can fly.

"Brent?"

"What?"

"Craig said he's not sure if he can cut your hair."

"What? Why?"

"I don't know. I think he's worried he might cut you."

"What?" Jesus, what a dork. All I wanted was to get a haircut from my brother. I thought it would be something we could do together. Dick.

I'm going to the Hair Cuttery. Mom says she'll drop me off and come back in a half hour. I really don't want to do this.

It smells weird in here, like bananas and hair spray. Someone's in the back, sweeping hair. The woman behind the counter is chewing gum and reading *Redbook*.

"Hi."

"Can I help you?"

"Um, I need a haircut."

"Do you have an appointment?"

"No."

"All right, I think Jill might be able to take you."

A woman calls out from the back, "I'm on my break."

"You've been on your break for an hour and a half."

"Oh Jesus, all right, I'll take him."

"She'll take you. Go on back."

"Thanks."

Jill is dressed in a black-and-white jumpsuit and wearing a hat with rhinestones and a bolo tie. She says, "Have a seat. What are we going to do today?"

"Um, I don't know, maybe take an inch off and cut around the ears." My mom told me to say that when I was in fourth grade, and I still say it.

"Okay, so you want kind of a layered thing?"

"I guess."

"Great. Why don't you come to the back and we'll give you a shampoo."

I always used to love this part, where they massage your scalp and use that shampoo that smells like dessert, but now it's kind of a hard stretch on my neck. It doesn't feel very good.

She's rubbing that stuff into my hair, and I can tell she's gearing up for some small talk. Shit.

"So, do you go to school?"

"Um, yeah."

"Where?"

"Um, I'm homeschooling right now, but I'm going to go to Marshall High School."

"Oh, really? I went to Marshall."

"Yeah?"

"Yeah, graduated in '86. Do you know Mr. Mensch?"

"No, I don't go there yet."

"Oh, right. If you get a chance to take his class, you definitely should. I think he teaches biology or chemistry or one of those science things. He's great." She's about to start asking me about my face. I can feel it, any second.

"Okay." Maybe if I think of something for her to talk about, I can stop her from talking about me. Maybe if I ask her about her kids. I think I saw a picture of a little girl in a cowboy hat at her chair.

"So what happened to you?" Fuck, I missed my opportunity.

"What do you mean?"

"What happened to your face?" I'll say the house fire.

"I was burned in a house fire."

"Really? That's terrible."

"Yeah."

"How'd it start?" Oh Jesus.

"Um, it was electrical." Did my voice just crack?

"Electrical?"

"Yeah."

"What do you mean?" Shit.

"Something happened in the electricity circuits."

"Really? How?"

"Um, the toaster."

"The toaster?"

"The toaster shorted out and the whole house just went up in flames."

"Did everyone in your family get hurt?"

"No. Just me."

"Just you? That's terrible. Did you sue?" Did I sue?

"No."

"Why not?"

"I don't know. I didn't ask."

"Oh. Well, I had a cousin that was burned really badly in an accident at the gas station where he worked, and he sued the company and got, like, a million dollars."

"Oh yeah?"

"Yeah, and he also said it was the worst pain imaginable. Was it really bad?"

"Yeah."

She's cutting around my ears now, and I'm sure she's going to cut me. She's just cutting and talking the whole time.

"My cousin said when he was on fire, he could really feel himself burning up, but then he found the fire extinguisher and put himself out and drove himself to the hospital."

"Oh."

"The doctors said it was a miracle he was still alive. He got this great tattoo of this bird on fire, what is that thing called?"

"The phoenix?"

"Yup, that's right, he got a tattoo of the phoenix on his right shoulder, which is so cool."

"Yeah."

Now she's got out the electric shaver to shave the back of my neck, and she's talking about her cousin the tattoo artist who does designs for all sorts of people. He did one for the drummer from KISS.

I wonder if it's okay to use that shaver on my scars. I'm not sure that she should use that on me. When she gets near the big hypertrophic scar on my right cheek, she stops talking and tries to be careful. I try not to look at what my face looks like, but I'm sitting here right in front of this mirror, and when she turns the chair, I can see all different sides of my scars that I've never seen before. There's so much redness on my face. So red and so heavy. The scars are so heavy they're pulling my eye down.

I don't really believe that it's me. Except for my eyes. I recognize my eyes.

She's brushing off my neck now. I guess that means we're done. She takes the twenty-dollar bill Mom gave me to give her and hands back a pile of ones. I'm supposed to leave a tip. I hand her two dollars, turn around, and walk out without saying anything.

278

Mom's waiting for me in the car when I come out. She says, "Your haircut looks good."

"Thanks."

"How was it in there?"

"Sucked."

"Why?"

"Let's just say, never get a haircut from a woman wearing a hat."

"What do you mean?"

"It's a joke. Can we go home?"

Today we're starting my new schedule. Mom's taking me to an elementary school for physical therapy. I'll do it twice a week here and twice a week at Children's. I have to go to see a therapist this afternoon, and next week I have to start with a tutor.

Mom walks in with me. School is in session, and it's only eleven o'clock, so all the kids are in their classrooms. I can smell the lunch cooking. Green beans and mashed potatoes.

We walk into a room down the hall from the cafeteria. There's a girl in a helmet drooling on a mat. This must be the place. A blond woman in tight jeans walks over to us. She's way too old to be wearing jeans that tight.

"You must be Brent. I'm Cathy, I'll be your PT."

"Hi."

Mom says, "Well, I'll be out in the car. Come out when you're done, okay?"

"Okay, bye, Mom." All of a sudden, I don't want her to go. Never mind, I'm not a baby.

"So, Brent, what kind of exercises have you been doing?"

"Um, well, I guess, up at duPont, this place I was at, I was doing a bunch of dorsal flexion to release the bands on my trunk. I'm a little tighter on my right side than my left." I show her how I can lift my left arm pretty high above my head but my right arm doesn't go as far. "With passive motion I can get almost a hundred degrees out of my left shoulder but only like eighty, eighty-five out of my right." I bet she didn't expect I knew all those medical terms.

"Well, that's pretty good. I guess we've got something to work on. How are your lower extremities?"

"About the same. My right leg's tighter than my left."

"Okay, why don't you take off your shoes and lie down on the mat, and we'll do some stretching?"

"All right."

She starts with my ankles, doing some heavy stretching on my right ankle. She's kind of straddling me with her legs, and she's got her butt facing me. That's nice.

After she's done stretching me, she goes and cuts some dark blue Thera-Band, that's the stretchy plastic band that you use to stretch and strengthen yourself. The different colors mean different strengths, like black is the thickest and white is the thinnest. So dark blue is pretty good.

She shows me my exercise I'm supposed to do at home,

wrapping the Thera-Band around my foot and pulling up on it. She shows me how to stretch it over my shoulders to work on my arms, and how to push against the tension to make me stronger. Yeah, right, like I'm ever going to do any of this shit. I might take it home and make a slingshot out of it.

Mom takes me to the appointment with my new therapist. He meets me in the waiting room.

"Hi, Brent. I'm Mark Nusbaum, you can call me Dr. Nusbaum." Another Mark, another mustache.

"Hi."

"I'm glad you could be here. We're just going to have a short session today, nothing too intense. How does that sound?" We walk into his office and sit down.

"Fine."

"Great. What I'd like you to do is take this Magic Marker and this paper and draw a few pictures for me."

"Oh yeah?" He must think I'm a total idiot.

"I'd like you to draw a house, a tree, and a person, okay?"

"Okay." Jesus, I am so fucking sick and tired of these fucking psychologists and their stupid little fucking games to try and figure out what's going on inside my head. If they really want to know, they should just ask me.

"Great, go ahead."

I shouldn't say anything, but I can't help myself. "Dr. Nusbaum?"

"Yes." He tilts his head like my dog when she wants a treat.

"You don't really expect this to tell you anything about me, do you?"

"Hmm?"

"You don't really think that these drawings are going to tell you anything about me, do you?"

"Well, Brent, all I'm asking you to do is draw some pictures. What they mean is up to you."

"Oh, come on, you and I both know that whatever I draw on this paper is supposed to tell you something about me."

"I think it's interesting that you think it's going to say something about you."

"I don't think that. You think that."

"Brent, all I'm asking you to do is draw a picture of a house, a tree, and a person, all right?"

"How about a boat, a bush, and a dog? How about I draw that?"

"Well, I'd really appreciate it if you'd draw a tree, a house, and a person, but afterward you're welcome to draw whatever you like."

"Does this work on little kids or something? Because it's pretty obvious to me what you're doing."

"What am I doing?"

"You're trying to figure out stuff about me."

"What am I trying to figure out?"

"Oh, Christ, just give me the paper." I sit down and draw

a nice little house with a door in the middle and a chimney. I draw a tree that kind of looks like a lollipop and a normal-looking person, standing off to the side.

"There," I say when I'm done, "how's that?"

"That's fine, thanks. Now, please draw a man and a woman."

"Fine."

They look like a bride and groom on top of a wedding cake and also a little like the drawings on the signs for restrooms.

I wonder if I tried hard enough if I could be an artist. Probably not, I've never been able to draw too well. Maybe I could be a writer, though. I'd like to write something, like a book or something.

When I was in fourth grade, when I was just starting with the acting classes, I used to tell people that I wanted to be a writer and an actor and that I'd write stories and then act them out, but I'm not really sure what I meant by that.

Anyway, it's about time for this fucking therapy session to be over. Jesus, what do I have to do to get out of here?

"Are we done yet?"

"Yes, we're done. Nice to meet you."

"Yeah, likewise." God, I hate psychologists. I hope I don't have to see him again.

Mom and Dad and I are driving in to Children's for a meeting with my old plastic surgeon, Dr. Boyagen. I like him. He's the one that did my hands.

I turn on the radio and go to Howard Stern. Mom and Dad think he's too crude, but I think he's funny.

He says, "So, what kind of shoes are you wearing?"

The woman he's talking to is a stripper. She says, "Black pumps."

"Oh, very nice. And you're wearing a little tube top. Stand up so I can see, and a little black miniskirt. Very nice. So have you done women?"

A bunch of people laugh.

"I've experimented."

"Oh, very nice, tell me about your first lesbian experience."

"I was fourteen, at a boarding school."

"Oh?"

Mom says, "Brent, this is terrible. Turn this off."

"Come on, Mom, it was just getting good."

My dad says, "Brent, listen to your mother." I think this is the first time they've yelled at me since I was in the hospital. I turn it off.

We're getting off the highway. "God, this is far."

"Yup."

"You drove this every day to come see me?"

"Yup."

There it is. I recognize the building. We park, and Mom says, "Okay, you guys, you go up to see Dr. Boyagen, I'm going to go give platelets. I'll meet you on the Burn Unit, okay?"

"Okay." Mom started giving platelets when I went into

the hospital. She said she wanted to do something for the kids that have cancer.

Dad and I get in the elevators and head up to the fourth floor. It's weird being back here. It seems like a few years since I was in here, but it's not, it's only been a few months. We follow the signs to Plastic Surgery and Dad signs us in at the desk. There's a TV with CNN on, but no sound.

"Mr. Runyon? Dr. Boyagen will see you now."

Dad and I go into the examining room. The walls are painted yellow. And there are a bunch of paintings of lions and tigers and other jungle animals on the wall. I sit up on the examining table and Dad sits in a chair right next to me. Dad brought a magazine with him. That was smart, I wish I'd thought of that.

Dr. Boyagen comes through the door with two young doctors in white coats. Dad and I stand up and shake his hand.

"Hello, Mr. Runyon, good to see you."

"Hello."

"Hello, Brent. You're looking much better than the last time I saw you."

"Thanks." When was that?

"Good. So today, let's just talk about our options for scar reduction, scar excision, and scar management."

Dad says, "Great." He takes a yellow legal pad out of his briefcase. Dr. Boyagen looks at me. "But what I first need to know is, how much do you want to have done? What are the areas that you find most problematic in your everyday life, and what do you want to do about them?"

I say, "Um, well, I guess I really don't like this scar on my left thigh. This one here." I unzip the Jobst garment on that side and show him and the young doctors. "I really don't like this one. This is the one that really bothers me."

Dr. Boyagen says, "Well, unfortunately, Brent, we don't have any recourse in that area. Mostly what we do here in plastic surgery is work with facial reconstruction, scar excision around the face especially."

"Oh."

"Why don't I tell you about your options."

"Okay." These paintings look like a kid could have done them because they're so simple, but the way the animals look, maybe an adult did them. The lion's eyes in the painting are so big and green.

Dad says, "That would be helpful."

"Well, the first thing we have to consider is the availability of donor sites for scar revision. This is different than what you've gone through before, where we removed sections of skin, meshed them out, and applied them to the open wounds. What we'll be doing now is using full-thickness grafts, excising the existing scar tissue and placing the full-thickness normal skin in its place. Now, the problem, obviously, is how much skin are we going to be able to use, and in Brent's case, in your case, we don't have a lot to work with."

The lion looks so lonely in the painting. He's just sitting there staring right at me.

"So, I can do a few things. Probably the most effective is

to insert what's called an expander, which basically is a balloon, and what we do is we insert the expander underneath a viable graft area and fill it slowly over a period of, say, two to three months, and so at the end of the process, we have two to three times the amount of skin as we did at the beginning."

I'm looking right into the lion's eyes and he's looking back. We're having a staring contest. I always win in staring contests because I don't care if my eyes get dry and start hurting. I can keep my eyes open with my willpower.

He goes on, "The other option we have is something called a Z-plasty, which is a fairly straightforward procedure. What we do"—he takes a ballpoint pen out of his pocket—"is excise the scar tissue in a Z shape, which is why it's called a Z-plasty." He draws what feels like a Z on my right cheek, like Zorro. "And what that allows us to do is release whatever banding might have accumulated in the area."

My eyes are starting to hurt. They itch and they're getting dry, but I'm not going to look away. I'm going to keep staring at the lion in the painting.

Dad asks a question. "So does the Z-plasty procedure include the expanders?" He always picks up the vocabulary quick.

"No. The Z-shaped excision takes the place of the expanders."

He grabs a big section of my right cheek between his thumb and forefinger and pinches it. "Now, unfortunately, we don't have a heck of a lot of play in here, so if you decide to go with the Z-plasty, we'll wind up with, probably, a series of three to five procedures over a number of years."

The lion isn't going to blink. I know that. But I don't care. It doesn't matter. I'm not giving up.

Now he grabs a big chunk of my left cheek, squeezes it hard, and draws another line across it. He outlines my scars with the pen. "But on the other hand, we can probably excise this side in one or two surgeries and really get rid of a lot of this ugly scar tissue."

I blinked. Shit. The lion won. I tried. I did pretty well. The lion was better, but I did pretty well. The lion looks a little nicer now than he did when I came in here. I wonder if he feels sorry for me having to go through all of this. Probably not, because he knows it's all my fault.

"So, as you wish, we can go ahead with the first surgery, sometime in the next year, not quite yet, just so we can see how the scarring matures and diminishes over time. How's that sound?"

Is the doctor talking to me? I don't know what to say. I wish the lion would help me.

Mom meets us in the waiting room. Now we're going down to the Burn Unit to see everybody. I wonder who's working. I'd love to see Tina, and Barbara, and the other Barbara, and Lisa. I'd love to see everybody.

We walk past my old room. Who's in there now? Some

baby in a crib. I don't see any nurses or anybody I recognize. My dad asks at the nurses' station if we can go back into Intensive Care and say hello. They say it's okay.

We go back through the double doors. All that alcohol and cleaning solution, it makes me feel like I just got a shot of morphine.

"Hey, Brent!"

It's Tina, she's wearing scrubs and her hair is back in a ponytail. She's so beautiful. "Hi, Tina!" She gives me a big hug.

"How are you?" I'd forgotten how high pitched her voice was.

"Great."

"God, you look great. You got so strong."

"I did?"

"How's everything? Are you back in school?"

"No, not yet."

"Oh, how's your skin?" She reaches out and touches the scar on my cheek.

"All right, it itches."

"Yeah, well, it's supposed to, but is it healing properly?"

"I guess."

"Jeez, if we had our way, we'd bring you into one of these rooms and strip you down naked."

I laugh. "Well, maybe some other time."

"It's so good to see you, Brent. I'm glad you're doing so well. Okay, keep up the good work and come back and see us more often." She hugs me.

"Okay. Bye."

"Bye."

She turns away, puts on a nurse's smock, and goes into someone else's room.

I don't belong here. It's not the same. I don't think I will be coming back.

I'm playing *Super Mario* in the basement. I warped to level eight because I wanted to try and beat the guy, but I didn't get enough lives on the earlier levels to beat him. So now I'm screwed. Mom calls from the top of the stairs, "Brent, your tutor is here." Oh shit, I completely forgot that the tutor was coming today. I was hoping I was going to get out of school for the rest of my life, but apparently not.

I come up the stairs. She's a nice-enough-looking woman, wearing a red coat and a funny little red beret. She says, "Hi, Brent, nice to meet you. My name's Maureen."

"Hi. Nice to meet you."

Mom says, "Is the living room okay for you, Maureen?"

"Yes, that's great, thanks."

"Okay. I'll leave you two alone, then."

Last year I had to go to a tutor's house to help me with algebra, right after I got caught for stealing school supplies. He had a lot of cats and his house always smelled like Indian food or something.

"So, Brent, we've got a lot of things to work on to get you caught up with your studies. I see that you've completed the eighth grade at, was it, the duPont Institute?"

"Yes."

"All right, so we've got the normal array of ninth-grade classes. Earth science, history, English, and algebra."

"I hate algebra."

"Hate is a strong word."

"Yeah, I know."

"So, I'm assuming that you would like to begin with

something other than algebra? Is that a correct assump-tion?"

"Well, you know what they say about assumptions?"

"No, what do they say about assumptions?"

"They make an ass out of you and umptions." I laugh at my stupid joke. She doesn't laugh.

"So, how does history sound?"

"Sounds like history." I'm cracking myself up.

"Let's read the first chapter in the history book and then talk about it."

"All right." We both read from our matching history books. It's about how the Greeks created democracy.

When we're done reading, she quizzes me with a bunch of questions and I get them all right. I wish regular school was this easy. If I got to do homeschooling all of the time, I'd get straight A's. I liked it better when I didn't have to do any schoolwork. Now I have to sit here with Maureen for a couple of hours three times a week. This sucks.

I'm naked, lying on the massage table at Children's, with a little towel covering my penis. There's a curtain pulled around me, but I can hear all the noises of the kids being worked over on the other side. Today's my first day with my new PT, her name's Nancy. She peeks her head through the curtain.

"You ready?"

"Yeah."

"Good. How are you?" She comes in and closes the curtain.

"Fine." She opens a jar of Eucerin cream. She's got big wide thumbs that look like she smashed them with a hammer about a million times. She starts down at my feet.

I don't have much to say. I just stare up at the ceiling and wonder why I did this. I can't even really remember anymore. I know I was sad or something, but what was I so sad about? School and girls? Megan and Stephen? Setting fire to that locker? None of it seems like a big deal anymore.

She's up to my thigh. When she rubs the top of my thigh, her hand goes in between my legs and rubs the inside of my leg. God, that feels good. Jesus. God, I'm getting a giant boner. I hope the towel isn't sticking straight up. Is it sticking straight up? Jesus, it is.

Nancy says, "You all right?"

"Yup." Is she trying to rub my balls? It really feels like it. It really feels like it. It feels like she's trying to rub my balls. Jesus.

"You can roll over now."

"Okay." I roll over with my hand over my penis so she can't see what a big boner I have. Now my butt is completely exposed. Now she's rubbing my butt. That feels good too. God, everything feels so good.

I'm going to ask her if she'll rub the inside of my thigh. I'm going to say that the skin is really tight between my legs, which it is, and I'm going to ask her if she'll rub it. That's what I'm going to do, and she's going to start rubbing it and maybe she'll see my big boner and she'll want to start rubbing it and touching it. Jesus.

"Okay, Brent, I'm done. Put on your Jobst and your clothes and we'll do some exercises." I sit up. I'm going to ask her, I really am.

"Um, Nancy?"

"Yes."

"I've got this really tight band that I was wondering if you could work on?"

"Where is it?"

"Um, it's sort of between my legs."

"Where?"

"Right here." She looks down and sort of raises an eyebrow.

"There?"

"Yeah."

"Well, that's a very sensitive area, maybe you could work on it when you're at home."

"Oh, okay."

"Get dressed and come out, okay?"

"Yeah."

She leaves. What's wrong with me? I feel stupid.

Mom and Dad and I are going to go see Dennis Miller at George Washington University. Since Dad works there, we've got really good seats. I'm so psyched. Ever since Dennis Miller left *Saturday Night Live* last season, I've been wondering what he'd do next. He's the funniest guy who ever did Weekend Update. Some people think Chevy Chase is the funniest, but they're wrong.

He walks on the stage like such a normal guy. How can he be so smart and so funny and still be so relaxed? I mean, he doesn't even look like he knows where he is. He says he's tired because he just flew in from Paris. I wonder what he was doing in Paris.

It's not just the things he says that are funny, it's the way he says them. The rhythm. I could be funny like that if I really tried. Life would be easier if I was funny. It's easier to get through life.

The whole drive home I keep thinking about how funny he was. God, that was funny. Wasn't that funny? He's such a funny guy. Dad says, "I'm sorry I couldn't get us backstage to meet Dennis."

I say, "That's okay, Dad. It's no big deal."

When we get home, there are two messages on the answering machine. I press play.

The weird computer voice says, "Message received at 10:21 P.M."

Then somebody's voice I kind of recognize, but not really. "Brent! Hey, what's up, babe, listen, I'm sorry I couldn't meet you after the show, but I was totally vamped from the flight in from Paris. Anyway, maybe I could meet you tomorrow, I've got some time to kill before my plane leaves. I could come out to your house, or school, or whatever. Anyway, catch you later, cat. Uh, call me at the Four

Seasons, room . . . Christ, what is the room . . . room 402. All right, hope you liked the show. Bye-bye."

Jesus. Was that who I think it was? Was that fucking Dennis Miller on my fucking answering machine? I look at my parents, they're smiling with their eyes open really wide.

I say, "Was that Dennis Miller?"

"I think it was."

"Did you give him our number?"

"We gave someone our number at the show, but we didn't know if he'd call."

"Wait, there's another message."

"Message received at 10:31 P.M."

"Brento! It's Dennis, where are you, cat? It's like ten-thirty, and I'm totally vamped, so call me soon, babe, as soon as you get home. All right."

Jesus, that really is Dennis Miller. I'm feeling a little light-headed. My dad runs and gets the phone book, finds the number, and brings it with the phone over to me in the comfy chair.

Out of habit, I turn on the TV. It's Comedy Central, and there is Dennis Miller doing Weekend Update.

I'm dialing the number.

"Four Seasons, how may I direct your call?"

"Room 402, please." Jesus, I'm so nervous.

"Just a moment."

It's ringing. It's fucking ringing.

"Yeah?"

"Um, Dennis?"

"Yeah, who's this?"

"It's, um, Brent, um, Runyon. You called me?"

"Brento! Hey, babe, what's happening?"

"Nothing. Um, you were really funny tonight."

"Thanks. Hey, so where do you live?"

"Uh, northern Virginia. Falls Church."

"Where's that."

"On the Orange Line."

"Okay, can you give me directions so I can come out and meet you tomorrow? Would that be cool?"

"Yeah, that would be great. Hey, you're on TV right now."

"What, *SNL*?"

"Yeah."

"What episode, do you know?"

"I think it's, like, really early. Damon Wayans is on with you."

"Oh yeah? God, that's like my second show."

"Cool."

"Yeah, so, can I get those directions from you?"

"Yeah, I'll get my dad. Dad, he wants directions to come out and meet me tomorrow."

Dad takes the phone and starts explaining how to get here.

Dennis Miller is coming over to my house. He's going to be here in five minutes. Dad's at work and Mom went out to get some groceries so he and I could have the house to ourselves. Christ, what will I talk about? What am I going to say? I've got to be funny. I've got to be funny. I've got to find a way to make him laugh.

There's the limo. The limo is right in my driveway. Oh my God, there's Dennis walking up to my front door. We don't usually use the front door, but that's okay.

I open it and walk out to meet him. He's kind of short, but he looks basically like he does on TV except for more tired and like he didn't shave this morning.

"Hi, I'm Brent."

"Great to meet you, babe." We shake hands.

"Your show was great. You were so funny."

"Thanks, man. Is this the pad? Can we hang inside?"

"Sure, come in."

"Are your folks here?"

"No, they're at work." We walk into the living room and he sits in the chair. I sit across from him on the couch. Dennis Miller is sitting in my living room. "Do you want anything to drink or anything?"

"No thanks. So, tell me, what happened?"

"What?"

"What happened to you?"

"Oh, um, you mean, like, the fire?" I didn't know he was going to ask anything like that. "Um, I was . . ." I point upstairs to the bathroom. "I was up there, and I had some matches. . . ." I can't say it. I don't know what to say. I look down at my hands and then up the stairs at the bathroom.

"That's okay, you don't have to talk about it if you don't want."

"Okay."

"So you want to go for a ride in a limo?"

"Sure."

There's a big fat Italian guy driving the car. He opens our door for us and we slide in. Dennis says, "Why don't you take us for a spin around town."

What should I say? Should I ask about *Saturday Night Live*? Should I ask what he's going to do now? Celebrities like to talk about themselves, I think. I should ask him something where he can be funny and tell a lot of jokes or something. If I was a talk show host, I would already know what to ask him, but I'm not sure.

I'm still trying to think of something to say when Dennis says, "I was talking to Franken, you know, Al Franken. He's got balls, man. We had Oprah on the show one time, and in the pitch meeting he asked her if she was willing to play Aunt Jemima." He laughs just like he does on TV. "That crazy motherfucker."

"Yeah, he's funny. Did she do it?"

"No, she was pissed. Hey, what time is it? Ten o'clock, that's seven in L.A., shit, too early. I was thinking we could call Leno and wake him up, but I think it's too early."

"Jay Leno?"

"Yeah, he's a good friend."

"Oh yeah?"

"Yeah, you like him?"

"Uh, yeah, he seems nice."

"But Hanksy is the nicest guy in showbiz."

"Who?"

"Tom Hanks. He's a genuine cat, man. A real sweetheart."

Jesus, I can't think of anything to say. I'm such an idiot.

He says, "Hey, want to see a picture of my wife and kid?"

"Sure." He pulls a photo out of his pocket with a picture of a pretty woman and a little kid.

"That's Ali. That's Holden."

"They look nice."

"Light of my life, man." We pass the Long John Silver's and keep driving through Falls Church. I've got to think of something to say, but I can't think of anything. He says, "So, do you go to school or what, man?"

"Um, I have a tutor right now, but I'm supposed to go back to regular school soon."

"How long have you been out of school?"

"Like, eight months."

"Yeah. Tough, man, listen, I feel for you. You're a tough kid."

"Thanks." It's a good thing he doesn't know what really happened, he probably wouldn't think I was so tough. He probably wouldn't even be here. I've got to find something funny to say. Jesus, anything, I have to make him laugh.

Now we're just driving, not even talking. God, I can't think of anything to say. Nothing.

Dennis says to the driver, "You can swing back around

now. Hey, does somebody know where we are, because I have no idea. Brento, where are we, man?"

I look around. I'm not sure where we are. I say, "Uh, I wasn't paying attention." I mean, I know I've been here before, but I'm not sure how to get back.

The driver just puts his hand up, like he knows what he's doing. Dennis seems worried. He says, "You know where we're going, right?"

"Yes, sir."

"Good, because I've got a plane to catch at some point."

The car swings around and starts back to where we came from. Now I know where we are. We're not even that far away.

We pull back into my driveway and Dennis opens the door. God, it's over so fast. I wonder if I'll ever see him again. He says, "Listen, I've got a show at George Mason University in a couple of weeks. If you want, I'll get you some tickets."

"That would be great."

"Yeah? I've got your number. I'll give you a call, okay?"

"Yeah, um, before you go, can I take a picture with you and get you to sign my tape?"

"Sure, man."

I run inside and grab my tape. He signs it, I'm Outta Here, Dennis Miller. And makes spirals with the pen, like he always used to do at the end of Weekend Update. We get the driver to take a picture of us with our arms around each other's shoulders.

He says, "Brento, it was really nice to meet you, man. Hang in there."

"Thanks, Dennis. Thanks for coming out here."

"No problem." We shake hands. He's got really small hands.

"And tell Luca Brasi I said good-bye." He laughs and gets in the car and drives away. That's so awesome. Dennis Miller laughed at my joke. He laughed at my stupid *Godfather* joke. God, he laughed at my joke.

Except I should have said Clemenza. Clemenza was the driver. I should have said Clemenza, that would have been so much funnier. Shit.

Mom comes home about twenty minutes later and makes me tell her the whole story, then she makes me call Dad and tell him the whole story. I should call Stephen. I wonder if he's back from Australia yet. I bet he would think it was cool. It's just so cool that Dennis Miller came over to my house and hung out with me for a while.

Maureen, the tutor, is here. I can't believe I have to do school stuff on a day like today. She wants me to read an article about a tribe of Africans that lived apart from society for thousands of years and then, just recently, somebody found them in the jungle. They're called the Yokemite tribe or something.

The phone is ringing. Mom answers. I can hear her talking in the kitchen.

"Hello? Yes. Yes. Okay, yes, I'll get him." She pokes

her head around the corner. "Brent?"

"Yeah?" She doesn't usually interrupt me when I'm in school.

"It's Jay Leno."

"What?"

"Jay Leno is on the phone for you."

"What?"

"It's Jay Leno. He wants to talk to you." She opens her eyes really wide to let me know she's serious. I run upstairs into her bedroom to get the phone. God, this is so weird. I can't believe this is happening to me.

"Hello? Mom, I've got it." She hangs up.

"Hey, is this Brent?"

"Yeah."

"Hey, this is Jay Leno."

"Hi." He sounds just like he does on TV, with the speech impediment and everything.

"So what's going on? Dennis gave me your number, just thought I'd give you a call, say hello."

"Uh, I'm just in school right now, like homeschool." God, I sound like an idiot.

"Oh yeah? What are you studying there?"

"Uh, this, uh, African tribe called the Yokemite."

"Huh. I must have been sick that day." I laugh.

"Well, there's a lot of stuff to learn, actually."

"Oh well, I must have been sick that week." I laugh again. He's funny.

"Yeah."

"Well, it's good to talk to you. Hope you feel better, and if I'm ever in town doing a show, I'll get you some tickets."

"Okay."

"Great, nice to talk to you."

"Okay, bye."

"Bye-bye."

I walk back into the living room. Maureen's still here. She wants me to keep reading about that Yokemite tribe. I'm not really in the mood anymore. I mean, I woke up this morning like a normal person, and now I've ridden in a limo with Dennis Miller and talked on the phone with Jay Leno. I'm not going to do any work today.

The phone is ringing again. Who's it going to be this time? Mom answers. She says, "Hello. Yes. Sure. I'll get him. Brent, it's Dennis Miller again."

"Okay." This time I take it in the kitchen. "Hello."

"Hey, Brento! Did you talk to Leno?"

"Yeah. He was really nice."

"Great. Great. Can't tell you how happy I am to hear that. Just wanted to check in, make sure you guys got in touch. So, I'll see you in a couple of weeks."

"Okay. See you later."

"Bye-bye."

"Bye."

I'm starting to feel a little dizzy. I have to lie down.

Mom and I are on our way home from Children's. She says, "Do you want to do anything special today?"

"No."

"Do you want to go anywhere?"

"No." What is she talking about? We never do anything special. We always just go home.

"You sure you don't want to do anything special?"

"I'm sure."

"Come on. Let's have a little fun."

"No thanks." She's driving a little faster than she normally does. She doesn't normally pass people like this, either.

We're supposed to get off at this exit to go home, but Mom keeps driving. I say, "Mom, that was our exit."

"I know."

"Where are we going?"

"You'll see." What the hell is going on? She's got a weird smile on her face, like she's got something up her sleeve.

"Mom, what are you doing?"

"We're doing something spontaneous."

"Spontaneous?"

"Yup."

"We never do anything spontaneous."

"I know. That's why we're doing it."

"You're crazy."

She laughs, opens her eyes really wide, and blinks a few times. I wonder if she's gone crazy. I mean, the whole time I've known her, she's never done anything spontaneous.

Craig and I used to joke that if she was going to do something spontaneous, she'd have to put it on her calendar at least a year in advance.

We're still driving. There's nothing out this way at all. We passed the mall and the movie theater. A sign says Dulles Airport. I look at Mom.

"Mom, are we going to the airport?"

"You'll see."

We are going to the airport. Why the hell are we going here? We don't have tickets. We don't have luggage.

She parks the car in the departures section and we walk into the terminal. Look at all these people in business suits.

We go over to the bank of television screens and stare up at the list of departures. Mom says, "So where do you want to go?"

"What do you mean?"

"Where do you want to go?"

"We can't go anywhere. We don't have any luggage." I think she has gone totally crazy.

"That doesn't matter. Where do you want to go?"

"I don't know."

"Do you want to go see Nanny and Grandpa in Florida?"

"I don't know."

"Do you want to go to California?"

"I don't know."

"Where do you want to go?"

"I don't know. How are we going to pay for the tickets?"

"I'll put it on my credit card."

"What about Dad?"

"We'll call him when we get there."

"Where?"

"I don't know. You have to decide."

We stand around looking up at the screens. There are flights to New York and Los Angeles. And Nashville. And Chicago. And Boston. But I don't really want to go anywhere. I've been away for too long. I just want to go home.

"Mom, I don't want to go anywhere. I just want to go home."

"Oh. Okay. Well, let's at least get a souvenir."

We go to the bookstore in the airport and buy a copy of *Where's Dan Quayle?*, which is like *Where's Waldo?* but with Dan Quayle, and walk back out to the car. I look at her face. I hope she's okay.

Mom and Dad are looking into programs for me before I go back to real school. They found one that's not too far away called Dominion, which is like an outpatient hospital for kids with problems. I'm not sure that I have problems, but I don't know, maybe I do. Anyway, Mom and I have a meeting with the director of the program today.

We pull into the parking lot, and just before we open the doors, Mom says, "Brent, I just want you to keep an open mind about this place, okay? This is just our first meeting, and if it's not the right place for you, then you won't come here, but just keep an open mind, okay?"

"Okay."

We wait for Dr. Mager to come meet us. We're the only ones waiting, but other people keep coming through and the lady behind the desk buzzes them in.

Some guy opens the door. Is this him? "Hi, Mrs. Runyon, Brent, I'm Michael Mager, you can call me Michael." His name sounds like major.

"Hello, nice to meet you." Mom shakes his hand.

"Hi." He shakes my hand too and looks me right in the eye.

He's got a nice-looking face, not handsome exactly, but kind. He leads us back through a hallway, past a cafeteria— I can smell the meat loaf—and into his office.

We all sit down and he starts talking. Apparently he already knows everything about me. "Well, to start, I'd just like to thank you both for coming. I'll tell you a little about our hospital and what we do here. We have two programs you may be interested in. The first is an inpatient program, in which we provide twenty-four-hour care for adolescents with a variety of mental health concerns. The second is an outpatient program, in which we provide mental health counseling in the morning and a one-on-one tutoring program in the afternoons. Brent, you'd be eligible for both of those programs."

There's something I like about this guy. Maybe it's the way he smiles when he talks, even though the stuff he's saying is the same stuff every other doctor says.

"Most of our patients here at Dominion fall into two

groups. We treat eating disorders and adolescents in drug rehabilitation. Now, Brent, I know that neither of those is your problem, but I think, in the right environment, it could be very helpful to have other kids around who are slightly different from you to give you a different kind of perspective. And to be honest, I'm sure, no matter where you look, it will be difficult to find anyone that fits directly into your diagnosis group."

He smiles at me, then at Mom. Most of the other doctors talk to Mom or Dad and don't pay any attention to me, but this guy, when he talks, looks right at me. He continues, "So, I think the most important thing is that if you decide to come here, we're on the same page as far as treatment goes. I think that if you come here, the focus shouldn't be on why you set yourself on fire because at this point you probably don't even know yourself."

Wow, that's completely right. I never thought of that.

"The focus should really be on making sure that it never happens again."

I say, "That sounds good."

Mom says, "Yes, that sounds good."

"Great, well, you think about it and get back to me." He shakes our hands and walks us out.

Outside in the car, Mom says, "What'd you think?"

"He seems nice."

"Yeah? Do you think you'd like to go there?"

"Well, yeah, I think I would."

"Great, honey. That's great."

The phone is ringing. Mom answers it. She calls down, "Brent, someone on the phone for you." Then she whispers loudly, "It's a girl." A girl? I wonder who that could be. I turn off the TV and pick it up. My heart is beating really fast all of a sudden.

"Hello?"

"Hi, Brent?"

"Yeah?" Who is this?

"Hey, Brent, it's Caroline. How are you?" She sounds so cheerful.

"I'm good. How are you?"

"I'm well. Hey, what are you doing tonight?" Caroline and I were in the same French class, but we were never really good friends before. I mean, I knew her and thought she was cool, but we weren't that close. Then when I was in the hospital, she started writing me all these letters and sending me cards all the time. She's just about the only one from my school that kept sending me cards. I don't know why she did that.

"I'm not doing anything. What are you doing?"

"Well, a bunch of us are going to the Marshall-Madison game tonight, and I was wondering if you would like to come."

There's big football rivalry between Marshall and Madison. Caroline goes to Madison now, and if I ever go to high school, I'll go to Marshall.

"Yeah, sure."

"Okay, so I'll meet you at eight in front of where they sell the tickets?"

"Okay. Great."

"See you then." We hang up.

I'm standing out front by the ticket booth. The game has already started, but I don't see her. There must be a thousand kids here. I'm wearing my old black winter coat and a hooded sweatshirt. I've got my hood pulled up because it's cold and also to cover the scars on my cheeks. So far I haven't seen anybody staring at me, so it's working. I told Mom to pick me up at ten, but what if I don't want to stay that long? I hope I recognize Caroline. Is that her? That must be her. God, I thought she was kind of dumpy when I knew her at Kilmer, but now she's looking pretty good. She looks older, but maybe it's the cheerleading outfit she's wearing.

"Hi, Brent!" She gives me a hug.

"Hi, Caroline."

"It's so good to see you."

"It's good to see you too. You look good."

"Thanks."

"So you're a cheerleader?"

"Captain of the freshman cheerleading squad. Go, Madison! Woo!" I laugh.

Caroline takes me into the stadium and we start walking around the track, looking for people we know. Suddenly I realize I don't want to be doing this. I really don't.

God, there's Vicki Kee. She was the girl I had to race in elementary school that one time, and she was so much faster than I was, I had to pretend I pulled a hamstring.

"Brent!"

"Vicki." The only problem with seeing people you know is that they know you.

"Oh my God, I'm so glad to see you. Brent, I'm so happy you're okay."

"Thanks."

"When are you coming back?"

"I don't know. Soon."

"I can't wait. Well, see you around."

"Yeah."

That was weird. There's Kevin Manz. He was the kid I stole school supplies with in algebra. Jesus, he's big. He must be a football player now.

He comes over to us and says, "Hey, Caroline. What's up?"

Caroline says, "Hi, Kevin. Look, it's Brent."

"I know. What's up, Brent?"

"What's up?"

"Nothing."

"Cool."

"Cool."

Caroline walks me over to the Marshall side to see if we know anyone over there. I haven't watched any of the game. I don't even know who's winning.

I say, "I'm starting to feel like Michael Corleone when he comes back from Italy."

"Do you mean from *The Godfather*?"

"Yeah."

"I love that movie."

"You do? That's so cool."

"That's the one with the horse's head, right?"

"Yeah." I do my Brando impression. "'I'll make him an offer he can't refuse.'"

She smiles.

"Do you remember this part?" I point my fingers into a gun like Sonny does and say in my New York accent, "'This ain't the army, where you shoot 'em a mile away, you gotta get up close and—bada bing—you blow their brains all over your nice Ivy League suit.'"

She laughs, "That's pretty good."

"How about this part." I scrunch up my face like Luca Brasi and make my voice sound really low and dumb. "'Don Corleone, I am honored and grateful to be invited to your daughter's wedding, on the day of your daughter's wedding. And may their first child be a masculine child.'"

She's not laughing as much at that one. I hope she's not getting sick of it. I can do an impression of almost everyone in that movie. Next I do Sonny in the closet with the bridesmaid. I pretend somebody is knocking on the door and then I pretend I'm having sex with a woman, slamming her against the wall. "Uh uh uh uh. Uh uh uh uh." I'm laughing now.

She's not laughing anymore. "It's a good movie."

"Yeah, a really good movie." Shit, I think I overdid it.

"Brent, you haven't changed at all."

That's my problem. I haven't changed at all.

I see Chris standing at the edge of the wire fence, watching the game. I walk over and tap him on the shoulder.

"Hey, Chris."

"Brent! I didn't know you were coming."

"Yeah. Here I am."

"Cool. Hey, I was talking to Jake and some of the other guys on the JV soccer team."

Oh shit, he's going to ask if I'm going to try out. I don't think I can try out. I can hardly run.

"Yeah?"

"And we were wondering if you wanted to be our manager when you come back to school."

"What do you mean?"

"You could help us carry the equipment and be up in the press box and announce our names when we come on the field."

I can tell he's trying to be nice, but I don't know, it makes me feel bad that he doesn't ask if I want to be on the team. I played soccer with him for seven years.

I say, "Okay. I'll think about it."

"When are you coming back to school, anyway?"

"I don't know. Not for a while."

"Okay. Talk to you soon."

The phone rings. Mom picks it up and yells downstairs that Caroline is on the phone. I pick it up next to the TV.

"Hello?"

She says, "Brent?"

"Yeah, hi."

"Hi. How are you?"

"Good. How are you?"

"I'm well. I just wanted to make sure you had fun last night."

"I did."

"You did?"

"Yeah, it was fun."

"Good, I'm glad. I was worried you didn't have any fun."

"No, I had fun."

"Okay, good. Hey, I was wondering if you wanted to go out on Halloween with Megan and me. We're going on the Haunted Hayride."

"Megan? The Megan I know? Um. Okay. That'd be fun."

"Great. Bye."

"Bye." Jesus, I'm going to see Megan. I wonder what she looks like now. I wonder if she's still going out with Stephen. I wonder if she still likes me. I wonder if I'll still be in love with her.

Stephen's back from his vacation to Australia. It's so good to see him. He doesn't look that different. He's maybe a little taller and a lot tanner, but other than that he looks the same. He gives me a hug.

"Hey, bro."

"Hey, bro."

"Great to see you, man." God, it's so funny to hear his Australian accent again.

"Great to see you too."

We go downstairs into the basement. I say, "So what have you been up to?"

"Not much."

"No? You still doing comedy?" Stephen and I used to do comedy together.

"I don't do comedy so much anymore, but I started doing some magic."

"Really, that's so cool. I started doing magic too."

"That's awesome."

"What can you do?"

"Well, I can't do too much, but I can do this." He holds up a quarter in his left hand, puts it in his right hand, and then opens the right hand and the quarter is gone.

"Wow. That was awesome. Show me how to do that." Stephen shows me just how to hold the coin in my hand so it makes it look like it's going into the right hand. It's kind of hard for me to do it because of the Jobst gloves on my fingers, but maybe I can do something else, like put the coin inside the glove.

I'm dying to ask about Megan. I wonder if he ever had sex with her. God, I bet he had sex with her.

"So, Stephen."

"Yeah."

"Are you and Megan still going out?"

"No, she and I broke up before I went back to Australia."

"You did?"

"Yeah."

"Why?"

"I don't know. I guess it wasn't really working out?"

"How far did you get?"

"Well, a lot of times, in the middle of the night, while my mom and dad were sleeping, I'd sneak over to her house, and, uh, we'd make out."

"Really?"

"Yeah."

"That's so awesome."

We just sit there, not saying anything. I can't figure out why he broke up with Megan. I'd give anything to be able to make out with her.

"Brent?"

"Yeah?"

"Did you know I'm moving?"

"You're moving?"

"Yeah, back to Australia."

"What?"

"Yeah. My parents are sending me back to a boarding school there."

"What?"

"Yeah."

"Why?"

"Um, I don't know. I guess they don't like it here."

"Are they moving too?"

"Not yet."

"So why are they sending you back?"

"I guess they don't like some of the things that have happened here."

"Like what?"

"Like what happened to you."

"What?"

"Yeah."

"They're sending you back to Australia because of what happened to me?"

"Yeah."

"That fucking sucks, man. I can't even believe that. That fucking sucks."

We play Nintendo for a while and then go outside and sit on the deck. I can't believe that they're sending him away. I say, "So did they, like, make you go to a psychologist or something?"

"Yeah, he was a real dick. But I borrowed this big book of magic from him and never gave it back."

"That's awesome. Man, I hate all my psychologists too. They're such dicks."

"I know. You know what I was thinking?"

"What?"

"We could go over to my psychologist's house, it's not too far from here, and we bring a can of gasoline with us and burn an anarchy symbol into his lawn."

"Are you serious?"

"Yeah. You want to?"

I know he's serious. I know there was a time when I

would have done something like that, but I don't really want to do crazy stuff anymore.

"Um, I'm kind of tired. Want to order pizza and play Nintendo some more?"

"Yeah, sure."

Mom drops me off at Caroline's house for the Haunted Hayride. I wonder what it'll be like to see Megan again. I haven't seen her for nine months. I wonder, I mean, I wonder if she's not dating anybody if she'd like to maybe go out with me. My heart is beating so hard.

I ring the doorbell. Caroline opens the door. "Hey, Brent. You guys, Brent's here."

"Hi."

The twins, Adam and Laura, are here. The last time I saw Laura, I told her I was going to set myself on fire. I wonder if she remembers that.

There's Megan. Something's different. It's like she doesn't know me anymore. She says, "Hi."

"Hi."

"Good to see you."

"You too."

Adam says, "Hey, man, it's so cool you could come tonight."

"Thanks."

"Yeah, we didn't know if we'd ever see you again."

"Yeah." I try to laugh, but I don't think it was a joke.

Caroline's mom drives us. There's six of us and only five seat belts. My mom would have a heart attack if she knew someone wasn't wearing a seat belt. Caroline sits up front and the rest of us crowd into the back. I'm next to Megan. Her leg is pressed up against mine and I let my hand rest gently against the side of her knee. I can smell her hair, it smells so good. She's even more beautiful than before.

Laura says, "So, Brent, did you get all our letters?"

"I don't know."

"What do you mean?"

"Well, I got some letters, but there's no way to tell if I got all of them." That was funny. Why didn't anybody laugh?

Caroline says, "Did you get the one I sent you from French class?"

Adam says, "Yeah, the whole class wrote you little notes, did you get them?"

"Um, yeah, I think I got that." Honestly, I don't remember, I got so many letters, it's hard to remember.

"Did you get that tape Jennifer made you?"

"Yeah, I got that." I remember it was kind of stupid. A bunch of girls screaming into a microphone.

Why isn't Megan asking me anything? I wish she would say something to me. Oh well, I'm just happy to be this close to her. I always wanted to be this close to her. Maybe I'll put my hand on her leg. Maybe I'll slide my hand under her shirt and feel her stomach and then move it up to her breasts. Maybe I'll just sit here quietly and not do anything.

Last year, when the three of us were friends, Stephen and I would always ask her what color underwear she was wearing when we'd talk to her on the phone. She wasn't like other girls, she actually would tell us. For her birthday, we bought her this sexy bra and panties, I think they were red, and she said she would model them for us. I never saw them. Stephen saw them, but I never did.

I wonder what would have happened back then if I'd just told Megan I liked her and I wanted to go out with her.

Maybe I could have had sex with her. I could have lost my virginity to her. We could have lost it together. Now all that's gone. There's nothing left of all that stuff we had together. There's nothing left but being scrunched into the same backseat, smelling her hair and wondering what color underwear she's wearing.

That balloon, the first balloon I ever got when I was in the hospital, the silver one that says Get Well Soon, still has air in it. All the other balloons deflated, but that one is still floating in my room. It just sits there, sometimes by the windows, sometimes in my closet, sometimes in front of the bathroom door. Mom calls it my guardian angel. I tell her she's wrong, but the way it just floats up in my room, it feels like it's taking care of me.

It's my birthday and I told Mom and Dad I didn't want to do anything, but I think they're planning something. I saw that Mom bought a whole bunch of those premade pizza crusts so you can make pizza at home. I'm sure they're going to do something, and I wish they wouldn't.

I was right. Surprise party. Stephen and Caroline just drove up. Megan's not with them. There's Chris and his sister Robin. They must have walked over from their house. There's Alida and her mom. I haven't seen her since she came to see me in the hospital.

   I guess it's nice that my parents had everyone come over,

but it seems so pathetic that my parents had to organize a party for me. Last year for my birthday Stephen and Alida and Cecilia, my girlfriend at the time, went with me to the Hard Rock Cafe in D.C.

It was so cool being out with my friends in the city. All night I kept trying to make eye contact with Cecilia, to smile and show her how much I cared about her, but she would never look at me. And then the next day she broke up with me in D-hall right before science.

Chris and Jake are talking about the JV soccer team. I guess Chris blew out his knee and is going to have to have arthroscopic surgery. Caroline and Stephen are talking about a teacher they both have.

Robin's sitting next to me, not talking to anyone. She says, "Hey, Brent, what foreign language are you going to take when you come back to school?"

"I don't know. What should I take?"

"Well, the Latin teacher is supposed to be good. I take Spanish and I hate my teacher."

"Yeah?"

Jake butts in, "Yeah, my French teacher sucks too."

Chris says, "Who do you have?"

"Madame Goldberg."

"She sucks?"

"She's the worst."

I say, "I guess I'll take Latin, then."

"Good idea."

This pizza really isn't that good. It's too chewy. Mom's

lighting the candles on my birthday cake. Alida turns out the lights. Everybody's singing, but there's something missing. Their voices sound disconnected, like they're not really trying. Wow, that's a lot of candles. Fifteen burning things coming right toward me.

Mom puts the cake down right in front of me. I can feel the heat from the candles. I lean back in my seat.

Stephen yells, "Make a wish."

I close my eyes for a second and think about what my wish should be. Should I wish that I have sex in the next year? Should I wish that Megan will fall in love with me? Should I wish to be funnier? Or that everything would go back to the way it was before?

No. I know what I'm going to wish.

I wish that everyone will be happy, that everyone gets through this okay. That's what I wish.

I open my eyes and look at all the faces lit up by the candles. They're all waiting for me. I take a deep breath, lean forward, and blow, but I don't have enough air in my lungs and one is still lit. I take another quick breath and blow again. This time the last flame goes out.

Everyone's gone, but there's still a few pieces of the devil's food cake Mom made from the box. She's stuffing all the wrapping paper and dirty paper plates into a big black Hefty bag.

"Hey, Mom," I say.

"Yes?"

"How come you didn't invite Megan?"

She looks up with a real surprised look on her face. She says, "I didn't know you would have wanted her here. I'm sorry, honey. I didn't know."

"That's okay. Forget it."

God, I feel like my whole life could fit in one of these trash bags. I walk downstairs and lie on the brown corduroy couch.

It's been nine months and I still don't know why I did it. I was so sad. I wanted to be funny and cool and I wanted everyone to love me, but I still don't know why I did it.

"Mom," I call out. She's upstairs. She's coming down. I think she can tell I'm upset.

"What is it, honey?" She sits down next to me on the couch. I start crying. I can't keep myself from crying. Where is all this crying coming from? She says, "It's okay, honey. It's okay. You can tell me. You can tell me. It's okay." She's hugging me and hugging me. And she's crying.

"I don't know why I did it. I was just so sad. I was so sad. I don't know why." I'm crying so hard I can't get the words out. I can't say any more. I can't talk anymore, I'm crying so hard.

She's crying hard now too. She's holding me. She's hugging me. "It's okay, honey. It's okay. We love you so much. We're just glad you're okay. We're just so glad that you're okay."

Oh God, I can't stop crying. I can't stop. The spit in my mouth is thick and my whole face tastes like salt. My face hurts from crying so hard.

I say, "I'm okay."

"I know, honey. I know."

"I'm okay, Mom. I'm okay now."

Today is my first day going to Dominion Hospital. I have on this cool blue-and-white shirt my mom got me at the Gap, white in the front with blue arms and a blue back, and a pair of jeans. I'm nervous.

I put a notebook in my black book bag. I put on my plastic face mask and sit at the kitchen table, waiting for the school bus. Mom wanted to make me lunch, but I guess they have a cafeteria there, so she doesn't need to.

Mom hands me a sheet of paper with all the rules of the Adolescent Day Treatment Program.

Safety Rules

Please do not bring any of the following items with you to the hospital:

1. Items with sharp points and edges such as knives, firearms, scissors, razors, nail clippers, tweezers, cans, wire hangers, keys, and other items that staff may feel is unsafe to the program

2. Cigarettes, lighters, matches, pipes, chewing tobacco

3. Gum

Fucking great.

The bus is outside. Jesus, it's a short bus, one of the ones that they take retarded kids around in. I walk out and the bus driver opens the doors for me. There are only two other kids, both about my age. There's one girl in the front seat who's wearing a helmet and looking out the window. What the fuck.

The bus driver asks me a question. "Where you going?"

"Dominion."

"All right, stay seated, young man."

"Okay."

I walk toward the back of the bus because that's usually where the cool kids sit, but what's the point of sitting in the back by myself? I haven't been on a bus in so long. It smells like motor oil and asparagus.

After a couple of miles, we stop and the retard gets off the bus. I stand up and start to get off too, but the bus driver says, "Sit down. Not your stop, young man."

"Okay." I sit back down.

Michael Mager meets me in the waiting room, and we get buzzed into the main part of the building. He leads me into a little room with four other kids. They all look a little older than me, two girls and two boys, and they all look like trouble.

Michael says, "You guys, I'd like you to meet our newest student. Brent, this is the group. Group, this is Brent. I'll leave you to your own introductions."

327

A chubby nurse who looks a little like that actress Shelley Winters comes over and shakes my hand. "Hi, Brent. I'm Suzanne. I'm the nurse around here." She's got that kind of syrupy Southern accent I can't stand.

"I take care of the day-to-day things, so I'll dole out your medication when you need it, okay?" I don't take any medication. Shouldn't she know that?

I shake her hand. A tall skinny kid with a green hooded sweatshirt and hair falling in his face comes over. He says, "Hey, I'm Owen. What's up?"

I say, "What's up." He looks like a skateboarder, I wonder why he's here.

The other boy stands up. He looks like he might lift weights. "Yo, wussup, man? I'm Steve."

"Hey." Oh, I see, he's white, but he acts like he's black. He looks tough, I better stay away from him.

A short girl in a long hippie skirt and dirty hair comes over. "Hi, I'm Calliope."

"Hi." She's kind of pretty.

The other girl comes over. "I'm Christina." I don't know what to make of her. She's pretty, but she's dressed like a real slob in torn jeans and a sweatshirt.

We all sit around in a circle in orange cafeteria chairs. The girls sit next to each other on one side of the circle and the boys sit on the other side with a chair between them. I sit down next to the nurse.

Suzanne, the nurse, says, "So, Christina, you were saying?"

"Yeah, I was at this party this weekend, and it was just,

like, you know, crazy. All these people were so fucked up, and I was like, should I get fucked up? And there was this kid there, and he took me into a room and showed me, like, forty sheets of acid."

Suzanne says, "Did you take any?"

"No. That's what I'm saying. I was like, should I get high? And then I was like, no."

What is she talking about? I mean, I've heard of acid, that's like LSD, but I didn't even know it came in sheets. This girl is fucked up.

Suzanne says, "Well, I think that's really good, Christina. Does anyone else want to tell us about their weekend? Steve?"

"Yeah, so I was, like, hanging out on my block, and this kid who's like a total punk ass came over, and he was like, 'Wussup?' and I was like, 'Nothin'.' Then he was acting fucking whack, man. Man, if I was strapped, man, I would have popped a cap in his ass." He laughs, pulls up his shirt to show where the imaginary gun would be, pulls it out, and pretends to shoot it.

Everybody laughs except for me and the nurse. I can't believe this shit. I'm hanging out with a bunch of druggies and gangsters.

At lunchtime, they open the doors and let us walk up the street to the Hardee's all by ourselves. I didn't know we were going to be able to do this. Owen and Calliope walk ahead of the rest of us. I wonder if they're dating.

Christina, the druggie, comes over to me. "Hey," she says.

"Hi."

"What's up?"

"Nothing."

"You in here for drugs?"

"What?"

"You in here for drugs?" I can't believe she asked me that. Do I look like a druggie? I thought it would be obvious.

"No."

A big truck drives by us and blows out a cloud of black smoke. The air smells like gasoline. I used to love that smell.

She's not going to quit. "So, why are you here, then, if you're not here for drugs?"

"Um." I don't say anything for almost a minute, trying to think of what to say. She's not asking what happened to me, she's asking why I'm in the hospital. She's still waiting for an answer. I say, "I don't know."

"You don't know?"

"No."

"Okay. Want a cigarette?"

"Um, okay." I've never really smoked a cigarette before, except for that one I smoked out by the shed that time, but everybody else here smokes, so what the hell, I might as well try it.

Christina lights the lighter and holds it out for me. I put the cigarette between my fingers and hold it over the flame. She says, "No, put it in your mouth."

"Oh yeah." I put the cigarette in my mouth and lean over the flame, but it's really hot, and I pull away. I try again, but I keep thinking it's going to set my hair on fire or my gloves or something. I pull away from the flame again and she pushes it closer to my face and I pull away again. Jesus, that's hot. She's just staring at me.

Finally I get the end of it lit and suck a little smoke into my lungs. I cough it out. The smoke is so hot and burning me on the inside, why would anyone want to do this? God, why would anybody do this? My hands are shaking.

I pretend to smoke it for a while and then put it out in the ashtray outside of the Hardee's.

When I get home, I go right to the basement and lie on the little bed we've got set up there. It's so cool and quiet down here. It feels like a little habitat for a snake or something.

I grab my new book, *101 Amazing Card Tricks*, that Mom got me at the bookstore. I find one that looks good and pretty easy. I separate all the cards and start practicing. I'm getting good at this.

Mom calls me up for dinner when Dad gets home, and they start asking me all about my day. I don't really have much to tell them.

Mom says, "So how was your first day?"

"Fine."

"What'd you do?"

"I don't know, stuff."

Dad says, a little gruffly, "Like what?"

"I don't know, sat around."

I can tell they're getting frustrated, but I don't really care. I mean, come on, fuck them. It's my life.

I get up to get some more milk and Dad asks me to get him another beer. I go over and pour it for him, and then I realize I shouldn't be standing this close to him. He looks up at me and asks, "Have you been smoking?"

"What?"

"Have you been smoking?"

"No."

"Have you?"

"No."

Fuck. I drink my milk standing up and go back downstairs.

I want to show my new card trick to Michael Mager. He's into magic too. He's great at the disappearing coin trick. I mean, you really think it's in the hand that it's not in.

My trick is simple, it doesn't take all that much doing, but it's still a good trick. To do the trick, first I had to separate all the black cards from the red cards, so it's really easy to tell which one is his because his is the only black card in with all the red ones.

Anyway, here goes.

"Pick a card, any card." My voice is shaking. I forgot what else I was going to say.

"All right." He picks one and looks at it. He gives me a

funny look as he puts it back in the deck, like he knows exactly what I'm doing.

Now I turn over the deck and start looking through them.

I say, "Is that your card?"

"Yup. Pretty good."

"Yeah?" My hands are shaking as I push the cards back together.

"One thing, though."

"Yeah?"

"Try not to make it so obvious that the red and black cards are separated next time."

Fuck.

Dad's outside raking leaves. We always rake them into a brown plastic trash can and then I get in and stomp on them. I told him to call for me when he needs me. Mom's making brownies from a box. I'm just sitting on my ass, watching *American Gladiators*. Nitro is trying to shoot this guy with a tennis ball gun. The guy is trying to shoot the bull's-eye behind Nitro's head, but he doesn't aim long enough to even come close. Nitro is pretty accurate with the tennis ball gun. I wish I had one of those.

I hear Rusty barking like crazy and then Dad calls out, "Brenner, come here."

"Wait a second."

"Come here!" Why does he always have to yell when it's not even an emergency? I fucking hate that.

I go outside to see what he's yelling about. He put Rusty on her leash, but she's still barking like crazy. He's standing on the fence looking down at something in one of the big brown trash cans. I climb up there next to him, I bet we look like those guys in the rodeo getting ready to ride the bulls.

At the bottom of the trash can is a possum, curled up into a little ball.

I say, "Is it dead?"

"I don't know."

"What are we going to do?"

"Let's see if it's alive."

Dad picks up a tennis ball from the yard, one that we throw around for the dog, and holds it over the possum. When my dad gets excited, he starts talking in this high-pitched voice with a funny accent that sounds like he's from Switzerland.

"All right, Brenner, get ready to run because when I drop this thing, man, we don't know what's gonna happen, budder."

"Okay." I laugh at Dad's accent, but I am actually scared.

Dad drops the tennis ball and we both jump back before it hits. The possum screeches, and my dad and I yelp too.

"What do you think, Brenner?"

"I don't know."

"Well, he's still alive."

"Yeah, what's he doing?"

"He's pretending to be sick so we'll leave him alone. I'm

not going to have a possum living in my trash can."

I follow Dad down into the basement. He grabs a wood splitter, which is just this heavy metal triangle you're supposed to use for chopping wood.

I say, "What are we going to do?"

"Get rid of it."

"Why?"

"So it doesn't get Rusty. And so it doesn't get you guys."

I pick up a bunch of weights that we have lying around. I don't think we've ever used these things for anything except maybe holding down science projects while the glue is drying.

We carry them up and stand on the railing with the weights and the wood splitter. The possum is still there. He hasn't moved. I wonder what he's doing.

Dad holds the wood splitter over the possum, lines it up, and lets it go. I pull my head back before it hits, but I can tell by the sound that he missed. It just bounced off the bottom of the trash can.

"Missed it."

"Give me a weight."

I hand him a five-pounder, which is pretty heavy, especially if you drop it on something's head.

Dad drops it. This time it hit. The sound is terrible.

The thing is squirming around in the bottom of the trash can. We hurt it. Oh God, we hurt it. We should stop. We should stop.

"Dad, shouldn't we leave it alone?"

"We can't stop now, Brenner, we already hurt it. We've got to put it out of its misery." He picks up the ten-pounder, holds it over his head, and lets it drop. I hear a squish, but no squealing. It's over.

Craig's home for the weekend. We're all sitting around the table, eating Dad's famous pancakes. He always makes breakfast on the weekends. His pancakes and his French toast are so good, and he makes the best coffee cake.

We each have a section of the paper. Dad is reading the front page. Mom is reading the *Parade* magazine section. Craig is reading sports. I like to read the comics on Sunday because they're in color.

I see something out of the corner of my eye. The silver Get Well Soon balloon just came out of my room. It's at the top of the stairs. Now it's drifting down the stairs.

I say, "Look."

They all look up from their sections of the newspaper. Craig says, "Weird."

The balloon comes down the stairs, turns the corner, and comes straight toward me.

I feel so calm. I can't explain it, I feel so calm all over my body right now. I know what the balloon is going to do. It's just going to circle around my head and go back upstairs, that's all. Nothing else. It's okay.

It looks so alive the way it's gliding along, moving in slow motion, working its way over to me.

It's coming around the breakfast table, not touching anyone else. It finally gets to me. The string circles around my head. I can feel it lightly touching my hair.

And then the balloon goes back around the table, back up the stairs, and into my room.

Mom looks at me and says quietly, "That was your guardian angel checking up on you, making sure you're okay."

"No, it wasn't."

I run up the stairs and into my room. The balloon is there in the corner, just sitting there, not doing anything. There must have been a draft that carried it downstairs. Maybe it's leaking air. It could have been anything.

I'm sitting at Hardee's with the other kids from Dominion. They're so pathetic. All of them are total drug addicts, it's all they ever talk about. Christina says, "We were at this party and this guy was there. He was totally burnt out. I mean, like, totally gone. Somebody told me he went out into the rain with about forty hits of windowpane in his pocket, and it sank into his skin, and he's been tripping ever since."

Owen says, "That's awesome. Before I got busted, I was hanging out at a friend's house, and this guy had the biggest bong. Dude, it was so big, you had to stand on a chair to take a hit."

Calliope says, "If I could, I'd smoke pot forever and lie underneath the stars listening to the Dead."

I think they know that I'm not like them. At first, they

asked me questions about what happened to me. I told them I was in a house fire, but I don't think they believed me. Now they pretty much just ignore me. I don't care. I don't really have anything to say. Steve's getting released on Friday, and Owen might too. Christina just has to pass her drug test and then she's gone. I don't know about Calliope, I think she might get released sometime soon.

I've been working on a new card trick. It's a cool one because it always works and you don't really have to do anything.

I ask Michael Mager if he wants to see the trick. He does.

"Okay, now, I want you to pick a card from one of these three piles." I can hear my voice shaking. Shit, that's embarrassing.

He says he's chosen the card. I say, "Okay, now, tell me which pile it's in." He says the center pile. I grab the center pile and pull it toward me, but my hands are shaking. Why are my hands always shaking?

I turn all the cards over. The nine of clubs falls out of my hands. Fuck, I'm such a spaz.

I lay all the cards facedown on the table in four piles. I say, "Okay, now, point to two piles."

He does, and I take them away. There are two piles left. I say, "Point to one pile."

He does, and I take that one away. Now I say, "Point to two cards." He does, and I take those away. There are two cards left. "Point to one card."

He does. I say, "Turn it over."

He does, and I can tell by his face that it's his card. Yes. Fucking yes.

All the other kids have been released. It's weird because no one made a big deal out of it. One day they just didn't show up. There's a new kid named Nick, and he's dressed like a skater, so I figure he's here for drugs. He's shy, so that's a relief. At least I won't have to talk to him.

Actually, he might be here for attempted suicide. It's hard to tell, but I noticed some bandages on his wrists. Maybe that was just a skateboarding injury. But there's something about him that's sad. I think it's the way he uses his hair like a screen to keep people from being able to see his eyes. I can relate to that.

I've been here at Dominion for one month and Michael Mager says that after a few more weeks, I'll be able to go back to regular high school. Jesus, that'll be scary.

I'll see all the people I know. And all the ones I don't know, and they'll all want to know what happened to me. Someone will probably shut me in a locker because I'm a freshman or beat me up, and then my skin grafts will break down and I'll go back into surgery and start the whole thing over again.

I'm lying on the bed in the basement. I notice a blue

thing underneath the pool table.

Oh my God, it's a Smurf. We got these when we were little kids and they're still hanging around in the basement. That's so awesome. Look at him, it's Papa Smurf, the one with the beard.

My friend Jake and I used to come down here and hold matches under his head. God, poor Papa Smurf. One side of his face is all black and melted. Sometimes we used to light a can of Lysol and spray him with fire, like a flamethrower. And now look at him.

We also tore the arms off of Cobra Commander and put his head in a vise. We took Duke, from G.I. Joe, and twisted him around until his spine snapped. Now he's in two pieces. And then we set them on fire too.

Why did we do that? I can't remember why we used to always be so mean. It seemed like fun at the time, but now I can't remember why.

Every Wednesday, at Dominion, we do a big group therapy thing. Mom and Dad, and sometimes Craig, come and sit around with the other kids and their families. There's only one other kid here now, Nick, who's got the worst haircut I've ever seen. His bangs are so long he can almost fit them in his mouth, but the rest of his hair is shaved like a buzz cut.

His dad comes to the meetings with him. Last time he came, he was completely bald, and now he's got a big fat toupee on his head. I want to say something to him about it, like, I like your hair, but I probably shouldn't.

Michael Mager is starting up the meeting. He's so funny. He's always got a little grin on his face like he's laughing at a joke or he's about to play a big trick on everybody.

"Thanks, everyone, for coming. I, uh, wish we had more patients here, but, um, I guess that's the way it goes. Okay, so, where shall we start? Runyons? Got anything you'd like to discuss here?"

Fuck. Why does he always have to pick on us?

Mom and Dad don't say anything. Neither does Craig. Thank God.

Michael keeps talking. "Well, I was wondering if you'd thought at all about Brent going back to high school. How does it make you feel? Are you concerned?"

Before anyone can say anything, I say, in the world's most sarcastic voice, "Well, I think it's the best thing since sliced bread." Craig smirks.

Michael looks at me. "You think it's a good thing, or are you being sarcastic?"

"I don't know."

"You don't know?"

"No." Fuck you, don't put me on the spot.

He says, "Well, Brent, you know, it's difficult to figure out what people mean when they're being sarcastic. I've noticed that your family communicates with sarcasm quite a bit."

"Oh really? I hadn't noticed." How's that for sarcasm?

I can tell Michael's getting annoyed. Good. "Let's change gears. Anyone ever read the book *When Bad Things Happen to Good People*?"

341

No one has.

"Well, the interesting thing about that book is that it outlines what happens when a family goes through a terrific trauma, like when a member of the family dies or almost dies." He gestures at me.

"I didn't almost die." Now everyone's looking at me.

Michael says, "Really."

"Yeah. I didn't almost die."

"Well, do you think you would have lived if, say, no one had called the ambulance and you'd never been taken to the hospital?"

"I don't know."

"Well, you wouldn't have."

"Whatever." He's so full of shit. Even if I did almost die, he doesn't have to say it.

Dad came in a separate car from Mom and Craig because he came straight from work, so I go home with him.

"Hey, Dad?"

"Yeah?"

"Can we go to the sporting goods store?"

"Sure. Why?"

"I want to look at some stuff."

I know exactly what I'm looking for. Two sets of red lightweight Everlast boxing gloves. That is exactly what I want.

At home, Dad and I strap on our new gloves and start

bouncing around the room. These things are heavy. Jesus, they're heavy.

Dad says, "No hitting on the head, okay, son?"

"Okay. Round one."

Dad covers up his stomach, and I take a couple of cheap shots at his belly. He's making noises like I hurt him, but I don't think I really did.

How about this? How about this? Did that hurt? Did that hurt?

He's not punching me back. How come he's not punching me back? Come on. Hit me. Hit me. I'm not made of glass. Hit me.

He's just covering up and letting me hit him in the stomach. Come on. Come on.

Jab. Jab. Right cross. Left cross. Uppercut.

Jab. Jab. Right cross. Right hook. Uppercut.

He's still not hitting me back. Hit me back. Hit me back. I'm not made of glass. Hit me back.

Right cross. Right hook. Uppercut. Uppercut. Right hook.

Oh shit, I knocked him down.

"Are you okay? Dad, I'm sorry, are you okay?"

"I'm okay."

We're both breathing heavy, and I'm standing over him. I'm standing over him. And I can't help it, I raise my hands over my head. I'm the champ.

Mom and Dad and I are going to the Falls Church Racquet Club to play Wallyball, which is exactly like volleyball except you play it indoors in a racquetball court, and the ball is blue and bouncy, and you can hit it off the walls.

We're playing with a bunch of their friends, including my old den mother from Cub Scouts. I'm the only one under forty.

I'm on the team with Mom and Dad. Bruce and Sandy and Chuck and Annette are on the other team. Mom gets so competitive at these games. Dad does too, but you don't expect it as much from Mom. Dad's wearing some shirt he got at a conference and an old pair of gym shorts, and Mom's wearing her fortieth birthday shirt tucked into her shorts.

Jesus, I hope I don't look that stupid.

Dad serves overhand and Bruce bumps it to Sandy. She gives him a set and he floats it over the net, right to me. Shit. I can do this. I get my arms above my head and send it back to their side. They can't get to it. It drops. Yes.

Everybody is clapping and hollering for me, like I just won the Olympics.

After the game, we go out to Sign of the Whale and get burgers. The meat is nice and juicy and drips down my hand into my Jobst glove. Good thing we can wash these. Nothing like a burger. Nothing like it.

I'm feeling pretty good. I didn't think I'd do so well at Wallyball. I mean, I know they took it easy on me and everything, but still, I was good, I think. I wonder if Wallyball will be an Olympic sport one day. Isn't Ping-Pong an Olympic sport?

344

I start playing the drums on the table. Pounding out a hip-hop beat. I'm pounding out a little beat.

Okay, so I can use my hands, arms, and legs. I can think. I can walk. I can talk. I'm fifteen. I'm alive.

Life's pretty good. It's pretty good.

Dad and I drive home together because he came straight from work. His car has seat warmers. I love seat warmers.

"Oh, Dad, on the way home can we stop at the bookstore?"

"Sure, sonner."

We go in together and I go right for the fiction section. Oh yeah, here it is, *The Godfather*. That's such a cool design on the cover, the guy holding the strings. Cool.

I go over and find Dad. He's browsing in the magazines. There's the new *Playboy* with LaToya Jackson on the cover. God, she's got a snake wrapped around her body. I heard about this on the news. She's so hot.

"Hey, Dad. Look, LaToya Jackson is in *Playboy*."

"Hmm. She's got a nice personality." I laugh.

"We should get it." I'm just kidding, I just want to see what he'll say.

"Okay, give me your book and wait in the car."

"Really?"

"Yeah." He slips me the keys and I go straight out to the car. I try not to look at the girl behind the counter as I walk by. Is he really going to do it?

I watch him through the window as he pulls it from the top shelf of magazines and brings it over to the girl. He's saying something to her. I don't even think he's embarrassed. He's got it. Here he comes.

He opens his car door and throws the magazine onto my lap. It's in a plain brown paper bag.

He says, "Don't tell your mother." We laugh.

It's almost Christmas. It's a week away. During breakfast, Mom and Dad ask me what I want and I tell them. I want a brand-new bathrobe. A black one, but this time with a hood, like the boxers wear. That's what I want. This year, I want a new black bathrobe with a hood. Last year, I asked for a black bathrobe for Christmas. A long, warm one that I could wear in and out of the shower. I guess it's kind of obvious what happened to that bathrobe.

When I think about it, it was after Christmas last year that everything really went downhill. We went to Florida to spend Christmas with Nanny and Grandpa, and I was feeling so good down there. So warm and so good. I remember I went out every day and sat on the beach with my cousins and worked on building that sand horse.

But I remember that I knew it couldn't last. It couldn't last, and it didn't. I knew it was going to get cold when I came home. I knew I was going to get in trouble somehow. I knew I wasn't going to make it through the winter because the winter is so long. I knew when I got to February that I wouldn't make it. February is the longest month.

Suzanne, the nurse, and I are sitting at the table, making Christmas cards. Nick was released from the hospital, and now I'm the only one here. It's kind of lonely, but it's also nice. It really is. It's so annoying when other people are here, always talking about their problems and their addictions.

I'm not very good at making cards. I do the same thing every time. I fold the green paper in two and put some glue and some sparkles on the front and write Merry Christmas. They're not beautiful. But who cares? I mean, who's going to care in a hundred years if I made beautiful Christmas cards or not?

I wonder what my skull will look like in a hundred years. I feel around my eyes. I feel the bones around my eyes and my eye sockets. There's the soft tissue inside them. That's where the holes would be if I was dead and someone was holding my skull. In a hundred years, someone's going to dig up my body and hold my skull in his hand, like Hamlet, and say that line that everyone always says.

Suzanne notices that I'm not working anymore. She says, "What are you doing?"

"Nothing."

"No, seriously, what are you doing?"

"Feeling my skull."

"Why?"

"I don't know. I just am."

"What do you mean?" God, here we go.

"Uh, I'm just feeling my skull bones, just kind of, you know, imagining my skull." I know what she's thinking. She's thinking I'm depressed, but I'm not depressed. I'm not depressed at all.

"Why do you think you're so interested in feeling your skull all of a sudden?"

"Oh Jesus. Give me a break."

She says, "What?"

"You know."

"What?"

"You know what you were thinking."

"What was I thinking?"

"Well, I'm not going to tell you."

"Why?"

"Please." I get up and go to the bathroom. This is such bullshit. I can't wait to get out of this place.

Michael Mager and I are in the classroom. I've got this new card trick I'm going to show him. I say, "Have you heard the story of the four thieves?"

"No."

"Well, I'll tell you. Once upon a time, there were four thieves that worked together to rob houses." I hold up the four jacks and put them on top of the deck. "The four thieves always entered the house from the roof. The first one went down to the first floor and stole all of the gold."

Half of this trick is just keeping the person interested in what you're saying so they don't notice all the sneaky things you're doing with the cards.

I put the first jack into the bottom part of the deck. "The second one went to the second floor and stole all of the diamonds." I put the second guy in the middle of the deck.

"The third thief went to the third floor and stole all the silver." I put him in the upper part of the deck. "And the last thief stayed on the roof to watch for the police.

"Now, normally, all the thieves were very good at their jobs, but this time, one of them tripped an alarm." I look at Michael's face. He's smiling at me.

"Over at the police station, the cops got into their cars and raced toward the scene of the crime.

"And the thief on the roof saw the flashing lights and sounded the signal that the police were coming." I knock on the deck three times. "And the four thieves came to the roof. And escaped down the fire escape." I turn over the top four cards one by one. Jack of spades. Jack of diamonds. Jack of clubs. Jack of hearts. I smile and give Michael a little wink.

He says, "Now, that was a good trick."

Yes.

Mom and I are on our way to the annual Burn Unit Christmas party at Children's. All those kids that have to spend Christmas in the Burn Unit and all of us that used to be patients come back to say hi. Mom parks the car in the underground garage and we go up the escalators to the main level.

I've been coming back here for physical therapy two times a week for months, but I haven't seen very many of the old Burn Unit nurses. This place feels so different now. It's just like, a whole different place.

There's a lot of people here I've never seen before. And lots of little kids with their hands all wrapped up in bandages. They probably have to spend Christmas here.

There're a few older kids. One guy looks familiar, kind of. Who is that guy? He's older, maybe sixteen, and he's wearing a hat. He's got scars on his arms, but he doesn't have to wear Jobst garments, and his scars are faded to flesh color. Mine are still all red.

Donna, one of the nurses, comes over and gives me a hug. She says, "Hey, hon! So good to see you!" I forgot she had a Southern accent. She says she wants to introduce me to some people.

She leads me over to the guy I was just looking at. She says, "Joey? Hey, honey. How are you? I want to introduce you to Brent. Brent was just here this last year."

He says, "Hey."

"Hi. How are you?"

"Good."

Donna says, "Brent, look at how his scars healed." She pulls up the sleeve of his shirt so I can see the scars better. "See how the redness faded? That's what yours are going to look like too, pretty soon." Donna's wearing sunglasses inside. I wonder why she's always wearing sunglasses.

"Cool. Thanks."

"Come on, I want to introduce you to some other people." She leads me over to a black kid in a wheelchair. "Brent, this is Douglas. Douglas, this is Brent." He's got one leg.

I say, "Hey."

"What's up." I remember this kid, he's the one that got his leg cut off by a freight train.

351

Donna says, "How are you, Douglas? You look good."

"I'm all right."

"Great."

I see some other nurses I know. But I don't see Tina. I don't see Barbara. I don't see Lisa. I thought they were all going to be here, but it's just a bunch of people I only kind of knew.

Suddenly I feel like I don't belong.

They're giving out presents now. They've got presents for all the kids, they picked them out special. I'll just sit here and wait my turn, and then I'll get my present and go. I don't even really want anything. I just want to go home.

They're calling my name from the podium. They've got a present for me. Eileen, one of the nurses, comes over and hands me a box and says, "We didn't know what to get you."

I say, "That's okay."

I sit at the table and open it with my mom. It's a set of Magic Markers, the kind that smell like different kinds of fruit.

Donna comes over. "How do you like your present?"

"It's great."

"You like it? Great."

"Yeah, it's really great. Thank you."

"We didn't know what to get you."

"I know, but it's really great. Thanks, I'll use them all the time." I'm lying, but that's okay. Now can we go?

On the drive home Mom's quiet. I don't know if she's not saying anything because of that party or if it's because she's thinking about something else.

I turn on the radio. It's "King of Pain" by the Police.

I say, "Hey, Mom, do you remember that time we drove up to Delaware and we played that game with the songs?"

She laughs. "And you knew all the songs, and the only one I got on the whole trip was Jim Croce—'Time in a Bottle'."

"Yeah. Would you say that's the only song that you know?"

She laughs. "Yes, that and 'Wheels on the Bus'."

"What do you think this song is?"

"This one?"

"Yeah, this one."

She tilts her head and listens really closely to the lyrics.

"Um, let me see." I don't think I've ever seen her concentrate this hard.

"Go ahead. Guess."

"King of Spain?"

I'm laughing. King of Spain, that's good. "That's good, Mom."

"Did I get it?"

"Yeah. You got it. Try another one."

The next song comes on. I think it's by Bob Dylan. "What's he saying, Mom?"

Early one mornin' the sun was shinin'

"'Early one morning the sun was shining'?"

> And I was layin' in bed

"'And I was laying in bed'?"

> Wond'rin' if she'd changed at all,
> if her hair was still red.

"'Wondering if I'd change at all, if my hair was still red'?" I say, "Hey, Mom, that's pretty good."

> Tangled up in blue.

"'Tangle nothing blues'?"

I say, "Yeah, that's not very close." I change the station.

> La la la la la la la la la la.

"'La la la la la la la la la la.' I'm good at this one."

> There is a rose in Spanish Harlem.

"'There is a rose in Spanish Harlem' or 'There is a road in Spanish Harlem,' I'm not sure which."

I'm laughing so hard I can hardly stand it. I don't remember the last time I laughed this hard.

Dad is going to read our traditional Christmas Eve book, it's called *Cajun Night Before Christmas*. He got it on some business trip about twenty years ago, and now we read it every year. He's so funny because he gets really into it and reads it in this terrible Cajun accent. Craig sits on one side and I sit on the other.

> 'Twas the night before Christmas an' all t'ru de house.
> Dey don't a t'ing pass not even a mouse.
> De chirren been nezzle good snug on de flo'
> An' Mamma pass de pepper t'ru de crack on de do'.

I don't know what half of this stuff means. Pass the pepper? It must be some weird Cajun thing. I scoot a little closer on the couch so I can see the pictures. Instead of reindeer, Santa has alligators pulling his sleigh.

> *Mo' fas'er an' fas'er de 'gator dey came*
> *He whistle an' holler an' call dem by name:*
> *"Ha, Gaston! Ha, Tiboy! Ha, Pierre an' Alceé!*
> *Gee, Ninette! Gee Suzette! Celeste and Reneé!"*

Dad is having a little trouble with all the names right in a row. I help him pronounce Celeste.

> *His eyes how dey shine his dimple how merry!*
> *Maybe he been drink de wine from blackberry.*
> *His cheek was like rose his nose like a cherry*
> *On secon' t'ought maybe he lap up de sherry.*

God, he's so into it. His voice has all these weird inflections in it. Craig is laughing. Mom is too. I lean a little closer so I can feel his voice through the back of the couch. I can't keep myself from laughing. Dad's face is getting all red. He's starting to look like the picture of Santa in the book.

I lean over to see the picture of an alligator on the roof, and Dad puts his arm around me. I put my head on his shoulder. He's so warm and soft.

> *An' I hear him shout loud as a splashin' he go*
> *"Merry Christmas to all 'till I saw you some mo'!"*

It's Christmas morning. I'm lying in bed, listening to the radio. I used to get excited about Christmas. I'd wake up early and lie in my bed and wonder what I was going to get. And then I'd go and climb into my parents' bed and wake them up. And we'd have our big Christmas morning. But today, I don't know, I don't really feel like it.

I can hear Mom and Dad making breakfast downstairs in the kitchen.

Anyway, I guess I should get up and see what's under the tree.

We open the stockings first. We each got a magazine and some Hershey's Kisses and an orange. My magazine is about movies, Craig's is about rollerblading, Dad's is about racquetball, and Mom's is about aerobics. I guess she's trying to lose some weight.

We take turns opening presents. Youngest to oldest. I get some videos I asked for and a couple of books about movies that I'll never read. Craig gets books and tapes of these bands I've never heard of. Mom gets kitchen stuff and Victoria's Secret underwear from Dad. Gross. Dad gets racquetballs and a new racket.

Now we're down to our big presents. This is the grand finale. I open my big box first. It's the bathrobe. Just like I wanted. Black, full length, with a hood and everything. Just like the one I got last year but with a hood.

Nobody says anything but I can tell that's what they're thinking. I can tell by the way they're looking at me when I put it on.

I say, "Thanks, Mom and Dad," and give them each a hug.

"Merry Christmas, bud."

"Merry Christmas."

After everyone is done opening their presents, Dad pulls a big box out from behind the curtains. What is that? It's a CD player. I can't believe it. I never thought we were going to be the kind of people with a CD player. I always thought we were more of an eight-track family.

Everything sounds so much better on CD. There's no tape hiss or background noise, it's like listening in a doctor's office.

We each got a CD too. I got *Aerosmith's Greatest Hits*. I used to listen to Aerosmith all the time, before everything, but now, I don't know, it's too noisy. I like the Beatles better.

I've been the only patient here at Dominion for five weeks. The only one. Two doctors, a nurse, a teacher, and me. All for me. That makes me laugh. They have all these people here just looking after me. Every time I cough, somebody puts it into the record. It's insane.

Mom and Dad and I have a meeting today with Michael Mager in his office. This is where Mom and I sat the first time we met him. Dad's dressed in his suit, and he smells like his pipe. I guess he's been smoking again. Both Mom and Dad have yellow legal pads on their knees and pens in their hands.

Michael starts, "So, thanks for coming in, Runyons."

Dad says, "No problem."

"Well, I just wanted to say before we begin that I think Brent has made an enormous amount of progress while he's been here. From my point of view, and from the rest of the staff's, we really feel that Brent has made some very significant strides. He's gotten more comfortable with us. He's expressed himself. He's gotten more confident with himself. So, having said that, it's about time to decide what to do next."

Dad looks very serious, jots something down, and asks, "Well, what are our options?"

"Good question. We've got two main options. Brent has been in our program for eight weeks now. He's been here about four times as long as any other patient we've ever had. And I think, we all think, that he's ready to get out of here. The only question is, where does he go from here? On the one hand, as we discussed when Brent came here, we could send him off to a residential hospital. Someplace like Woodburn, where they do a good job with severely depressed and suicidal teens, but I'm not convinced that's an appropriate place for him anymore."

I love it when people talk about me in the third person.

He pauses. "Or we could take a chance and start main-streaming him."

Mom and Dad both move a little in their seats. Does that mean what I think it means?

Michael keeps talking, but now he's looking at me. "That would mean going back to school. Taking classes.

Doing homework. Studying. And, I think most importantly, interacting with your peers." He nods at me like he wants me to say something.

I say, "Am I supposed to say something?"

He says, "Well, what do you think about that?"

"I think, well, I think I don't know." I don't know. I wasn't ready for him to say that. "I think that it could be good."

It could be terrible. What if it's terrible?

Michael smiles. "I think it could be good too."

I say, "I think, I don't know, I think that it seems a little scary, actually."

Michael smiles even bigger and nods. "I think it seems a little scary too."

"Could I do it, like, a little at a time?"

Mom says, "If we start to mainstream Brent, and we decide that it's not the right thing at that moment, would there be a way to change it?"

Michael nods. "Well, your contact in the school system seems to be very supportive of your choices. And I think that with a little elbow grease, you could get them to design a program around Brent's needs."

He turns back to me. "But, Brent, we need to be clear. This means that you will be going back to school. You will be in with the other students. You will be forced to interact with them. No one will be able to control what they say to you. You'll be on your own. Do you think you're ready?"

There's this big heavy bowling ball in my stomach, rolling up into my throat. Fuck. Fuck. Fuck.

What am I going to say? What am I going to say? They're all looking at me.

"Yes."

It's official, I'm going back to school in two weeks. Marshall High School. I'm going to start part-time, going to a few classes every day, and then I'll ramp up into being a full-time student.

I'm ready. I think I'm ready, but what does that mean, that I'm better? Does it mean that I'm all okay now? Jesus, I don't know. I can't tell. I don't know if I'm going to be okay or not.

I mean, I don't think I'm going to do anything crazy, but I really can't tell. What if something happens? What if somebody says something, or I get mixed up in something that gets me all screwed up and I start to think about death and all that stuff I used to think about all the time? I just don't know what's going to happen when I go back to school. I really don't. I really don't.

I really don't.

The thing about going back to school that I'm most worried about is the plastic mask I have to wear on my face. I mean, okay, I've got to wear the Jobst garments all over my body, from my toes to my neck, but they're skin colored, so they're not as noticeable.

But the mask is a little more apparent. Because it's on my face. Technically I'm supposed to wear the plastic mask all the time, except at night while I'm sleeping. But when I go to school, that will make me look even weirder than I actually am.

Mom says I don't have to wear it if I don't want to, but the truth is I've gotten kind of used to how it feels on my face. I like how it's always cold when I put it on in the morning and the way it smooshes down the scars and makes them flatter and change from red to white. It somehow makes me feel a little better about having scars on my face.

But I guess I'm not going to wear it if I don't have to. I mean, God, I don't always have to look like a total freak.

Chris invited me for a sleepover at his house tonight. I think it'll be fun. Anyway, he's got a lot of video games. He's wearing this big brace on his knee. He just had surgery the other day, and he's not going to be able to play soccer for months.

We sit down at the computer and play this cool new *Star Trek* computer game he has. Chris's whole family are *Star Trek* freaks. They've got every single episode of the TV shows and all the movies too.

Chris is playing first. He's fighting a Klingon warship somewhere in the neutral zone. I've been thinking about this whole high school thing.

I say, "So what period lunch do you have?"

"Sixth. What about you?"

"Sixth."

"That's cool. So you'll have lunch with me and my friends."

"Who are your friends?"

"A bunch of girls from Kilmer that you know and Steve from our soccer team."

"Cool. So, when you go in the front doors at Marshall, where's the cafeteria?"

"Oh, just take a right at the mural, go all the way down to the end of the hall, and turn left, and the cafeteria is right there. I'll meet you out front."

"Okay, so just turn right at the mural?"

"Yeah, and make sure you don't step on the school seal."

"What do you mean?"

"The school seal is like this tile thing on the floor right when you come in. Don't step on it or the seniors will beat you up."

"Okay, so don't step on the school seal." Wasn't there something like that in *Rebel Without a Cause*?

"Yeah, and if anyone tries to sell you an elevator key, don't do it because there's no elevator."

"Okay. No elevator."

"Yeah, and there's no pool either, so don't buy a pool pass from anyone."

"Okay. Right at the mural. Don't step on the seal. No elevator. No pool. Is that it?"

"Yeah, and if anyone messes with you, just tell me and I'll get the soccer team to take care of it."

I laugh, but I'm actually glad he said that. "Okay. Thanks."

He shoots the Klingon warship with a photon torpedo and it explodes across the whole screen.

There's this new kid at Dominion. His name is Joe and he's fat and wears glasses. He's wearing a Beatles shirt, with that famous picture of all four of them walking across the street.

Michael is going to do group with us. "Brent, have you met Joe?"

"Hi."

"Hey."

Michael says, "So, Joe. Would you like to talk about why you're here?"

Joe says, "Sure. Well, I'm here, basically, because I'm severely depressed. I've been suicidal. I almost killed myself four times. And I'm thinking about doing it again." He says that shit like he's proud of it. Give me a fucking break.

I can't help it, I'm going to say something. "Are you serious?"

"Yes, I'm serious."

"Why are you going to do that? Why are you thinking about doing that?"

"Because I'm depressed."

"So?"

"It's very depressing. I don't want to live like this."

"So? Get used to it."

"I don't want to. I want to die."

"Shut the fuck up."

"What do you know about it?"

"I know about it, okay? I know about it."

"You don't know shit."

"Fuck you. You're a fucking asshole."

Michael interrupts, "Guys. Guys. Take it easy. We've all got our own problems. We all go at our own speed, okay?"

That shit really pisses me off. Jesus Christ. Don't fucking talk to me about that shit.

Michael gets up and turns the light off. "Guys, let's calm down a little, okay? Let's do a little breathing exercise. Close your eyes. Breathe in through your nose. Slowly. Slowly. Hold it. And push it out through your mouth."

I push the air out through my mouth, and it does make me feel better. I just felt my whole chest relax. We breathe in again. In through the nose. One. Two. Three. Out through the mouth. One. Two. Three. In through the nose. One. Two. Three. Out through the mouth. One. Two. Three.

I feel better. I always feel better doing that breathing exercise. I shouldn't have gotten so upset. I just have to remember. In through the nose. Out through the mouth.

Craig is home for the weekend. He's hanging out in his room. I stand outside and listen for a second. I can't hear anything. I knock.

"Come in." He's sitting at his desk holding a notebook, writing or something.

I say, "What are you doing?"

"Drawing." I didn't know he drew.

"What are you drawing?"

"Stuff. Want to see?" I walk over to him, I wonder if he's going to punch me. No. He doesn't do that anymore.

I look over his shoulder at his drawing. It's just a few straight lines and a stick figure, but it looks like a guy jumping off the top of a really big building.

He says, "Can you tell what it is?"

"A guy jumping off a building? Or is he falling?"

"I don't know. I don't know if he's falling or jumping." He turns the page.

It's a picture of a man hunched over, holding his knees to his chest. All around him are bricks, everywhere, like he's built himself inside a wall. You can't see his face or anything, but there's something really sad about it.

I say, "What's that supposed to be?"

"A guy."

"I know, but what is it supposed to mean?"

"It's not supposed to mean anything. It's just a guy I drew."

"Cool. Why is he inside a brick wall?"

"I don't know. It's just how I feel sometimes. Sometimes I feel like there's a brick wall all around me."

"Cool." There is something so sad about that. I didn't

know he felt that way. I used to feel that way. I walk back out of the room.

He says, "Hey."

"What?"

"You going to school tomorrow?"

"Yeah."

"Good luck."

"Thanks."

I go back upstairs to my room.

I sit down at the desk and pull out some paper.

I click the pen and draw a circle. That's good, that's the head. Then I draw the body. The arms look like he's holding them behind his back. He's facing away from me.

I draw a rectangle around him because it looks like there should be one. He looks like he's standing in a doorway.

January 26, 1992
Falls Church, Virginia

I'm awake. Today's the big day. I go to Dominion for a half day, and then I go over to the high school for two periods. Lunch and home economics. It should be pretty easy. I'm going to meet Chris outside the cafeteria doors. I just have to find him when I go to lunch.

I get up and go into my parents' room and turn on the shower. I take off my boxer shorts that I wear over my Jobst. I guess I don't really need to wear boxers, but it just makes me feel more normal. I unzip the jacket and the pants and throw them outside the door so Mom can wash them. I feel like I'm taking off my skin when I do that.

I get into the shower. I turn the shower nozzle to pulse and let it bang off the back of my neck. I'm tired, but I'm so nervous my hands are shaking. I make my hands into fists and pretend there's somebody in front of me. I hit him with a right and a left and another right and a right and a right. Come on. Come on. Come on. Fuck.

I wash my hair with the Pert Plus and get out as fast as I can. I take the towel and wipe a space clear on the mirror. There I am. I lean close to the mirror and stare right into my own eyeballs. See that? That's me. Not the rest of it.

Not the rest of it. But right in there, right in my eye, the green and the little fleck of gold. That's me in there. That's me.

It doesn't matter if the rest of me looks different. None of that matters. I can still recognize myself. I'm still that person in there. Inside my eyes.

I walk out and go lie on my parents' bed. Mom comes in and spreads the cream quickly over my legs. Even if she's not that good at this, at least she's gotten faster. I get my own Jobst garments on and grab a pair of blue jeans and my favorite blue-and-white shirt from the hamper. I don't care if it's a little dirty.

I go downstairs and pour myself a bowl of raisin bran. Dad's reading the newspaper. He looks up. "Hey, sonner."

"Hey."

He looks over at the calendar. Mom's written in red pen, Brent to High School, on today's date. He looks back at me to see if I know what day it is. He says, "Big day today, huh?"

"Yeah."

"Big day." Dad always repeats what he says. I keep eating, and when I look up again, Dad's still looking at me. He looks like he wants to say something else. "Brent," he says, "it's a big day today for all of us. We've all worked real hard to get where we are right now. Real hard. And we're real proud of you and all the work you've done. Real proud."

He reaches over and puts his big hand on top of mine. His eyes are filling up with tears. "And we're your family, and we love you, sonner. And we want you to know that we're here for you whenever you need us. And we just love you and think you're a great kid. And whatever happens, we're with you. Okay, son? We're with you."

"Okay, Dad. Okay."

I give him a little hug. I can't stay around and talk about this right now. My bus is here. I grab my book bag and head toward the door. Mom gives me a brown bag with a peanut butter and jelly sandwich in it and a dollar for something to drink. She hugs me and kisses me on the cheek. I look into her eyes. She's about to cry. Her eyes get extra green when she's about to cry.

"We love you, sweetie."

"I love you too."

Dad gives me another hug and pats me on the back as I go out the door.

Michael Mager's called a special meeting because today is my last day. Suzanne is here. And the fat kid, Joe.

Michael does the talking.

"Well, Brent, I don't usually do this, but because you've been here for so long, we decided to get together to see you off."

"Thanks."

"You're welcome. I'm sure you'll do well going back into the world, but there are a few things that I'd like you to take with you. The first is that there's always help. There's always someone out there who knows how to listen. The

371

second is that if you ever feel like there's something you can't deal with, if you feel like you're panicked and trapped and there's nothing you can do to get out, just remember to breathe. Remember your breathing exercises. Remember to stay calm. Remember you're a smart kid and you can get through anything. Okay?"

"Yeah, okay. I'll remember."

"Is there anything you want to say to us before you go?"

"Um, I don't know, I really appreciate all the help you guys have given me over the last couple of months. I know that it's almost a year since I've been in school, and I know that it's going to be weird, and hard, but I think I can do it. I mean, I do think I can do it. So I guess I just want to say thanks. So, thanks."

Suzanne gets up and gives me a hug. Michael Mager shakes my hand and pats my shoulder.

I walk out of the meeting and head toward the door. The receptionist buzzes me out and I walk outside to wait for the little bus. Okay, here I go. Going back to school. I know it's only for two periods and one of them is lunch, but still. It's a big deal. It's a big fucking deal. It's a gigantic fucking mess of a giant fucking deal.

Because when you think about it, I mean, I really haven't been to school in, well, almost a year. And it's high school, and I don't know if I'm okay. I don't really know if I'm going to be okay.

Fuck. Fuck. Fuck.

Fuck.

The bus is here. Jesus. This is it. This is it. The bus is going to take me to school and the whole thing is going to change. I'm going to walk into school and I'm going to be a different person and they're all going to see that I'm a different person.

I'm getting on the bus. Okay, get your cameras out. Thank God there's nobody else on the bus. Thank God. It's just me on a little short bus that retards ride on. I used to make fun of people that rode these buses, but now I'm one of them.

Jesus. I hope I can find Chris. I hope I can find the cafeteria. I hope no one picks on me or says anything to me. I hope no one notices me and the way I look. I hope no one who used to know me wants to talk to me about anything. I hope school's not too hard.

I'm just going to lay my head against the window. I'm just going to put my forehead against the window and lean against it. That feels good. That feels so good. I'm going to be okay. I'm going to be okay.

I breathe in through my nose. One. Two. Three. Hold it. Out through the mouth. One. Two. Three. In through the nose. One. Two. Three. Out through the mouth. One. Two. Three.

Okay. Okay. I'm going to be okay. That sounds like a song. Maybe I should sing to myself. Maybe that'll make me feel a little better.

Okay, okay, you're going to be okay.
Okay, okay, you're going to be okay.
It's going to be all right.
It's going to be all right.

Okay, I feel a little better. I feel, at least, a little better.

Oh God, there's the school. They plant those bushes in a big M on the side of the hill like that every year. The sign says Marshall High School. Congrats, JV Field Hockey.

Jesus. The bus is stopped. I've got to get off the bus. I'm getting off. I'm walking up the steps. I'm opening the door.

I'm standing in the doorway.

Okay.

I'm here.

Acknowledgments

All the Runyons and Parseghians, especially Nanny and Grandpa.

The Boston Red Sox.

Ira Glass and Julie Snyder at *This American Life*.

Andrew Solomon and Kay Redfield Jamison.

Spalding Gray, Lucy Grealy, and Elliott Smith.

Judith Haut and Nancy Siscoe.

Tina Dubois, Margaret Halton, Kate Jones, and Margaret Marr.

Lisa Bankoff, my agent at ICM.

Sarah Hughes, my editor at Penguin.

My brother, Craig, and his wife, Deb.

And my mom and dad, who continue to live through all of this with me.